I0793426

IMAGES
of America

FOREST HILL

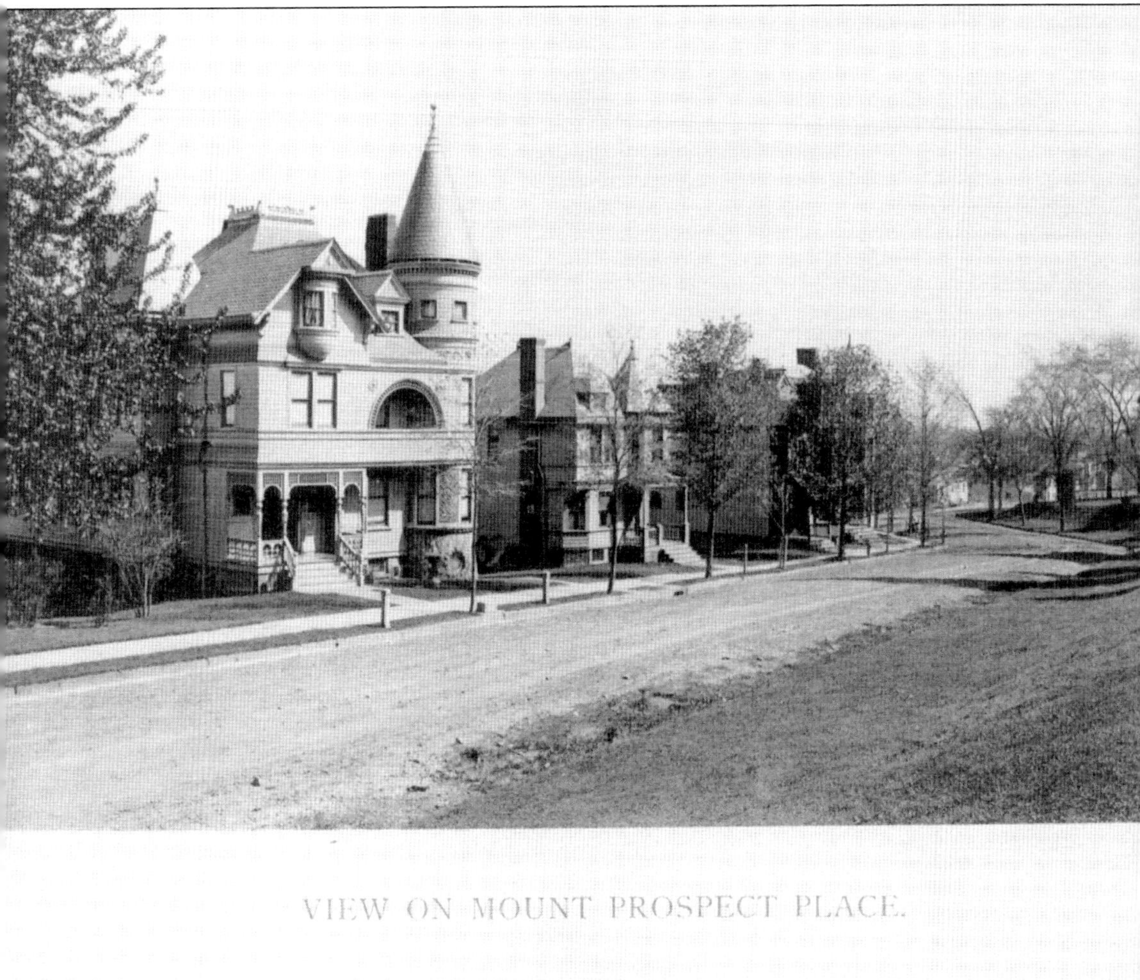

The Queen Anne residence at left in the photograph would have been almost directly opposite the Clark estate. Mount Prospect Place merges into Mount Prospect Avenue at this point. The latter was a major thoroughfare, yet as shown in the foreground, it was unpaved and, in 1892, did not yet have streetcar tracks. (City of Newark, Office of the City Clerk.)

On the Cover: Adrian Scharf built this residence around 1850 at 390 Mount Prospect Avenue. Scharf's estate was situated on Bloomfield Road near Harvey's Garden and ran from what is now Branch Brook Park down to what is now Broadway. William Clark acquired much of the land, and the Scharf residence passed to the Turnbull family. An apartment building now occupies the site. (City of Newark, Office of the City Clerk.)

IMAGES
of America

FOREST HILL

Catharine Longendyck and
Kathleen P. Galop

ARCADIA
PUBLISHING

ISBN 978-1-4671-2060-9

Published by Arcadia Publishing
Charleston, South Carolina

Printed in the United States of America

Library of Congress Control Number: 2013938248

For all general information, please contact Arcadia Publishing:
Telephone 843-853-2070
Fax 843-853-0044
E-mail sales@arcadiapublishing.com
For customer service and orders:
Toll-Free 1-888-313-2665

Visit us on the Internet at www.arcadiapublishing.com

In memory of Carol Baron, an Iowa farm girl who moved to the "big city" but eventually discovered Newark and spent her happiest years in Forest Hill.

—Catharine

To my coauthor, Catharine, whose dedication to our Forest Hill neighborhood and to completing this book have been an inspiration to me. Cathie, thank you for inviting me along for this journey!

—Kathleen

Contents

Acknowledgments

We salute the people of Forest Hill and everywhere who care about historic preservation and work so hard to maintain our neighborhoods and landmarks. Elizabeth Del Tufo, who was an invaluable resource to us in compiling this book, spearheaded the effort to achieve "Historic District" designation for Forest Hill. The nomination to the New Jersey and National Registers of Historic Places was submitted by the Newark Preservation and Landmark Committee.

The Newark Public Library was extraordinarily generous in providing images. Special thanks are due to its director, Wilma Grey, and the staff of the Charles F. Cummings New Jersey Information Center, particularly George Hawley, Tom Ankner, and Dale Colston, as well as James Lewis. Thank you for sharing your knowledge and archives with us. The Newark Museum also made its collections available to us.

The records of the City of Newark were vital to our research. We thank Robert Marasco, city clerk; Joyce Lanier, city archivist; and Jose De Silva, archives supervisor. They uncovered much helpful material for us, including the spectacular photograph featured on the cover.

The Essex County Parks Historic Documents Library was a tremendous resource, and we thank Daniel Salvante, parks director; Joseph Lanzara, parks archivist; and Kathy Kauhl, archive consultant, for providing images.

The New Jersey State Department of Environmental Protection, Historic Preservation Office, assisted us with locating photographs. We thank Kinney Clark and William Roger Clark for their help.

We are very grateful for the time and talent donated by Israel Ehrisman and Robert Hartman to advise and assist us with our technological challenges.

Many thanks to the Forest Hill Community Association for referring this book project to us and for its assistance and support throughout the process. Particularly helpful were Paul Agostini, Russ Anderson, Charles Bell, Byron Clark, Mark Covey, Flora Del Valle, Rose Gordon, Dan Karslake, and Ken Kroll.

We thank our many friends for providing us with historic information and photographs. Unless otherwise noted, images in this volume appear courtesy of the Newark Public Library (NPL); City of Newark, Office of the City Clerk (NCC); National Register of Historic Places (NR); Library of Congress (LC); or personal collection of Catharine Longendyck (CL).

Introduction

The name *Forest Hill* was first used in the northern part of the city of Newark, New Jersey, in 1890, when Elias Heller and his sons incorporated a real estate development company and named it the Forest Hill Association. As late as 1873, this land was just part of the Woodside area of Newark and was mostly farmland, but the Hellers and several other wealthy businessmen began purchasing large tracts of acreage for the purpose of building suburban residences for themselves and their fellow industrialists. The primary developers of this scheme were Peter Ballantine of the Ballantine Brewery, William Clark of the Clark Thread Company, and the Hellers, who owned Heller Rasp & File Works and Heller Steel Mill. The Clark and Heller manufacturing facilities were both located within walking distance of their owners' new residences. The Ballantine family continued to live "downtown," closer to their brewery. Tiffany & Co. owned another large parcel of land, although that property and that business were adjacent to the area that became known as Forest Hill.

Ballantine, Clark, Heller, and Tiffany all donated large tracts of their land in Forest Hill to the County of Essex to be incorporated into Branch Brook Park, which formed the western boundary of Forest Hill. The first county park in the United States, Branch Brook Park was envisioned by the firm of Olmsted & Vaux in their 1867 "Report on the Site for a Park at Newark," prepared for the Newark Park Commissioners. Today, the park is listed in the New Jersey and National Registers of Historic Places.

Clark and Heller built large mansions for themselves or to be sold with restrictions on further development. In 1890, the Hellers' Forest Hill Association proceeded to develop the land owned by them. Improvements in public transportation during this period made it attractive for wealthy businessmen, professionals, and upper-middle-class managers to travel downtown or into New York City to their places of business from their new homes in suburban Forest Hill.

In the late 1880s and early 1900s, Forest Hill was being developed and marketed as an exclusive residential enclave. Promotional brochures touted its proximity to Branch Brook Park and the Forest Hill Field Club, with all their recreational activities. While Branch Brook Park was a county park open to all, the Forest Hill Field Club was a paid membership club; again, this feature was emphasized to add to the exclusivity of this residential area. Today, the park still offers many facilities for athletic and recreational activities. Forest Hill residents have access to tennis courts that have evolved from the grass courts of 1900 to a complex consisting of asphalt and composite clay courts. The Branch Brook Park tennis complex at Heller Parkway has been dedicated to tennis great Althea Gibson. A life-size statue of her in action greets visitors to the tennis courts. And while the Forest Hill Field Club has moved to another location, its former golf course is now called Hendricks Field and is part of the Essex County Park System. The golf course begins at the northern edge of Branch Brook Park, within easy reach of Forest Hill residents.

Turn-of-the-century Forest Hill residents also enjoyed cultural pursuits. In 1896, Dr. Frank Gilman founded the Forest Hill Literary Society of Newark, New Jersey, which is still in existence today. Originally, the Forest Hill Literary Society was a social club that met twice a month for programs featuring literature, history, music, art, science, and current events. Each year's program was printed in advance with details of each meeting's host, location, topic, and featured speaker or performer. A theme was chosen for each year, and every program was structured around that theme. The meetings were described as casual, but gentlemen wore black tie and the ladies wore gowns. One of the society's highlights surely must have been the lecture by the Grand Duke Alexander of Russia on April 13, 1929. Exciting at the time, no doubt, but how ironic that a member of a deposed monarchy would entertain wealthy Americans on the eve of the stock market crash of 1929.

Interestingly, there was another literary group, this one organized in 1904 as the Forest Hill Reading Club. This group seems to have functioned more as a book club, and its membership was exclusively female. And even earlier, when the wealthy residents of North Newark lived in Woodside, there was a Washington Irving Literary Society. Today, the Forest Hill Literary Society is a traditional book club, meeting monthly to discuss their reading selections and occasionally entertaining authors.

In 1990, the Forest Hill area of the city of Newark, New Jersey, was designated a Historic District and listed in the New Jersey and National Registers of Historic Places. There are two National Register–listed buildings within Forest Hill: the Sydenham House (1712) and the Clark Mansion (1873). In addition to Branch Brook Park, there are several other listed properties nearby.

Today, the Forest Hill Historic District is still primarily a residential area. Most of the residences are single family and owner occupied. There are several churches of various faiths and both public and private schools within the boundaries of the historic district and adjacent to the residential area. The area designated as Forest Hill in the nomination to the National Register contains approximately 1,900 buildings, of which there were 104 "key" structures. Most were built during the period of 1890 to 1925. A wide variety of architectural styles are represented, including Colonial Revival, Georgian, Dutch Colonial Revival, Craftsman, Tudor, Shingle, Italian Renaissance Revival, Romanesque Revival, Spanish-Mediterranean Revival, Neoclassical, Prairie, and Queen Anne. There is also one Beaux Arts–style residence in the district. Several of the structures were designed by noted architects of the day.

Despite the various hardships Newark has weathered over the past 45 years, Forest Hill has remained a stable residential neighborhood. It has experienced a resurgence during the past decade, and its homes are once again becoming showcases. It has strong community groups, and its homeowners care about their neighborhood. They host walking tours and garden tours and support activities such as the Essex County Cherry Blossom Festival held every spring in Branch Brook Park.

This is the story and the history of Forest Hill in Newark, New Jersey. It is also the story of how a city grew and developed from a farming community to an industrialized city. In other words, it is the story of most large American cities. But it is unique to us, and we hope it will inspire other communities to preserve their historic districts, too. Not everyone wants to live in a modern house in the suburbs. Many of us appreciate the convenience of city living, with a short commute to business and easy access to cultural centers. We treasure our past and are willing to work at preserving it.

One

The Legend of Woodside

First, there was Woodside. The entire northern part of the city of Newark was called Woodside and encompassed the area that later became known as Forest Hill.

When Robert Treat came from Connecticut in 1666 and purchased land on the Passaic River from the Hackensack Indians, the area claimed by the settlers was approximately 61 square miles. This number reduced over time to 15.5 square miles as the land was sectioned to form other areas, such as the Oranges, Belleville, Bloomfield, and Montclair, and other towns that eventually became the bulk of Essex County.

In 1743, Newark separated "the Inhabitants of Second River"—basically, Woodside. But in 1871, Newark again annexed Woodside, and the rural character of Woodside began to change. Entire sections disappeared, including Bird's Woods, Woodside Park, and Blue Jay Woods. Roads that had been place names—River Road, Gully Road, and Back Road—were given street names and shaped into a city grid. Streets were paved, and streetcar rails were installed. Life became easier, but not everyone welcomed the changes.

Part of the push north was to enable workers easier access to the stone quarries located at Bloomfield and Clifton Avenues. Since 1668, there was a grain mill at the foot of Woodside, and more mills were built, along with sawmills, limekilns, and a calico print mill. The last blacksmith forge to operate in the city of Newark was also located in Woodside. And then copper was discovered along the Second River. As industry moved north into Woodside in the mid-1800s, the Passaic River became more polluted, the roads became more congested, the farms gave way to the demand for development, and families of means began to move away from the river and up the hill into what became Forest Hill.

Charles C. Hine wonderfully documented the good life in Woodside, from 1867 through the decline following annexation, in the book *Woodside*, edited by his son C.G. Hine from his father's papers. This engrossing history provides a comprehensive picture of the Woodside lifestyle in the last half of the 19th century.

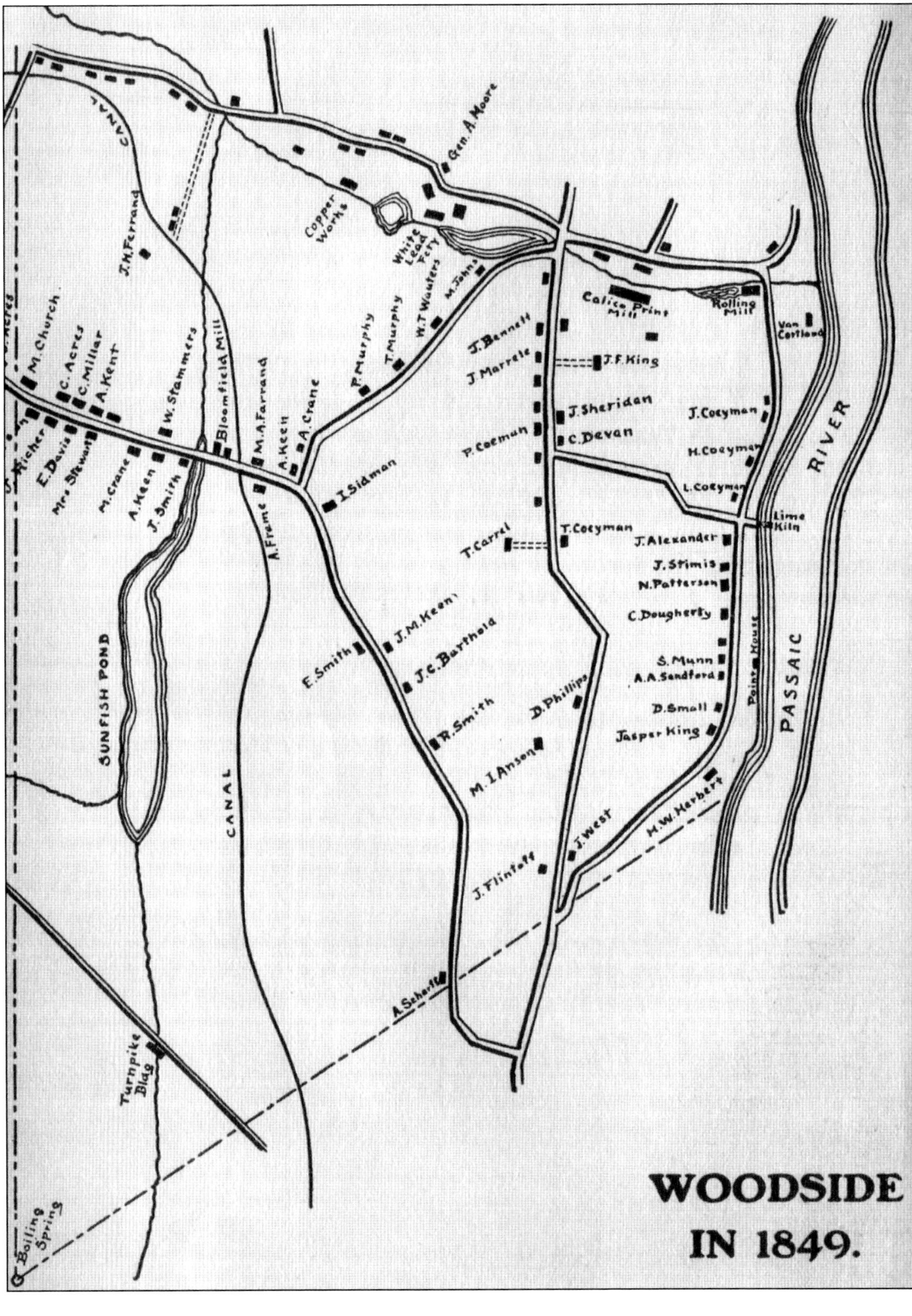

WOODSIDE IN 1849.

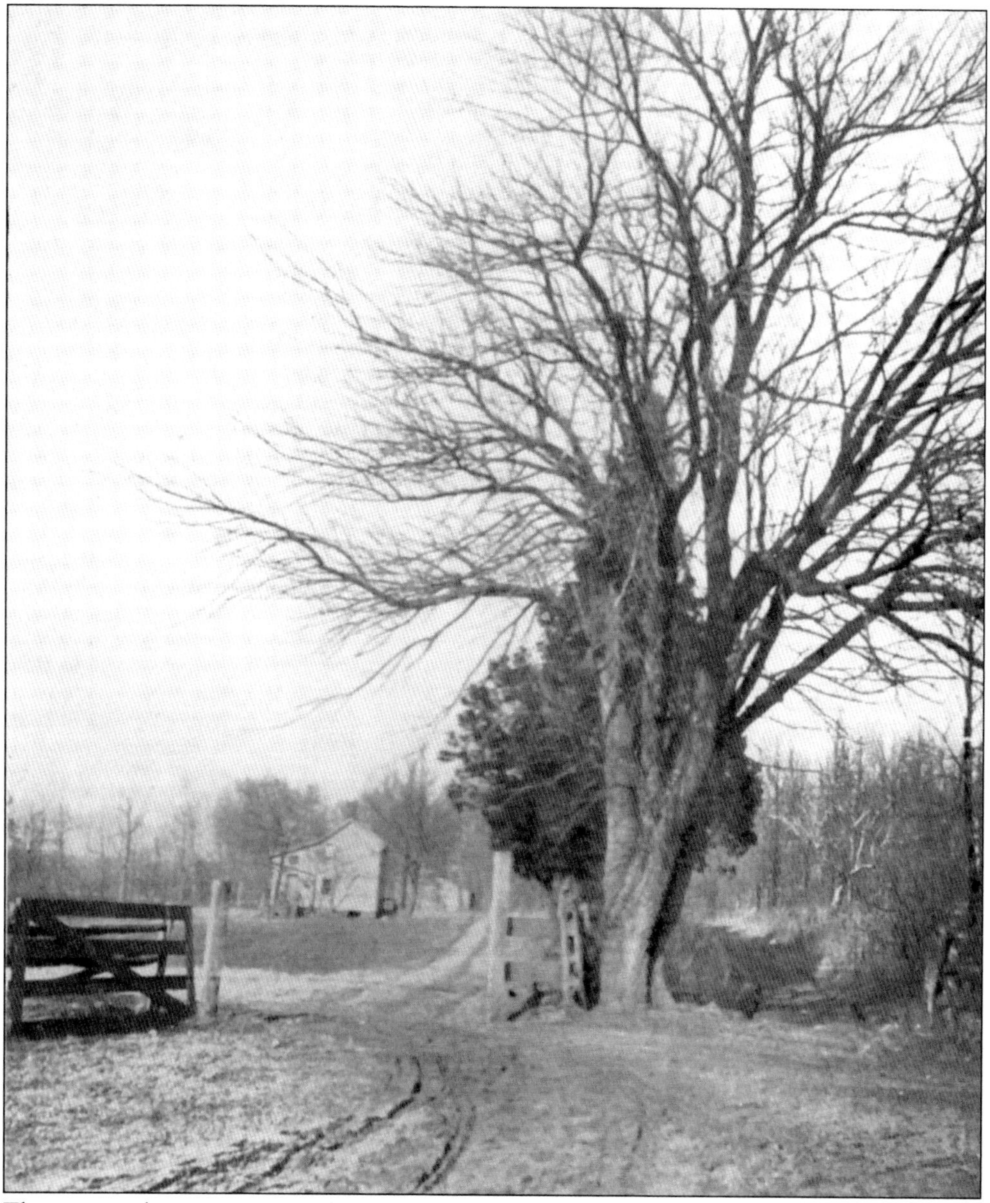

The map on the opposite page shows Woodside when it was part of Belleville. Names shown on the map were landowners at that time. Its western boundary lay beyond the Morris Canal, and the Passaic River formed its eastern boundary. Its northern boundary was the Second River, and the southern boundary was just north of Clay Street. The four main roads were the Old Road to Bloomfield, which was originally a toll road and ran on a northwest diagonal; two north-south roads, River Road and Belleville Avenue, which became Washington Avenue and is now Broadway; and Murphy's Lane (shown in the c. 1880 photograph above), which branched off the Old Road and ran northeast down to the Passaic River. There was another crossroad, known as Division Road (or Bootleg Lane), which eventually became Halleck Street and Grafton Avenue. Murphy's Lane was the site of the Shield Guards, a pre–Civil War armory near Mount Prospect Avenue. It also ran alongside Bird's Woods on the Second River. This area was later called Woodside Park, most of which was acquired by Tiffany & Co. (Both, NPL.)

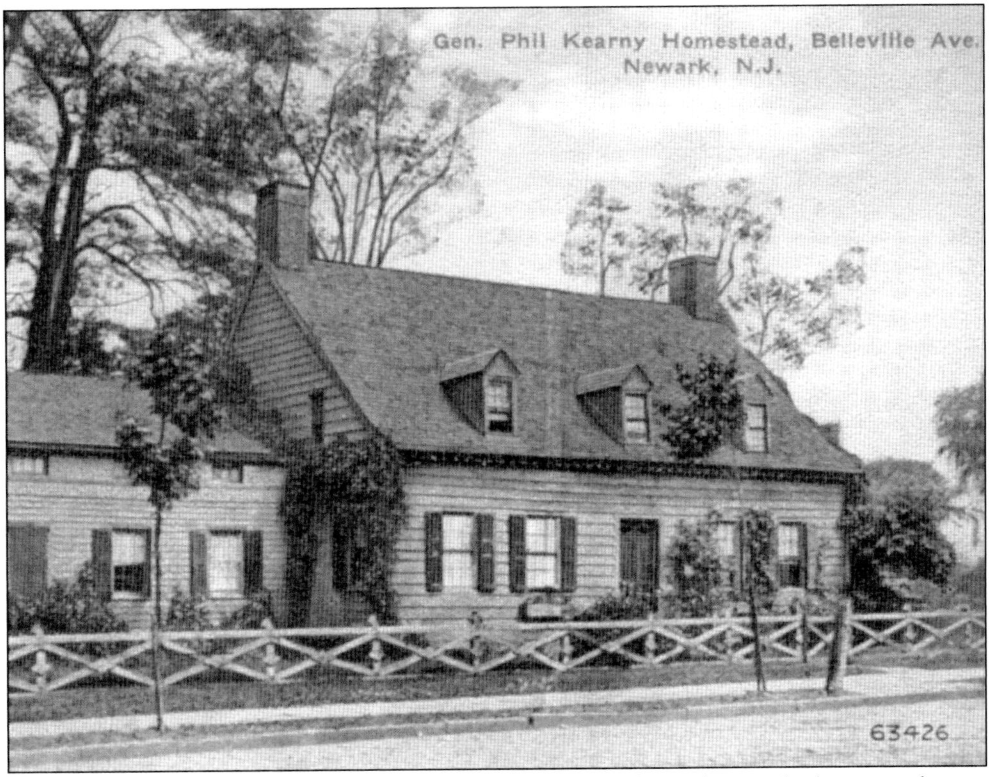

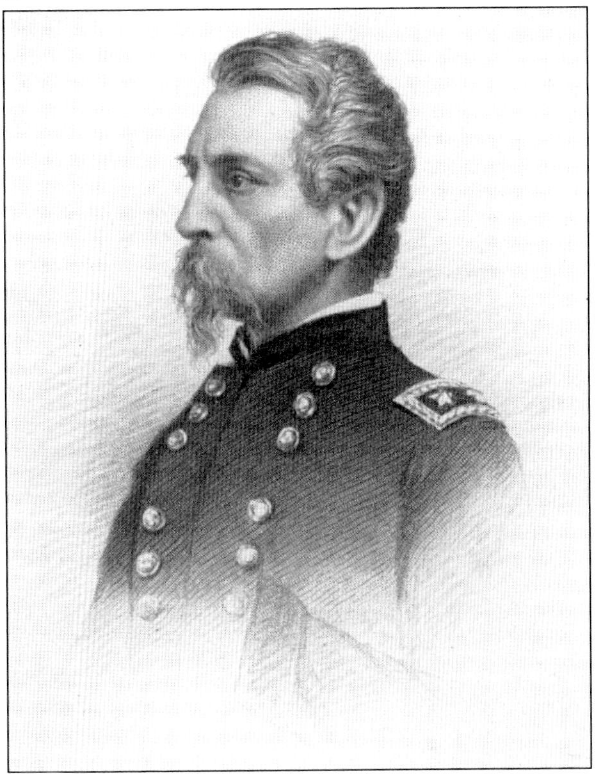

Shown here is the homestead of Philip Kearny Sr., whose son Stephen W. Kearny was career military, serving in the War of 1812 and eventually as military general of New Mexico. Stephen Kearny's nephew Philip Kearny Jr. (left) was born and raised in New York City but spent his childhood summers at his grandparents' Woodside farm. Philip Jr. also dedicated himself to a military career. He lost his left arm in the Mexican-American War, but reenlisted to serve as a major general in the American Civil War. He was killed in action in the 1862 Battle of Chantilly, and his statue stands in Newark's Military Park. (Both, CL.)

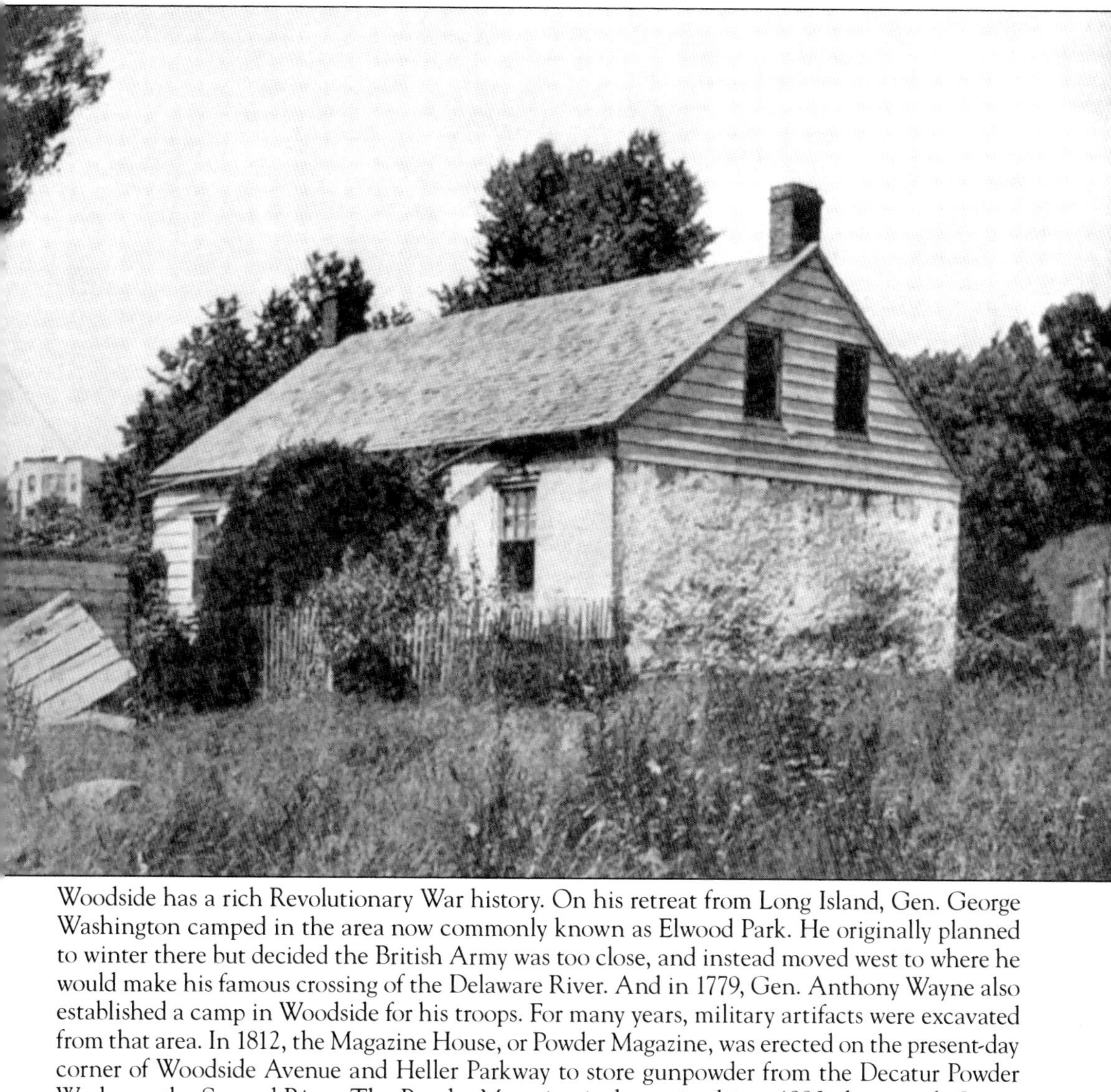

Woodside has a rich Revolutionary War history. On his retreat from Long Island, Gen. George Washington camped in the area now commonly known as Elwood Park. He originally planned to winter there but decided the British Army was too close, and instead moved west to where he would make his famous crossing of the Delaware River. And in 1779, Gen. Anthony Wayne also established a camp in Woodside for his troops. For many years, military artifacts were excavated from that area. In 1812, the Magazine House, or Powder Magazine, was erected on the present-day corner of Woodside Avenue and Heller Parkway to store gunpowder from the Decatur Powder Works on the Second River. The Powder Magazine is shown in this c. 1890 photograph. It was torn down in the late 1800s, when Woodside Avenue was laid out. Our Lady of Good Counsel Grammar School was built on that site in 1913. (NPL.)

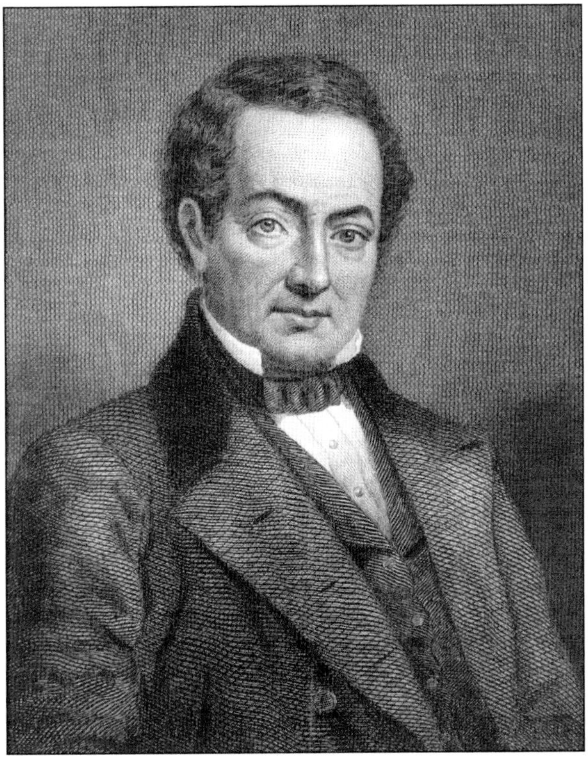

As a young man, writer and diplomat Washington Irving spent time at the Woodside estate of his friend Gouverneur Kemble. He and his companions called themselves "the Lads of Kilkenny" and usually stayed in a summerhouse on the Kemble estate that they nicknamed "Cockloft Hall." Irving immortalized this site in his work the *Salmagundi Papers* and based the Cockloft family on his friends the Kembles. (LC.)

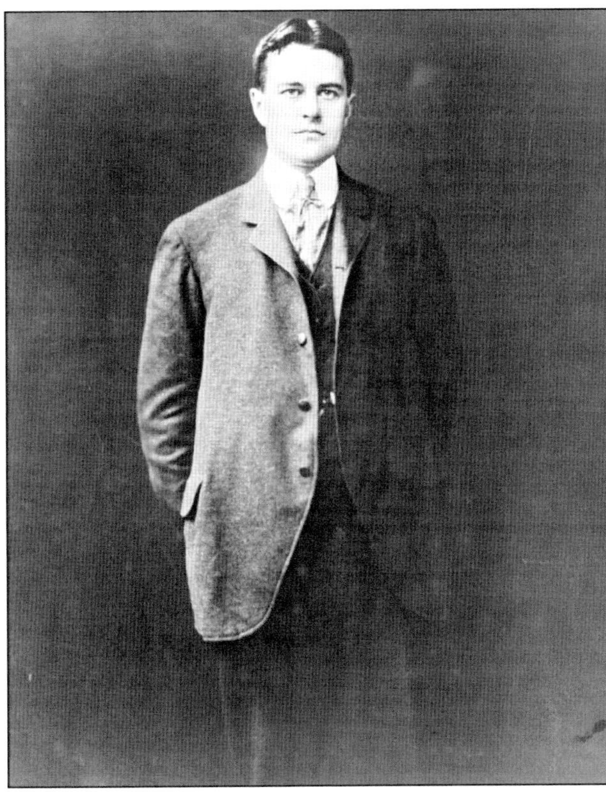

Albert Payson Terhune was born and raised on his family's Woodside estate. He became an author, journalist, and dog breeder, best known for his novels featuring his Rough Collies. He eventually moved to his family's summer home, Sunnybank, in Wayne, New Jersey, now a public park. His Sunnybank Kennels produced championship lines, and at Sunnybank Park are the graves of many dogs featured in his novels. (LC.)

Henry William Herbert was an eccentric, tragic Englishman who is best known as a writer and sportsman. The Cedars (below), his Woodside estate on the Passaic River, was the scene of many hunting parties. Under the pen name Frank Forester, he is acknowledged as the first newspaper sportswriter in America. He contributed to the *Spirit of the Times* newspaper and authored works such as *Frank Forester's Field Sports of the United States and British Provinces of North America* and *The Dog*. He also penned novels and historical studies. His first wife died, and his second divorced him after just three months. Shortly thereafter, he held a dinner party for his friends, and only one guest showed up. After dining, Herbert left the table and committed suicide. His tombstone bears his chosen epitaph: *Infelicissimus* ("The Unhappiest"). (Right, LC; below, CL.)

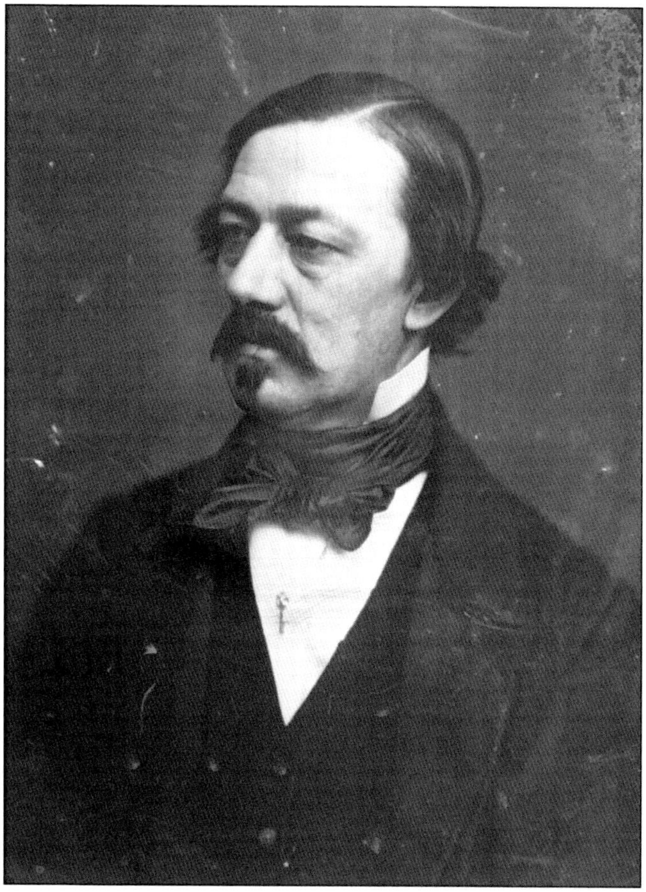

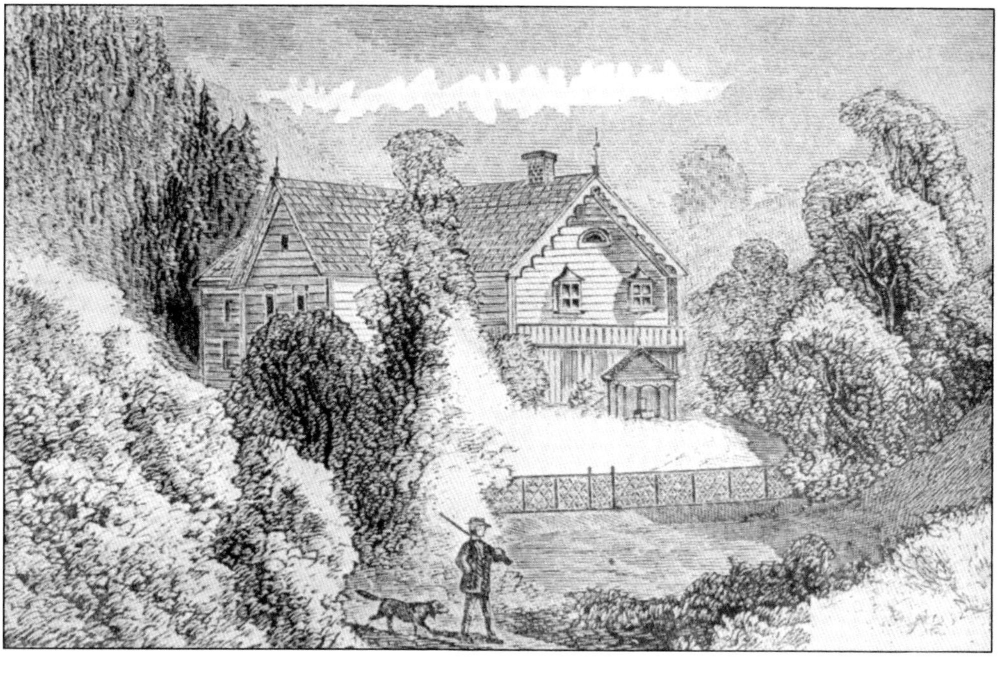

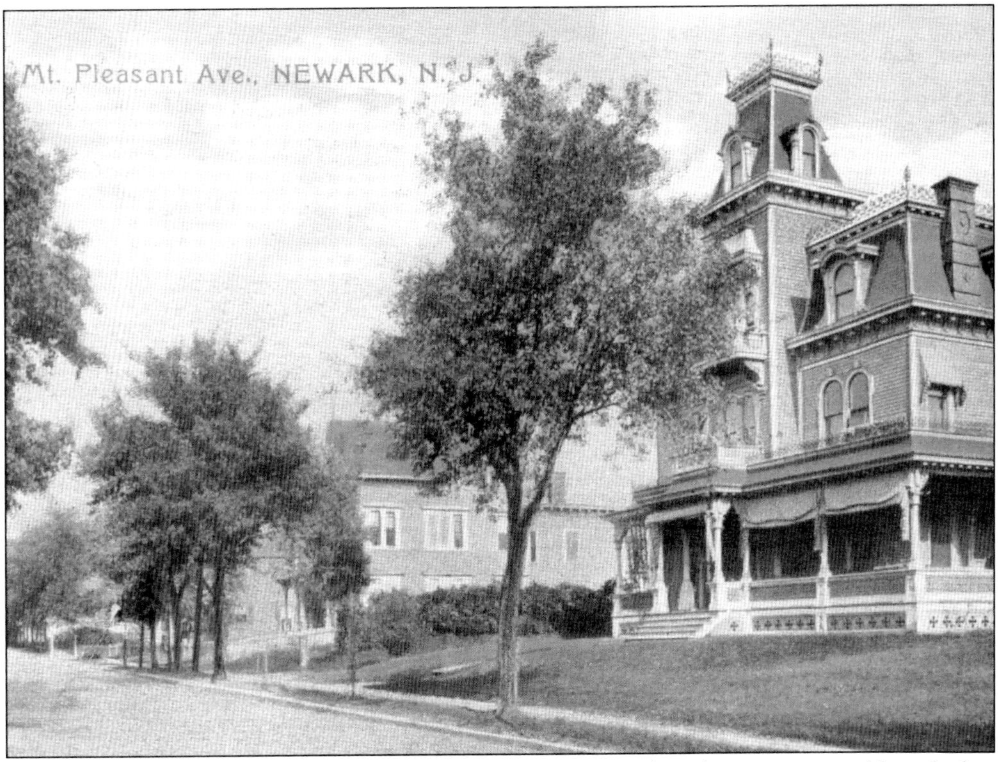

Once Newark annexed Woodside, the City laid out a street grid to eliminate some old roads that had evolved from Indian trails. Shown here is Mount Pleasant Avenue, which began around Clay Street and ran parallel to Belleville Avenue. Mount Pleasant Avenue was a very fashionable street, as evidenced by the homes shown on this postcard. (CL.)

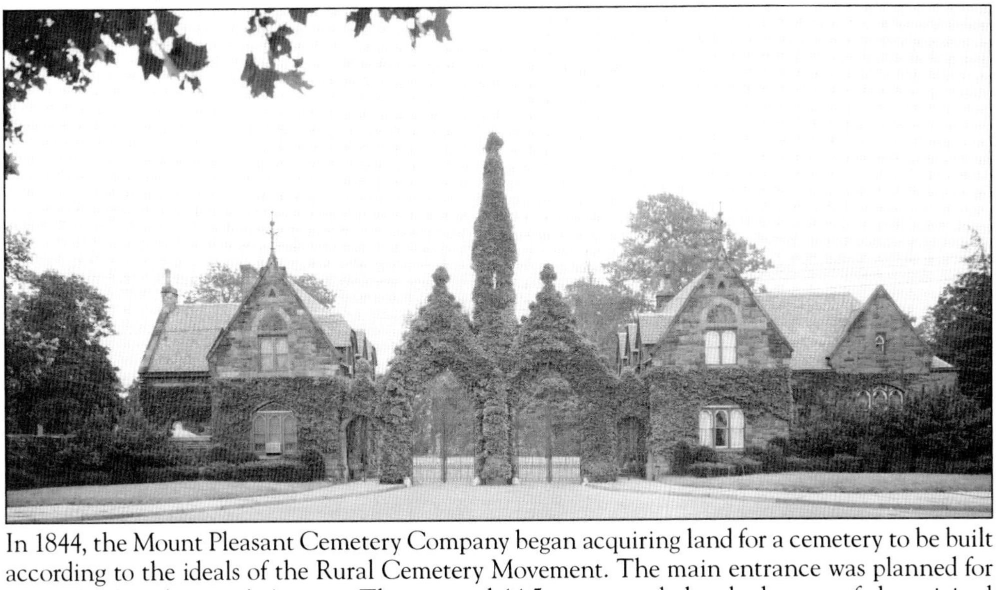

In 1844, the Mount Pleasant Cemetery Company began acquiring land for a cemetery to be built according to the ideals of the Rural Cemetery Movement. The main entrance was planned for Belleville (Washington) Avenue. The original 14.5-acre parcel absorbed many of the original Woodside estates, such as the Kembles' Cockloft Hall and Henry Herbert's The Cedars, and grew to over 32 acres. (LC.)

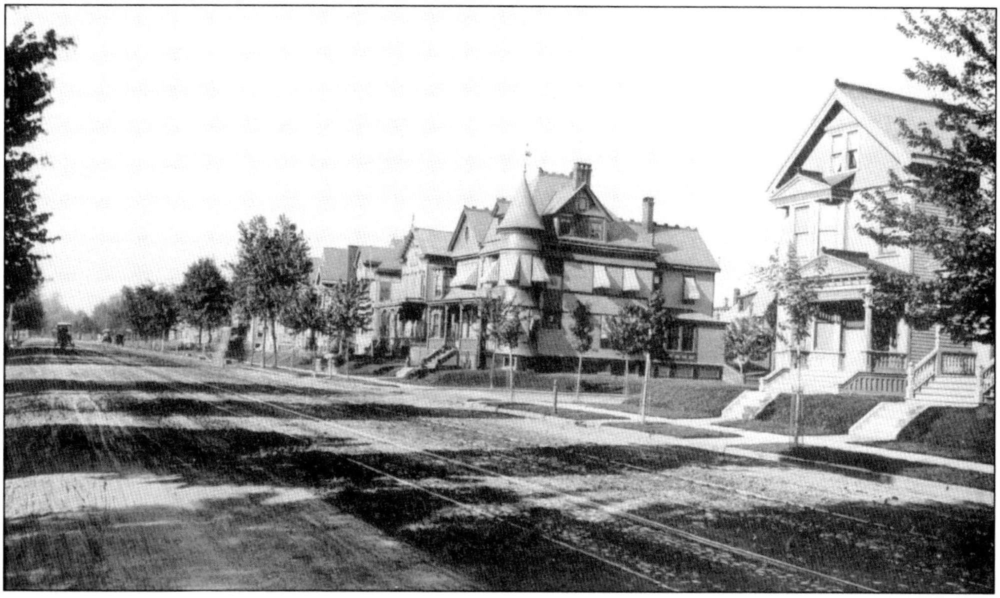

The main north-south road through Woodside was Belleville Avenue, but its name changed to Washington Avenue (now Broadway) when the City established the street grid in 1865. After annexation, the City graded the main roads and established regular transportation services, eventually laying rails for streetcars, first horse-drawn and then electric. Washington Avenue is shown above around 1892 and below around 1910. In those 20 years, the street surface improved, and there are more mature trees. (Above, NCC; below, CL.)

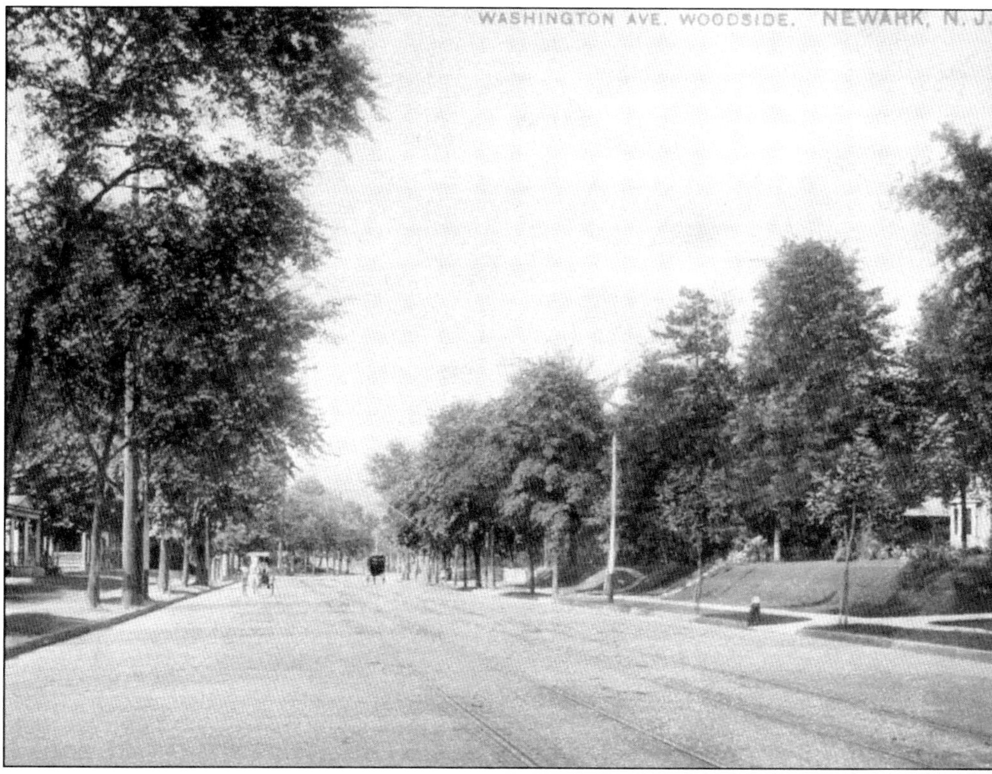

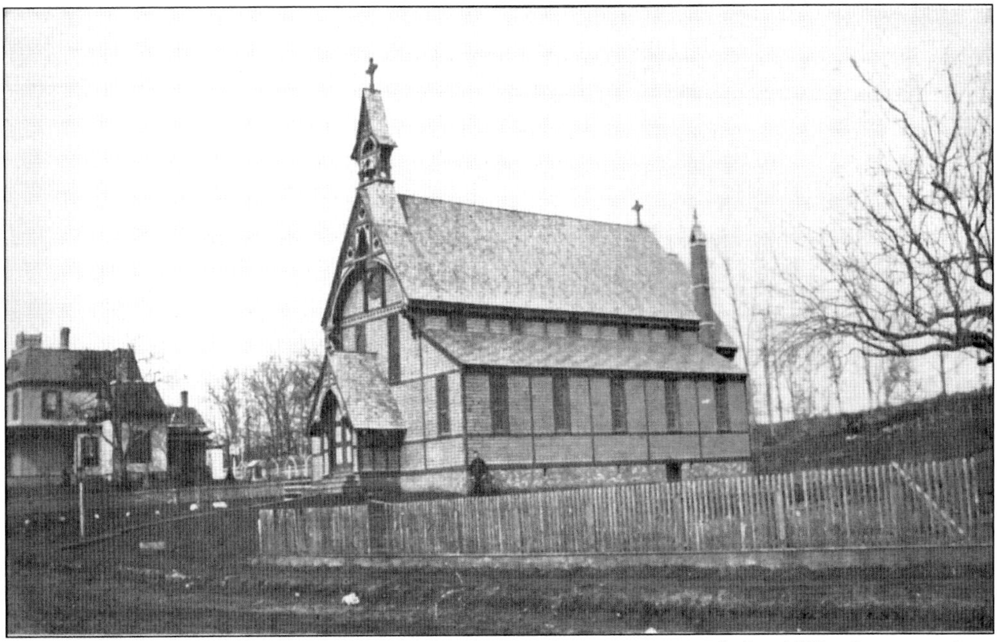

Woodside Presbyterian Church was built on Carteret Street around the 1870s. It was a plain wooden structure, the objective being to get a church built as quickly as possible. When Forest Hill was developed in the 1890s, the Heller family led the initiative to build a new church. Forest Hill Presbyterian Church opened in 1910, and the Woodside congregation abandoned its Carteret Street building and moved up the hill. (NPL.)

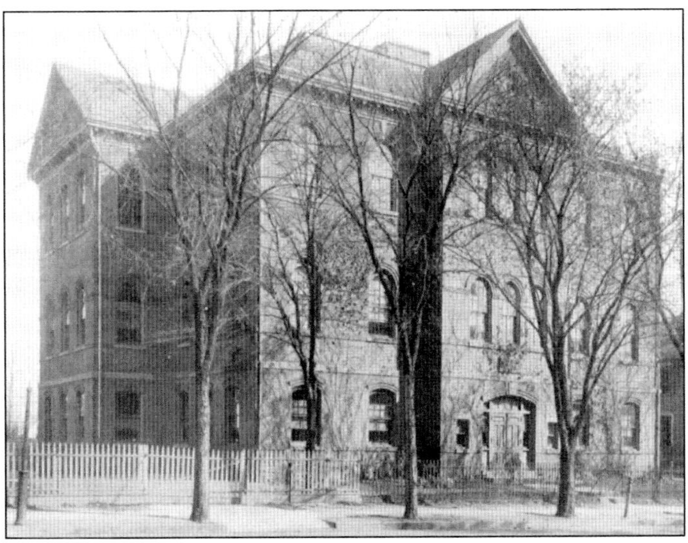

The demand for public school education was growing in the late 1800s and early 1900s. Up in Forest Hill, the Heller family was instrumental in having the Ridge Street School built. Down in Woodside, Elliott Street School had been built on Summer Avenue. Several years ago, Elliott Street School was struck by lightning and sustained structural damage so severe that this historic Victorian building had to be demolished. (CL.)

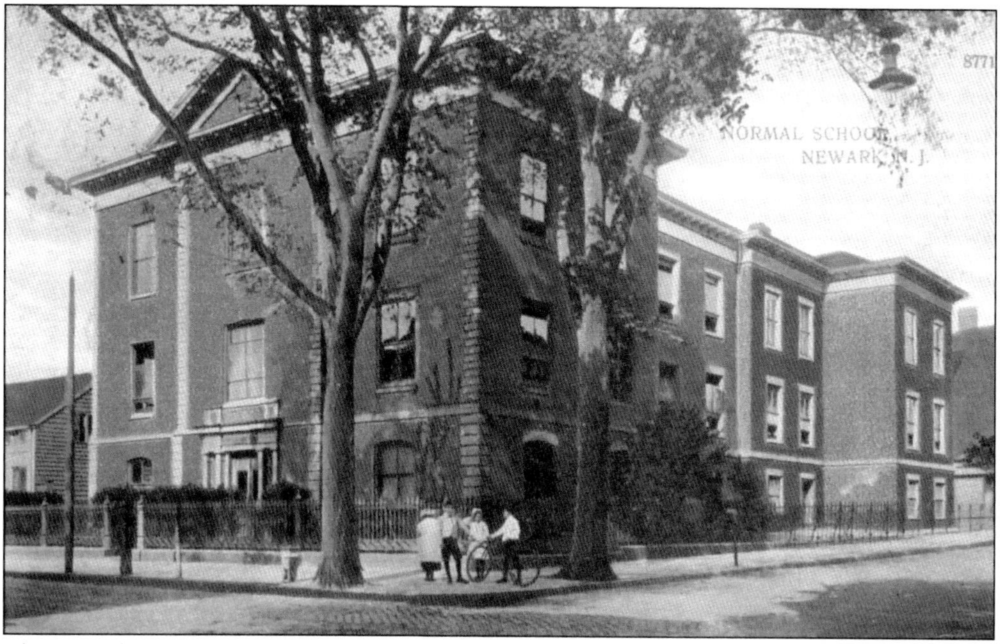

The Newark Normal School was founded in 1855 as a teacher-education college, one of the earliest in the country. The original building, shown on the above postcard, was built on the site of the Kearny Homestead. Beginning in 1863, graduates were required to teach in the Newark public schools. The Normal School relocated several times but, in 1913, was renamed New Jersey State Normal School at Newark and moved into a new building at its original location, shown below. The program gradually extended from one year to two, then three, and finally, in 1934, became a four-year college authorized to grant bachelor's degrees in education. It remained in Newark until 1958, when it moved to Union and later became Kean University. The Broadway building is now home to Newark's Technology High. (Both, CL.)

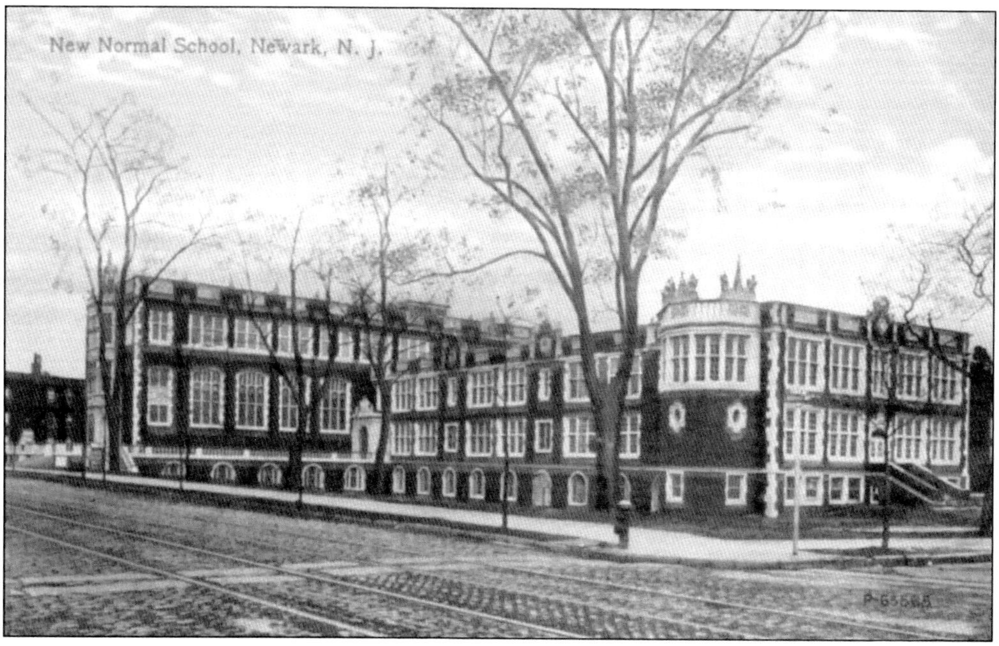

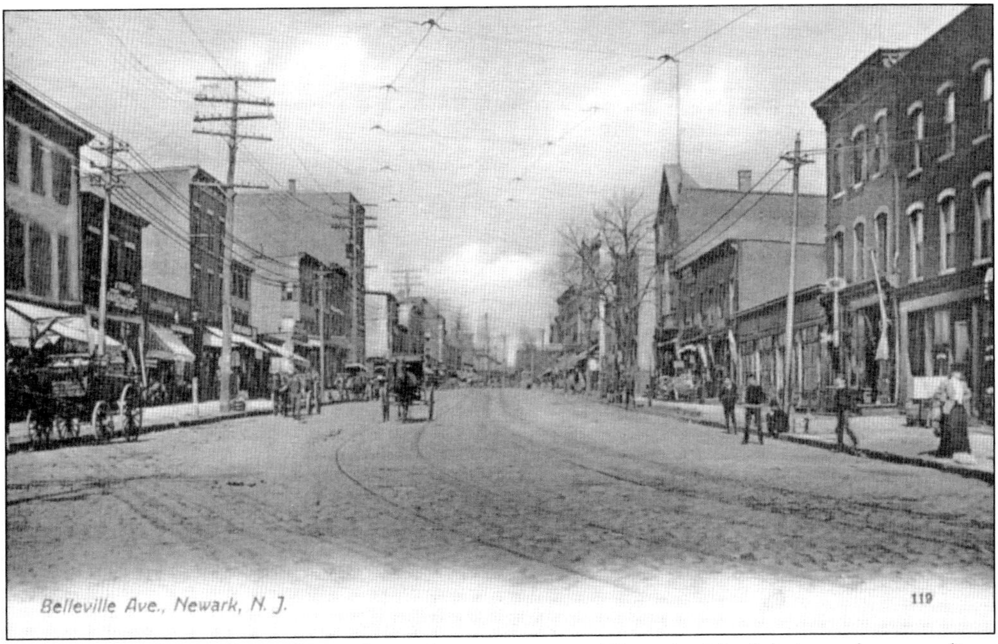

Woodsiders had a love-hate relationship with transportation. They cherished their rural surroundings but were fairly isolated until annexed by Newark. Commuting was difficult, whether for business or shopping. Even so, Woodsiders bemoaned the fact that Newark wasted no time in grading Woodside's main roads and installing streetcar tracks. And while they appreciated the new conveniences, they paid a steep price in the gradual change in Woodside's character. The 1909 postcard above shows Woodside's streets still with horse-drawn buggies and wagons; the 1909 postcard below shows streetcars on the streets of Woodside. The improved transportation prompted more manufacturers to move their operations up the Passaic River to the Woodside banks, and so began the gradual deterioration of the rural nature of Woodside. (Both CL.)

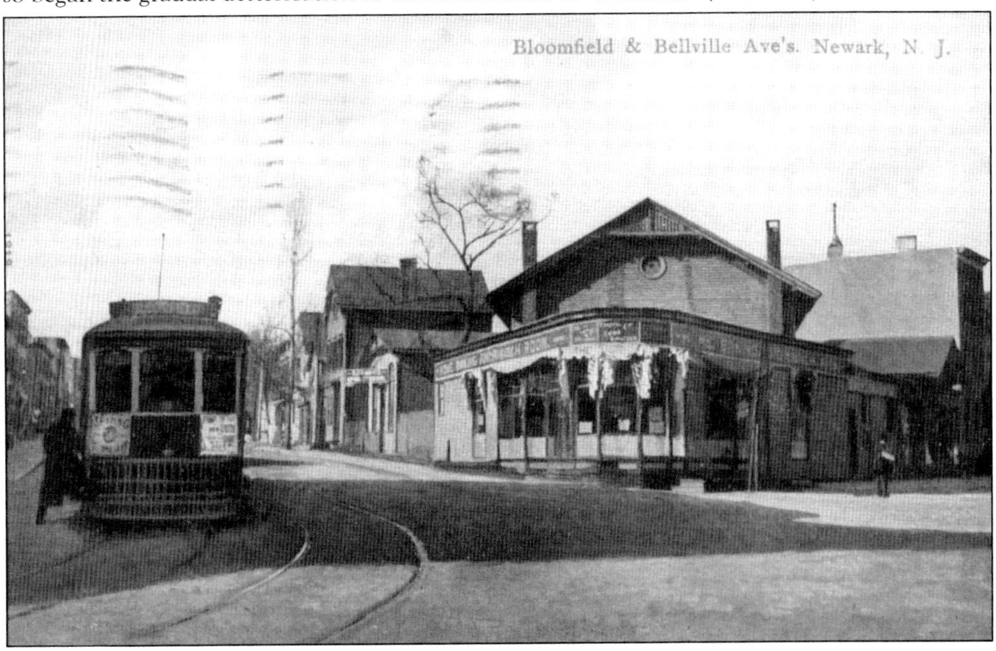

Two

From Farmland to Mansions

When the City of Newark annexed Woodside in 1871, it was during a time of great change in our country. Woodsiders might have bemoaned the changes that annexation brought, but their rural lifestyle was going to change anyway—it was inevitable. As industry established a position on Woodside's Passaic River, manufacturers took over more land, and as the air and water became polluted, the area became less desirable.

Above Mount Prospect Avenue, the farming families realized that the younger generation had been decimated by the Civil War. With the Ballantine, Clark, and Heller families making offers, they reluctantly sold the land that most of them had worked for generations.

Land acquired by Ballantine, Clark, and Heller was marketed to investors with the promise of suburban living within easy commuting distance. Mostly industrialists purchased the earlier mansions, but there were other prospective buyers as well. When life was simpler, professionals, such as attorneys and physicians, maintained home offices. But as more people required their services, it became less appealing to have all those people frequenting their houses, so these professionals established office spaces in a centralized location and bought new homes in purely residential Forest Hill. The service industry was also growing—newspapers and other printers, for example—so middle management numbers were increasing, and people could now afford to buy nice homes.

The Hellers cleverly applied the suggestion of exclusivity in their marketing materials. The Ballantine family followed their lead and, in 1899, began selling off parcels of their holdings.

Forest Hill homes were marketed through real estate offices in both Newark and New York City. Newspaper ads ran regularly on the same pages as stock market news, and by the early 1920s, most of the land previously held by the Ballantine, Clark, and Heller families had been sold and developed. Homes did not change hands frequently because Forest Hill was considered a premier residential area.

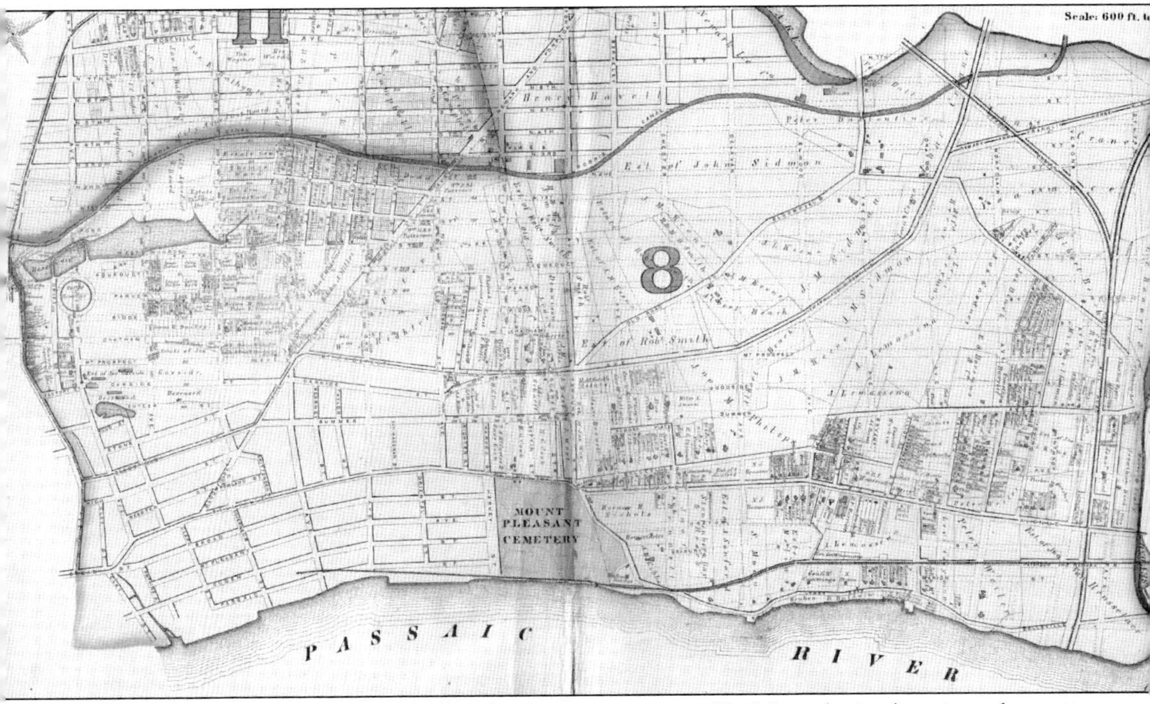

This 1873 map shows Woodside shortly after it was annexed by Newark. At that time, the entire area was still called Woodside, and while main roads are well delineated, the bulk of the land is still identified as farmland. Mount Pleasant Cemetery had been built, and the lower portion of the map shows the beginnings of a street grid. But above Belleville Avenue are only the names of the old Woodside settlers: Crane, Sidman (Sydenham), Coeyman, Keene, and Righter. It is clear where William Clark and Peter Ballantine have begun to acquire small land parcels, but the Heller or Tiffany names are not yet apparent. Branch Brook Park had not yet been created, but on the extreme left of the map is the reservoir that eventually formed the park's southern boundary, near the Orange Avenue border of the Eighth Ward, as it was known then. Bloomfield Avenue appears for the first time, as well as the Old Road to Bloomfield and Murphy's Lane. Mount Prospect Avenue is also listed as the Newark and Bloomfield Horse Rail Road. (CL.)

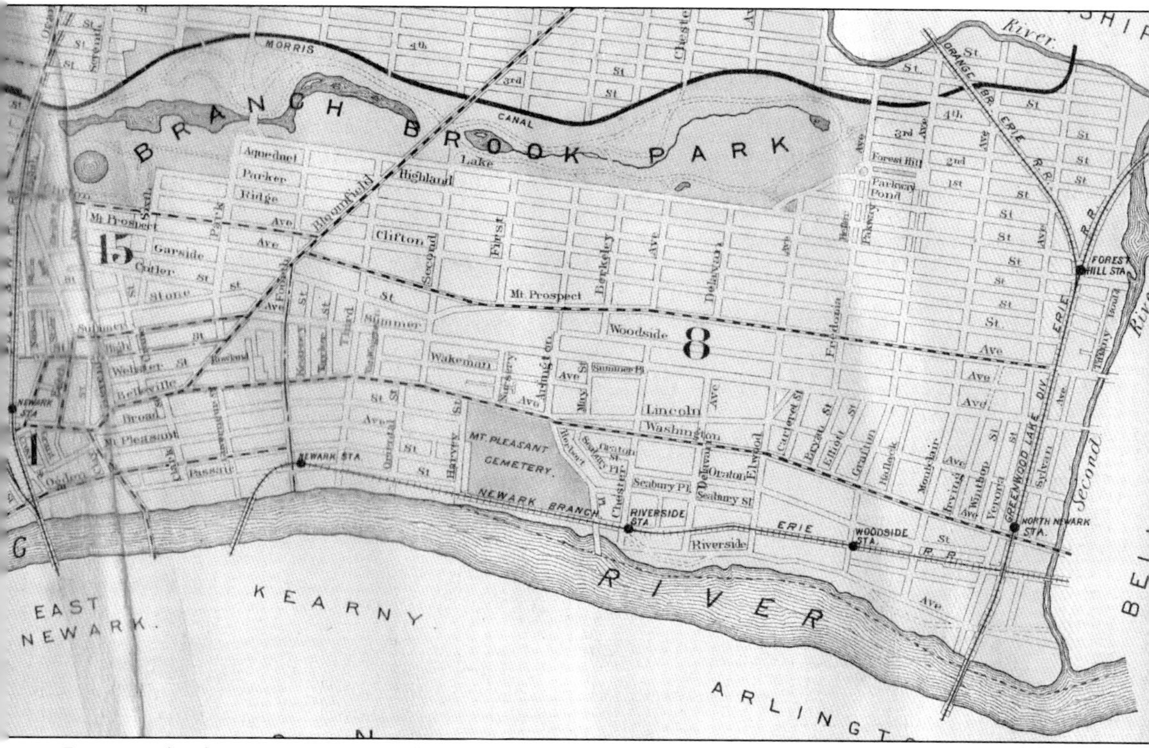

By 1910, the farms were gone, and the street grid was completed. Branch Brook Park had been laid out as far north as Heller Parkway (still shown as Fredonia Avenue here), with most of the land for the park having been sold or donated by the major landowners shown on the 1873 map (opposite page). Although the 1910 map does not include the names of property owners, the 1889 and 1901 city tax maps show large tracts being acquired by Peter Ballantine; William Clark, who named his estate New Park; a Mr. Tiffany and his business partner, Mr. Cook, who bought all of Woodside Park along the Second River; and the National Newark Land Co., which was the Hellers' real estate venture. On this c. 1910 map, the Old Road to Bloomfield and Murphy's Lane have disappeared, as has the Newark and Bloomfield Horse Rail Road. The eastern portion (shown at the bottom of the map) has more street density, while above Mount Prospect Avenue, the blocks are larger to accommodate the mansions being built there. (CL.)

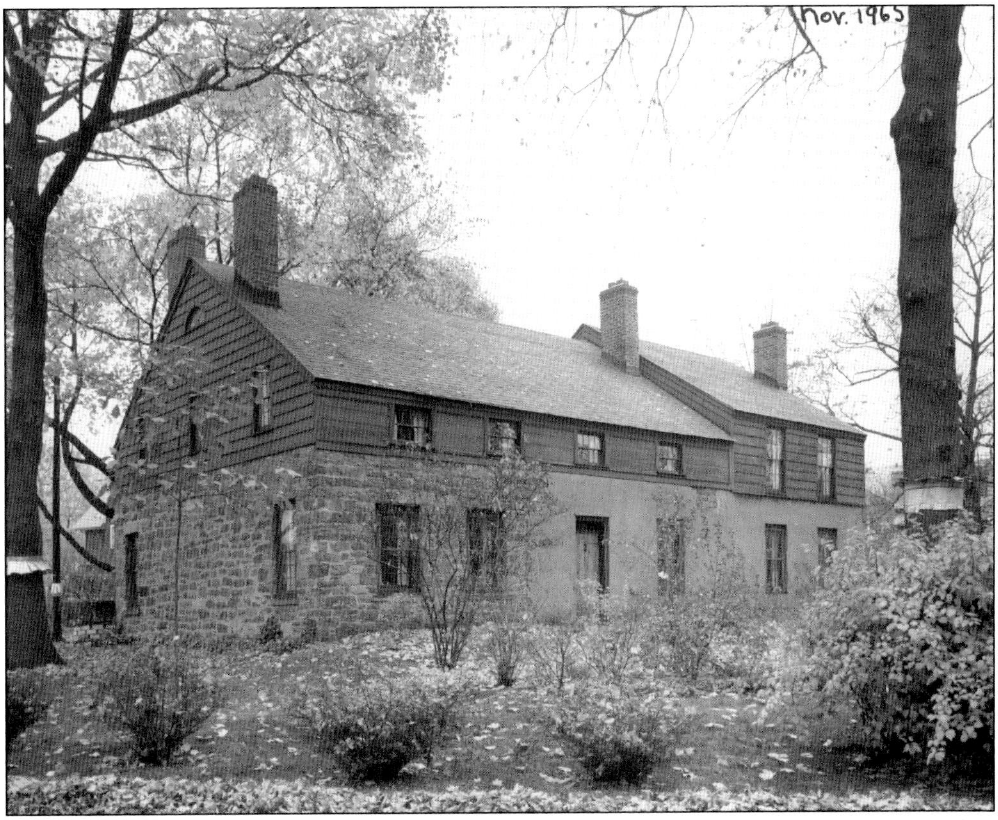

The Sydenham House, built in 1712, stands as Newark's oldest private residence. Having passed its third century mark, this 14-room farmhouse has witnessed dramatic changes in the neighborhood, from a predominantly farming community to one with architecturally significant homes and mansions. Standing sentinel on the edge of Branch Brook Park on the Old Road to Bloomfield, the house was rescued from dilapidation by Dorland J. and Elizabeth B. Henderson when they purchased it in 1954 and lovingly restored it. The builder-owners of the original farmhouse were John and Susannah Sydenham, who were married in 1711. The last of eight generations of the Sydenham family lived in the house until the 1920s, when it was sold to Dr. G. Rae Lewis. The Sydenham House was placed on the New Jersey and the National Registers of Historic Places in 1970. (Both, Francis Crespo.)

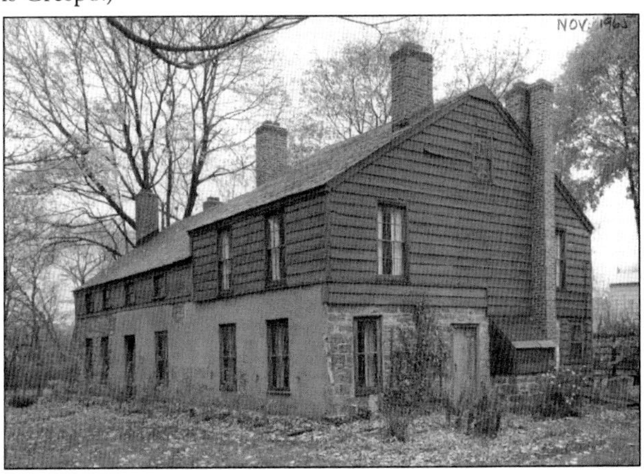

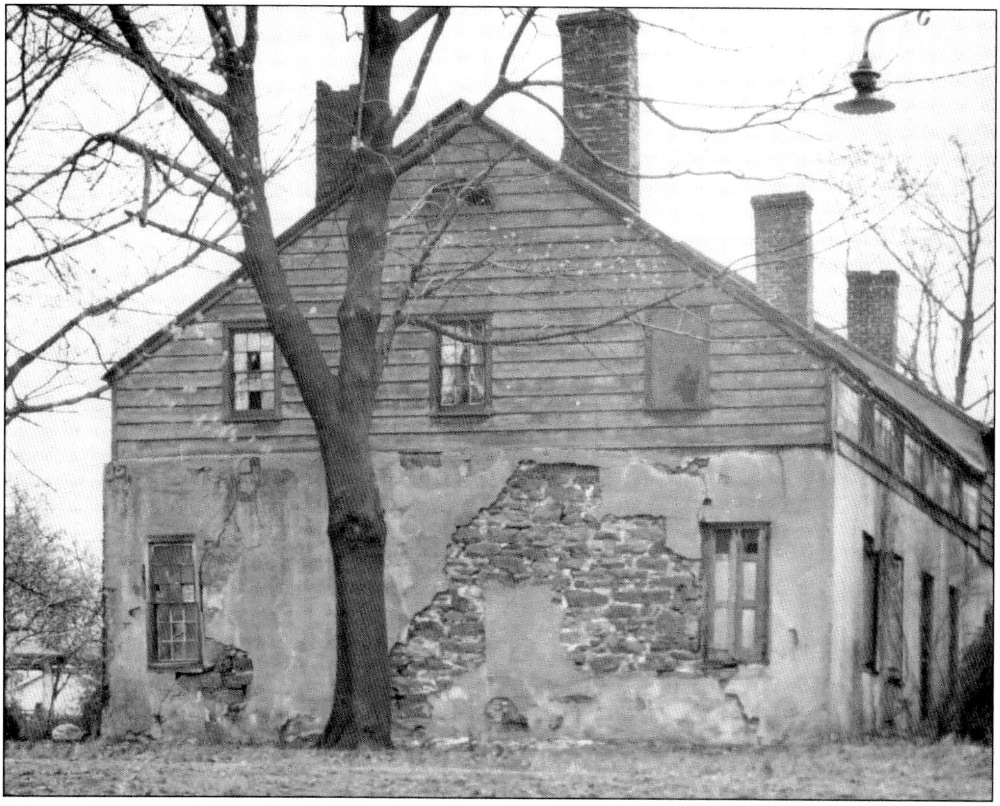

John and Susannah Handcock Sydenham eloped in 1711 but eventually received the blessing of her parents, who gifted the young couple with four acres of land in an area originally known as Watsesson. In 1712, John and Susannah built what is still known today as the Sydenham House. By the time the Hendersons purchased the house, it had become a neighborhood eyesore. Somehow, the Hendersons could see past the home's disrepair. By pouring their hearts, souls, and much sweat equity into it, D.J. and Betty transformed the wreck they had purchased into a showpiece of early-18th-century charm. Looking closely at this view of the structure, what appears to be an attached outhouse is visible at the back of the house. (Both, Francis Crespo.)

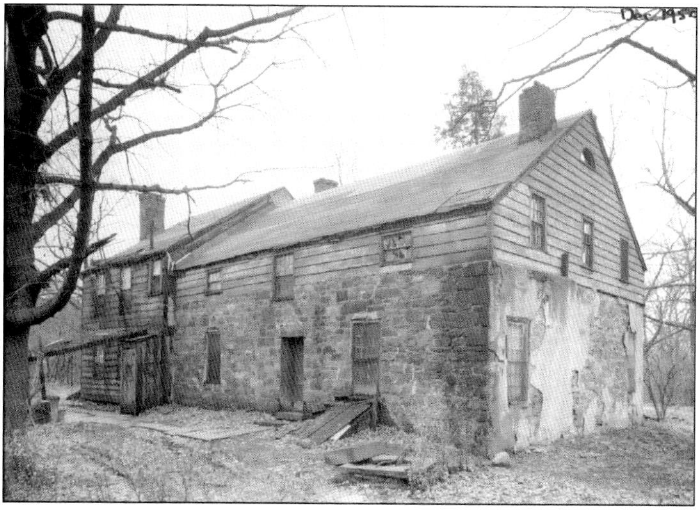

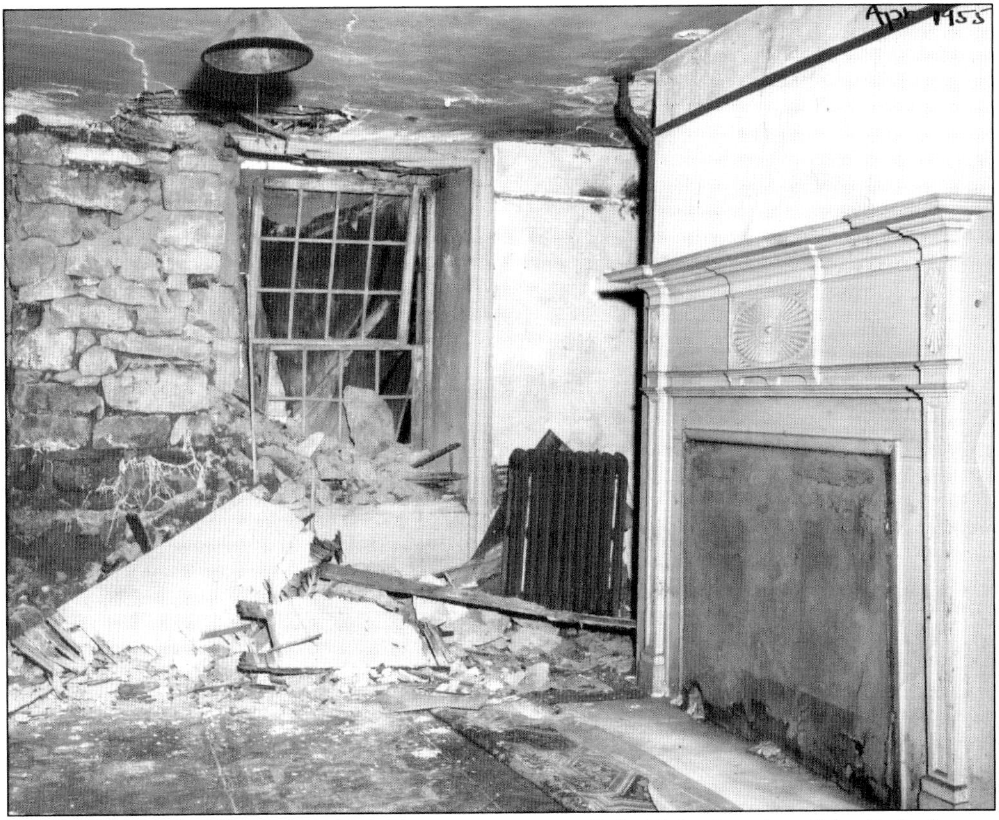

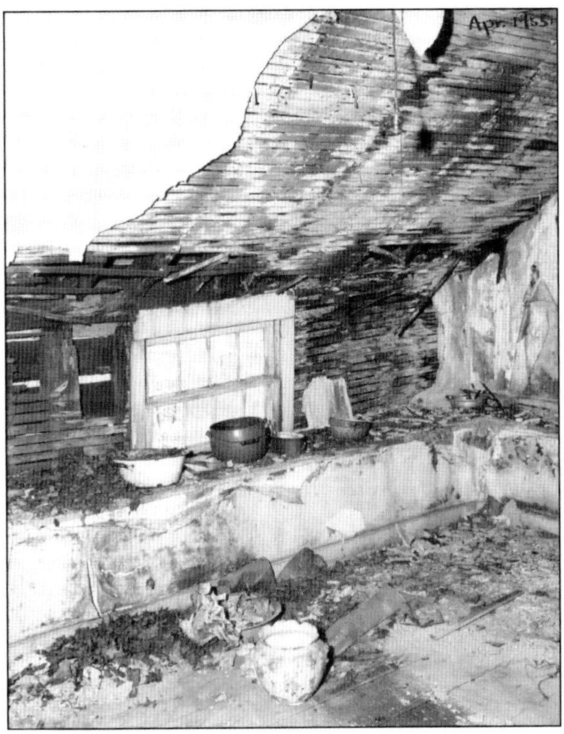

Behold the interior of the Sydenham House when purchased by the Hendersons. The above view shows the crumbling stone walls and nonexistent window glass, yet there is the architecturally significant mantle, which most likely inspired the Hendersons as they undertook their restoration. To the left, pots and pans are scattered throughout an upstairs bedroom, catching water pouring through what is left of the ceiling. Only the most dedicated of preservationists could see the potential here. The house was built of sandstone and wood, and through the efforts of the Hendersons and, beginning in 2005, Francis Crespo and Lance Drucker, further upgrades were made to the Sydenham House, always with attention paid to maintaining its historical integrity. (Both, Francis Crespo.)

Joined by their neighbor Helen Wallace (right), former president of the Newark Garden Club, Betty is shown in the image to the right enjoying a cup of tea as D.J. tends to the fireplace in their restored kitchen with its wide-plank flooring. Shown below are the original stove, coal bucket, and hot-water heater that the Hendersons inherited in 1954. While a good cup of tea could be brewed here, this room was one of the features that needed significant upgrading. D.J. kept meticulous notes on the restoration, including the gallons of paint remover used, the storm doors built, the windows reglazed, and the hundreds of structural repairs. Betty made Irish linen curtains for the windows to hang on wooden brackets fashioned by D.J.. Together, D.J. and Betty became Newark's most devoted preservation couple, demonstrating through their pioneering spirit that the 18th century still has a place in present-day Newark. (Both, Francis Crespo.)

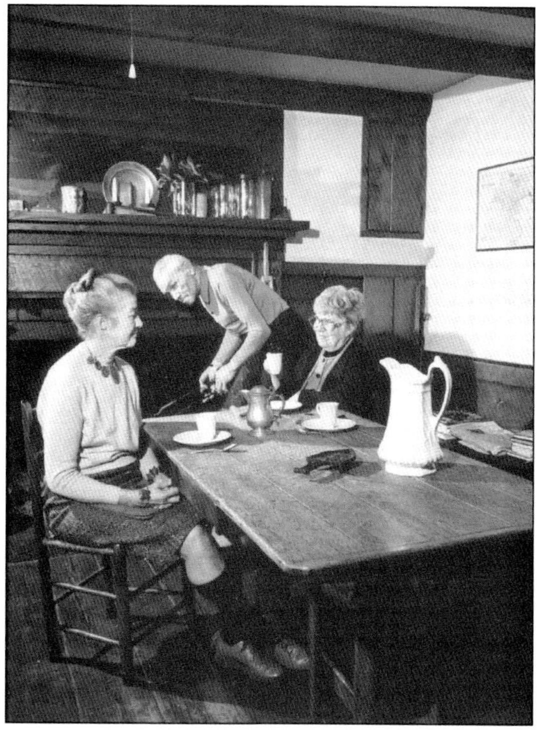

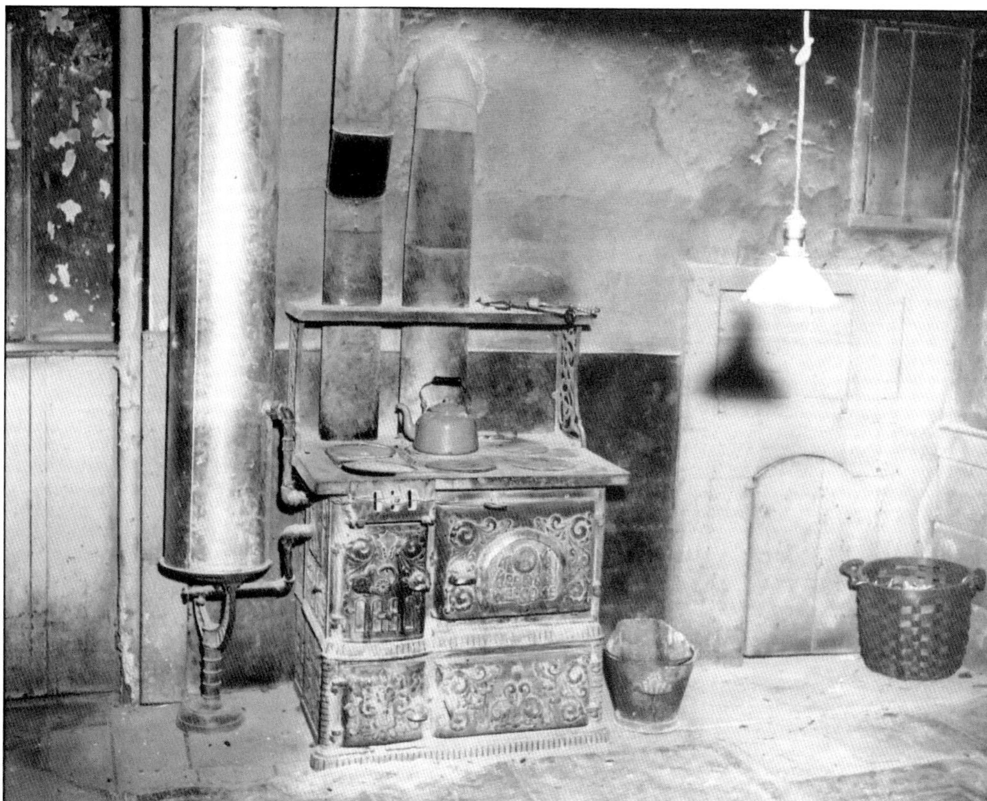

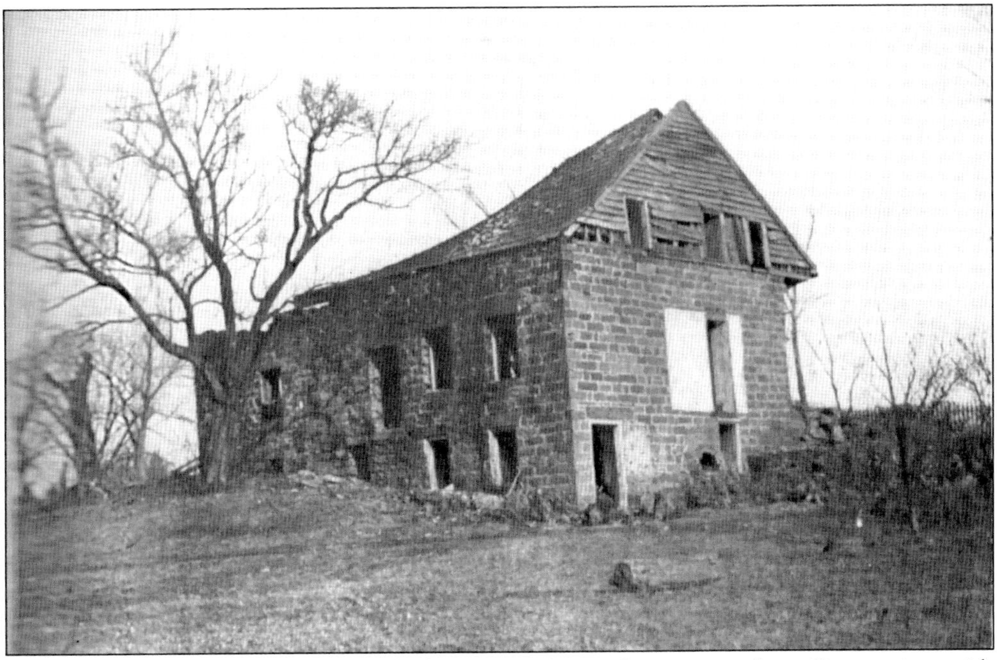

There were Cranes in Newark from the beginning. Jasper Crane came from Connecticut with Robert Treat in 1666 and was among the first to receive a land grant. As his descendants multiplied, they received more land, eventually reaching north to the Second River. The 1873 map on page 22 shows extensive landholdings by the Estate of Isaiah Crane. The Hellers purchased most of that land. The photograph above shows the Crane homestead, which dated to 1760. When it was demolished, the building stones were used to construct the Forest Hill Presbyterian Church. The c. 1924 photograph below shows the last Crane family to live in Newark; the child in the forefront was Constance Ward Crane, whose Forest Hill home was situated on land that was formerly part of the Crane farm. (Above, NPL; below, CL.)

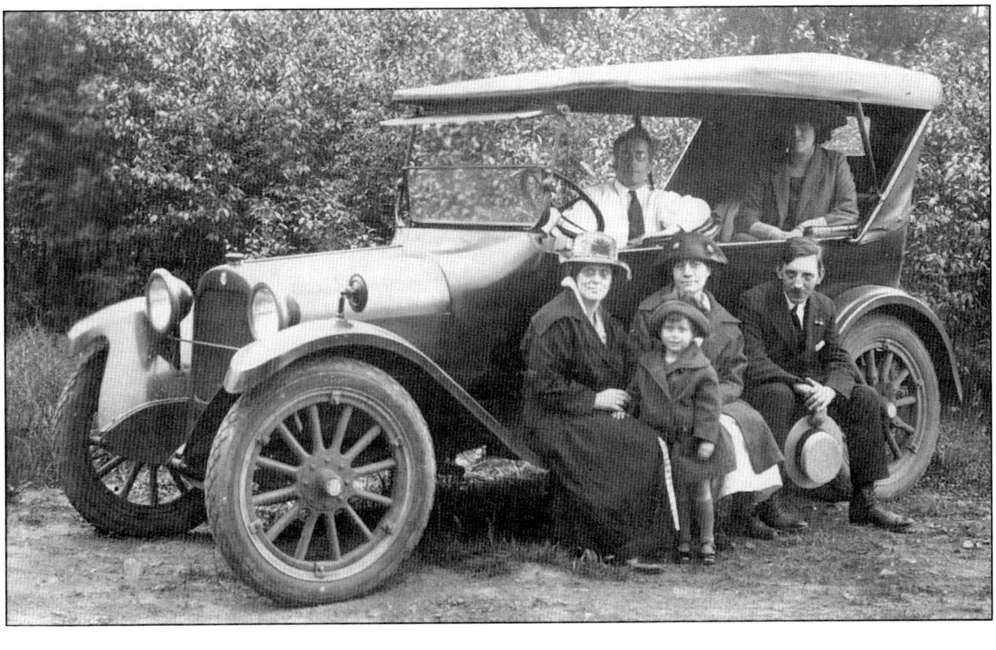

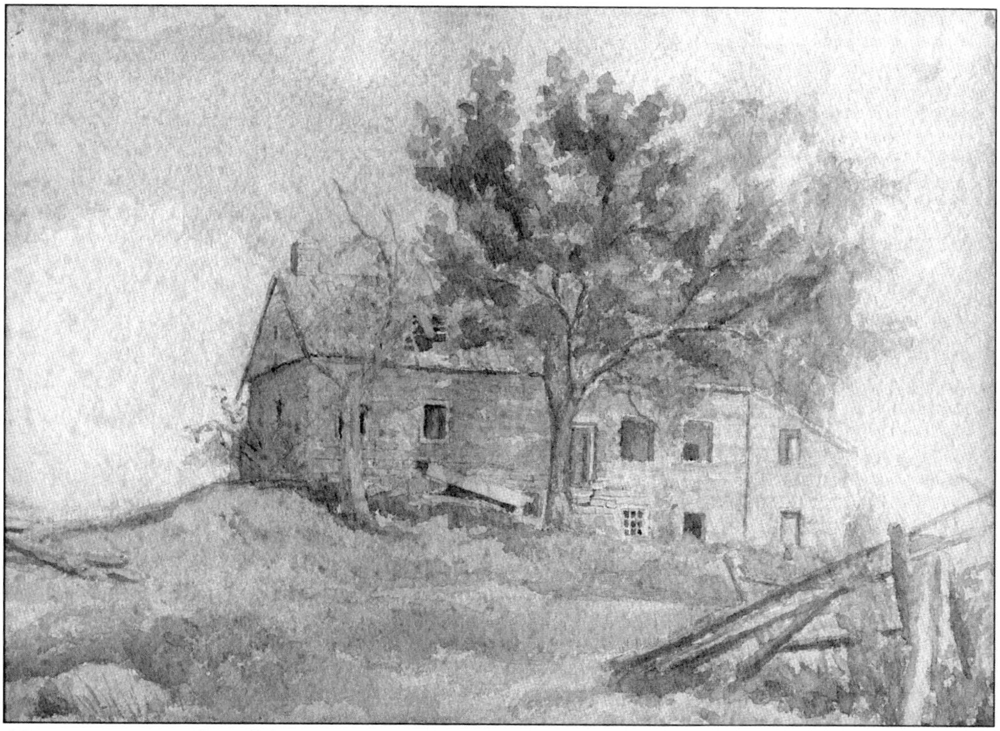

Above is a watercolor of the Crane homestead by S.W. Ward, a relative of Constance W. Crane. The Wards were also among the original Newark settlers, and Connie was proud to claim ancestry from two of the original Newark families. Connie was a very talented artist, having graduated from Newark Arts High School and the Newark School of Fine and Industrial Arts, where she later taught. During World War II, she served in the US Navy and drafted topographical maps. Later, Connie was a freelance illustrator for Norcross Cards and worked as an art therapist at Overbrook Hospital. She also volunteered at the New Jersey Historical Society, working on the restoration and preservation of old maps. Connie lived in Forest Hill until 2004, when she moved full-time to Long Beach Island to concentrate on her painting. (Both, CL.)

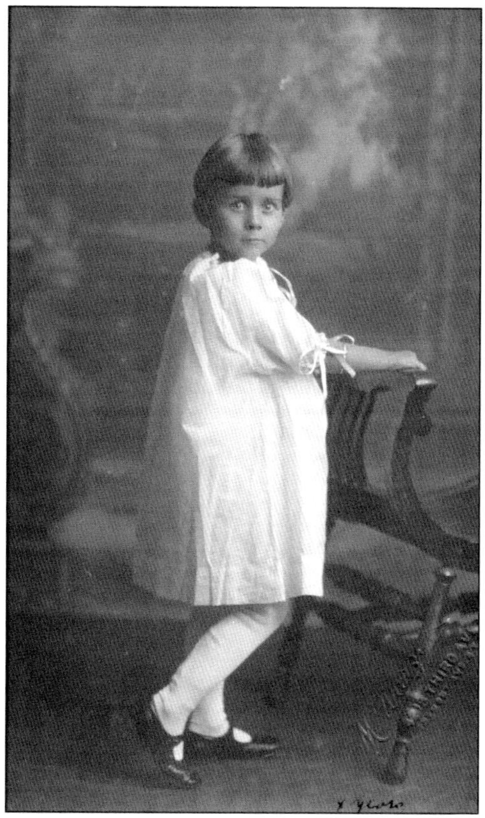

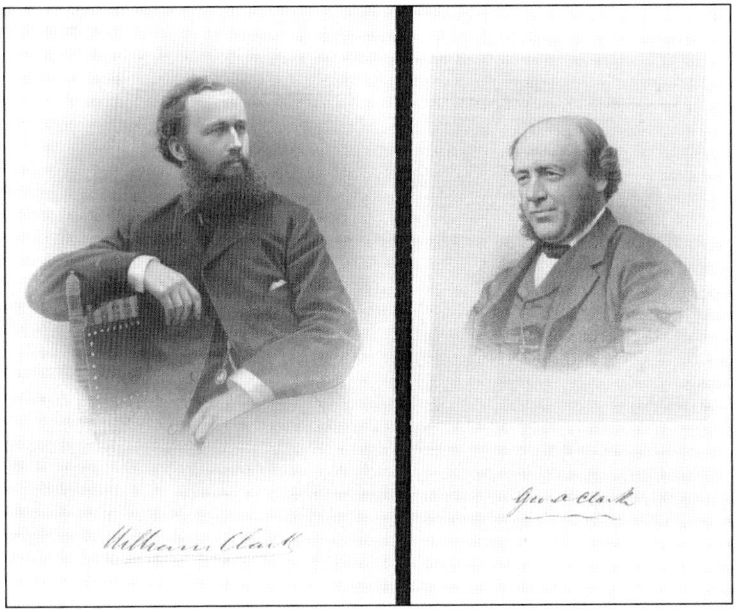

The Clark Mansion is a symbol of the grandeur and wealth representative of Newark in the late 1800s and early 1900s. The Clark family had been spooling thread in Scotland since 1812. The eldest son, George A. Clark (born in 1823), came to Newark in 1855 as an agent for the Clark factory. Joined by his brother William, they capitalized on the demand in America for sewing machine thread. (CL.)

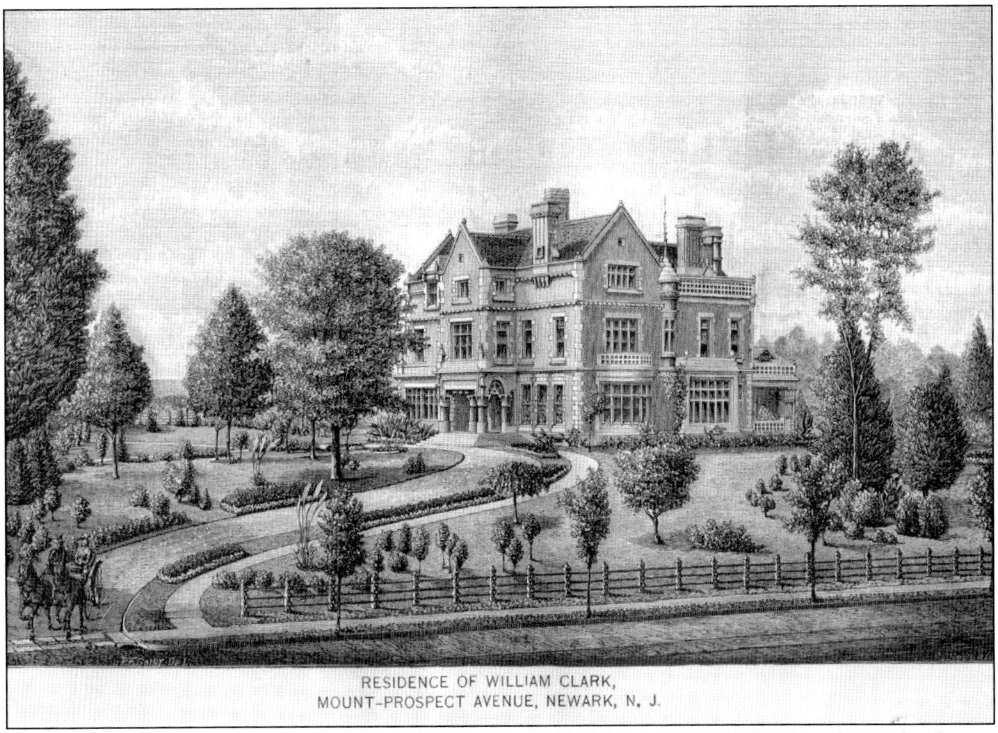

After George's sudden death in 1873, William retained William Halsey Wood to design his home at 346 Mount Prospect Avenue. Built in the Jacobean style, its historical integrity is still evident. Completed in 1879, the 28-room mansion retains its original wood paneling and fireplaces, as well as its imposing staircase with a magnificent leaded-glass window. The Clark Mansion was placed on the New Jersey and National Registers of Historic Places in 1977. (CL.)

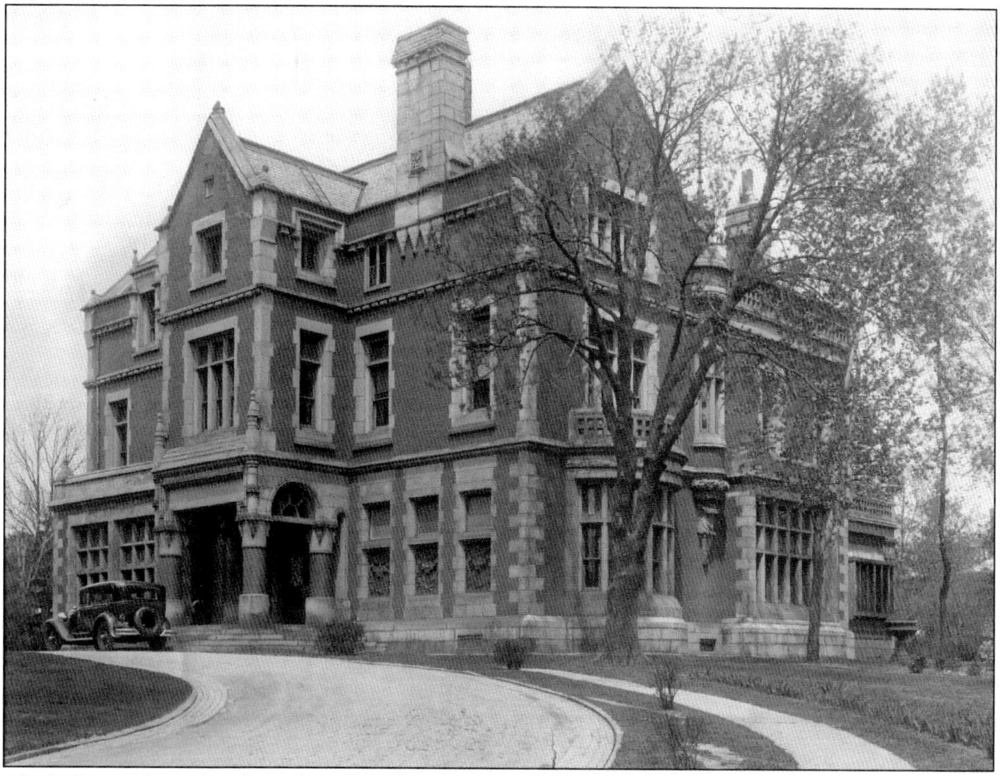

Clark descendants lived in the mansion until 1912, when it was sold to a member of the Heller family. It remained a private residence until 1924, when it became home to the exclusive Prospect Hill Country Day School. Its intricately carved staircase was a popular spot for photographs. On the eve of its 50th anniversary, the school closed in 1973 due to dwindling enrollment and financial considerations. (NPL.)

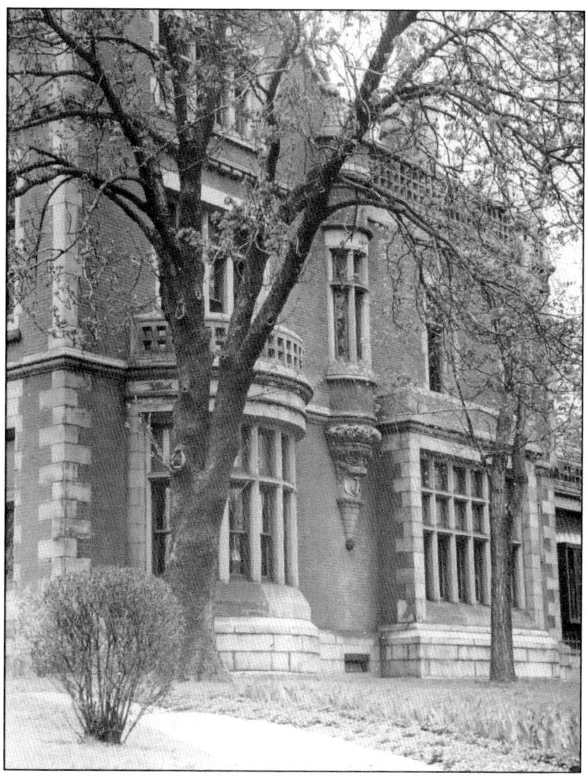

William Clark sent architect William Halsey Wood to Scotland to study its castles. This exterior photograph is evidence that the opulence of Scottish castles was not lost on the architect. Materials were even shipped from abroad for use in the home's construction. Shortly thereafter, Wood would become the architect for the 1890 First Baptist Peddie Memorial Church in downtown Newark. Another of his clients was Andrew Carnegie. (NPL.)

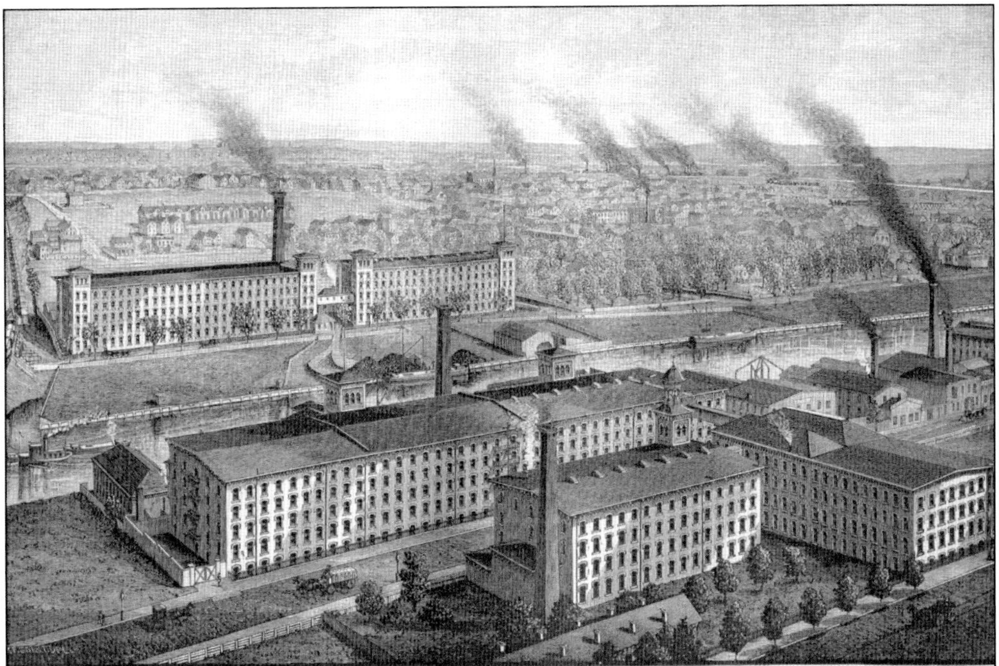

WORKS OF THE CLARK THREAD CO.,
NEWARK, N. J.

The Civil War brought increased demand for cotton thread and caused the Clarks to open a larger factory on Bridge Street, employing 1,000 workers by 1870. After George's death, William took over the operations and expanded, with factories on the opposite Newark and East Newark shores of the Passaic River. The above engraving is dated around 1915. Clark Thread introduced many innovations to sewing thread, including the one developed by George in 1866 and marketed as Our New Thread, or ONT. The phenomenal success of ONT catapulted the Clarks to become the largest manufacturer of cotton sewing thread in the country. The Clark Thread Company thrived until the 1930s, when labor and operating costs necessitated a move to Atlanta. Eventually, a merger with the J&P Coates Company resulted in Coates & Clark, Inc. In 1947, Newark's factory closed in favor of the Georgia operations. (Both, CL.)

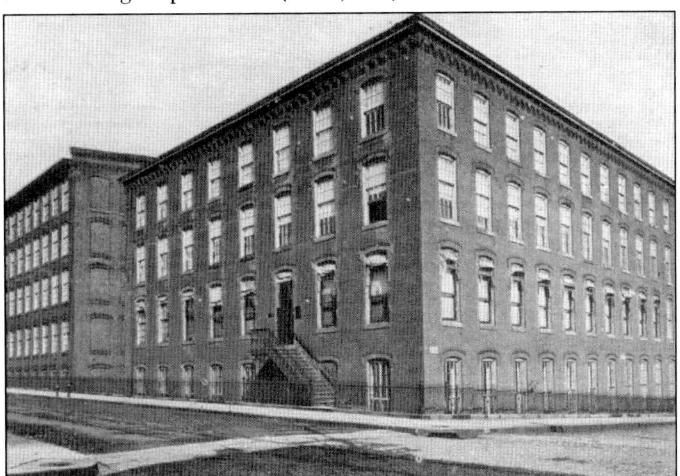

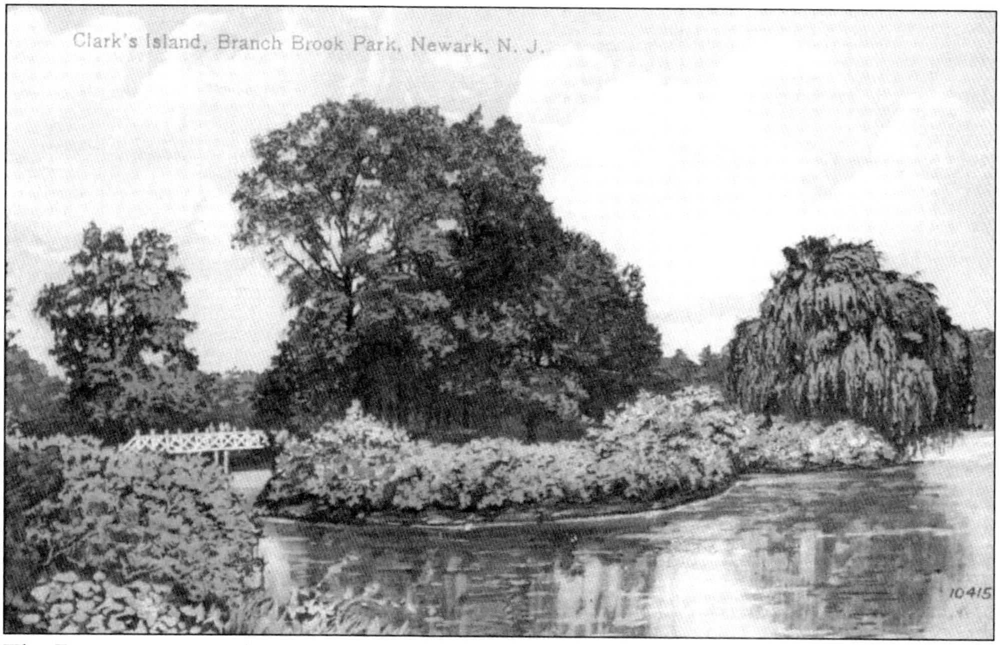

The Essex County Park Commission began development of Branch Brook Park in June 1895. Large landholders from the Forest Hill neighborhood donated much of the land included in the park. The Clark family gave a significant tract of land for the Middle and Northern Divisions of the park. Other prominent families who gave their land for the park included the Hellers and Ballantines as well as Z.M. Keen and William A. Righter. Tiffany & Co. also donated land adjacent to its silver factory. Pictured above and below are two views of Clark's Island, which was named to recognize the generosity of the extensive lands given by the Clark family. In the photograph below, the rustic bridge to Clark's Island is an example of the pastoral ambiance envisioned for the park. (Both, CL.)

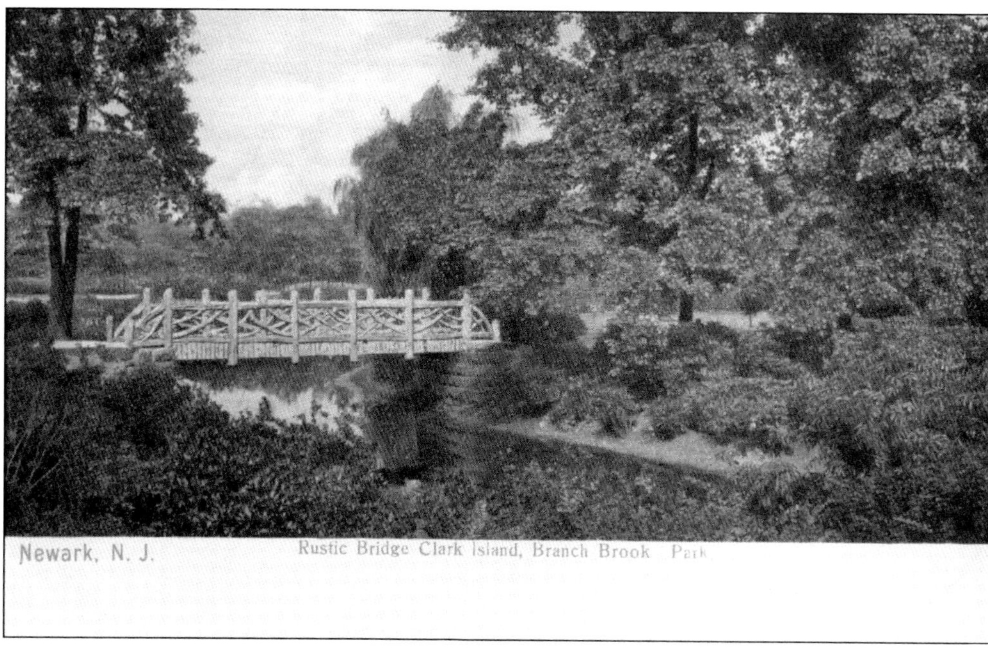

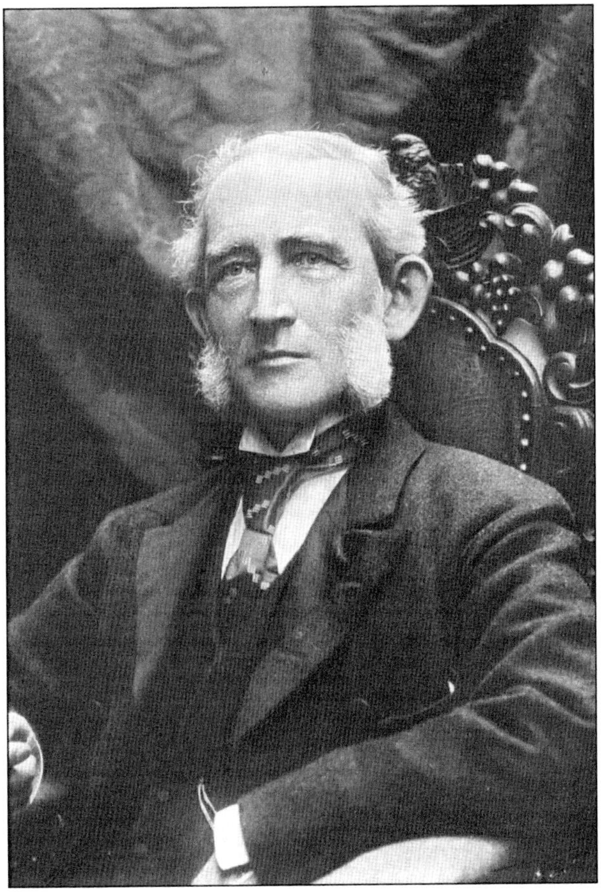

Robert F. Ballantine was the son of Scottish immigrant Peter Ballantine, who started the P. Ballantine & Sons Brewery in Newark in 1841. By the 1860s, the factories covered whole city blocks in Newark's Ironbound neighborhood. Robert served as a member of the Essex County Park Commission from 1901 to 1905 during the construction of Branch Brook Park and facilitated large donations of family land for the park. (NPL.)

Robert's most significant contribution to Forest Hill was the donation of a grand entrance into Branch Brook Park. In 1899, the Ballantine Gates were designed by Carrere & Hastings, architects of Branch Brook Park's Sand Court and Octagon Shelters and known nationally for their design of the New York Public Library. The architects drew on Scottish castles for inspiration. The $27,895.23 cost represented a small fortune at that time. (CL.)

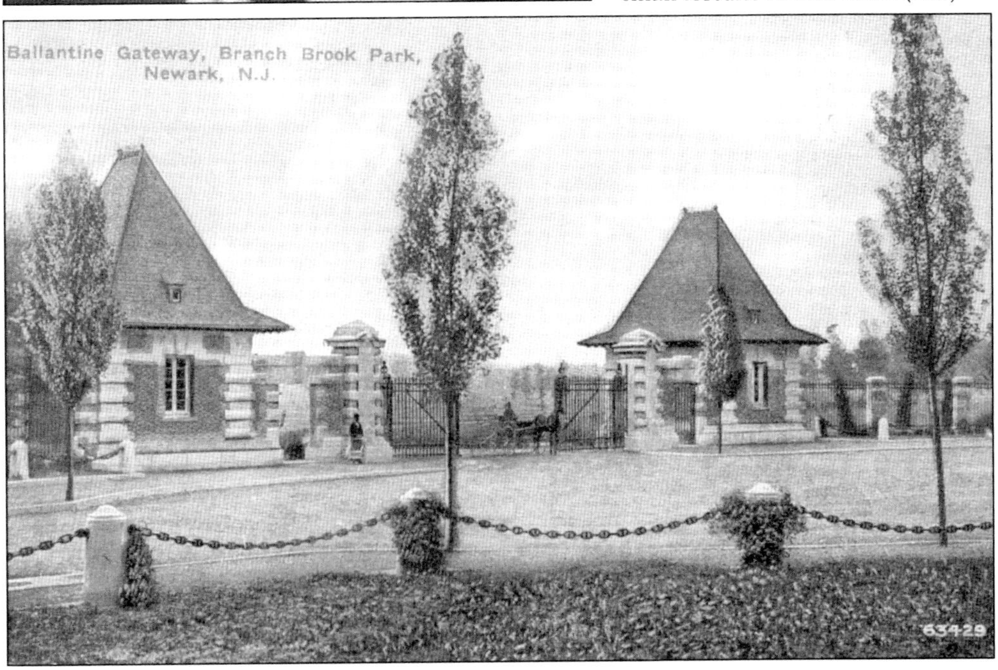

The Ballantines never built in Forest Hill, preferring to live near their plant. The Ballantine House on Washington Park is now part of the Newark Museum. In 1985, the US Department of the Interior designated it the first National Historic Landmark in the City of Newark. Designed in 1885 by architect George Edward Harney in the Renaissance style, the house is constructed of Philadelphia pressed brick and Wyoming sandstone. (NPL.)

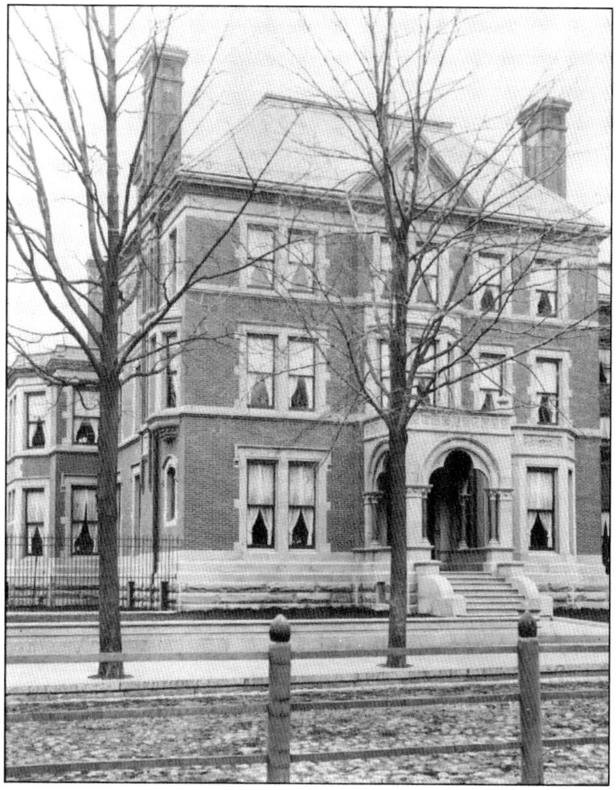

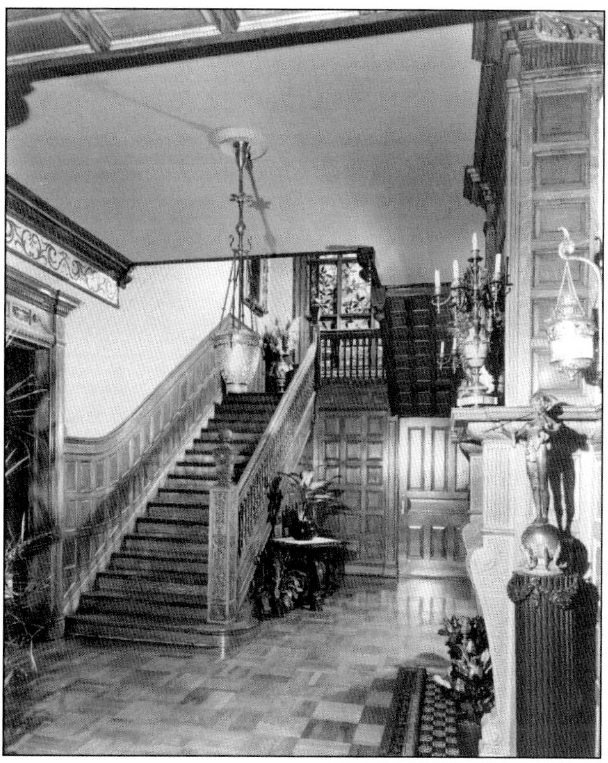

The entrance hallway is dominated by a five-foot-wide grand staircase backlit by a soaring stained-glass window comprised of 12 panels in the Japanesque style popularized during the Aesthetic Movement. Facing west, this window magnifies the setting sun with streams of jewel-colored light featuring turquoise and lavender. The hallway also features a Renaissance-inspired massive oak mantelpiece bearing the initial *B* in an oval cabochon at the center. (NPL.)

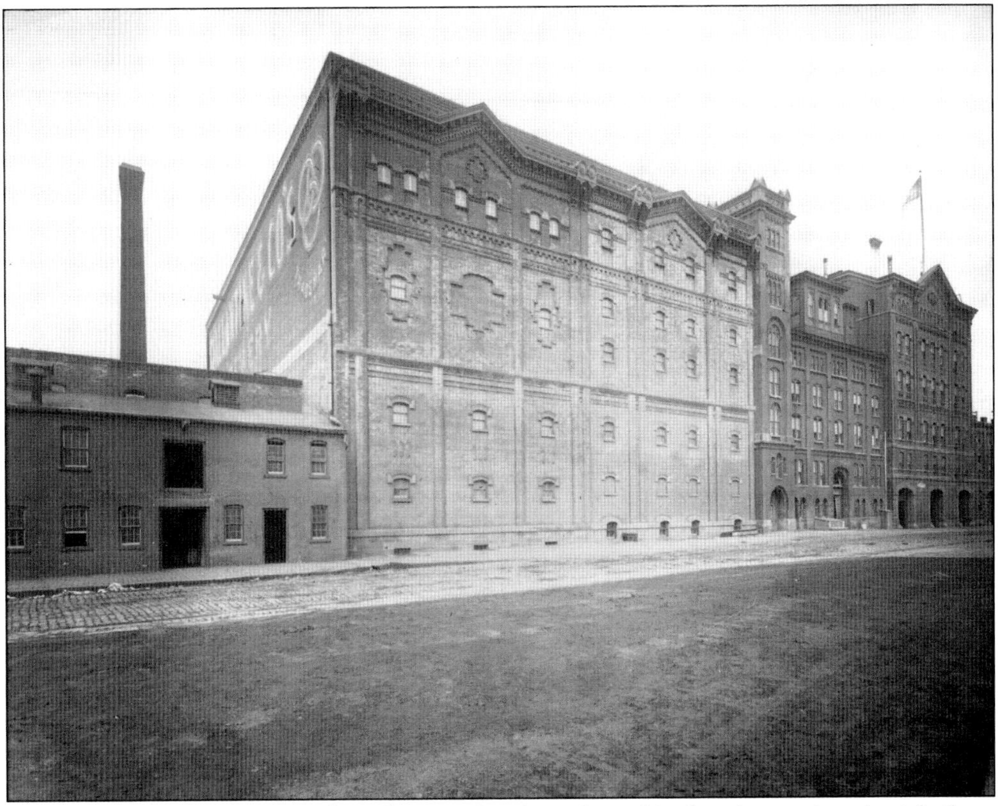

The Ballantine Brewery (above) in the city's Ironbound neighborhood contributed mightily to the rapid industrialization of Newark at the end of the 19th century. Breweries contributed to Newark's importance as a manufacturing city as many other brewers came to Newark, attracted by its pure water supply. As the brewing business expanded, the city's population grew dramatically from 17,000 in 1840 to over 105,000 in 1870 with the first wave of European immigrants. The three rings representing purity, body, and flavor became the trademark for Ballantine Beer & Ale. Deliveries from the Ballantine Brewery in horse-drawn wagons, such as the one shown below, were a common sight. (Both, NPL.)

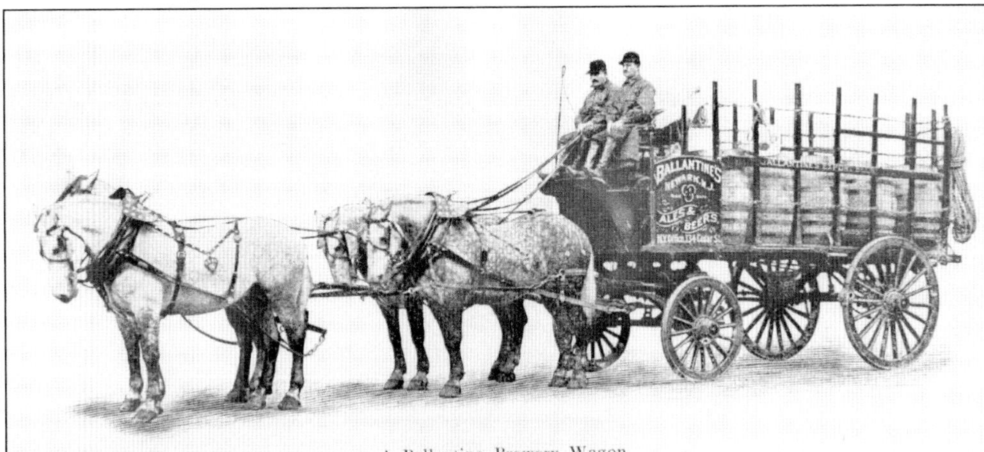

A Ballantine Brewery Wagon.

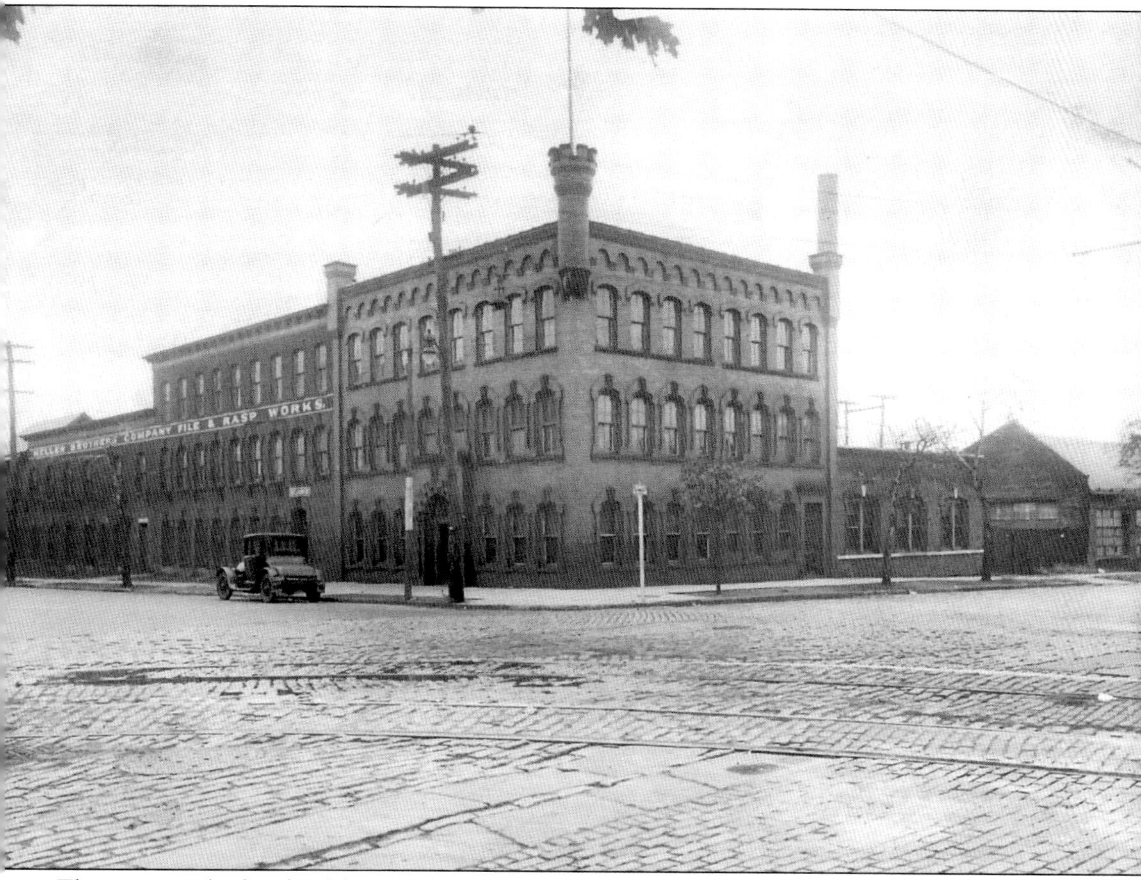

The name on the facade of this 1874 building, which still stands on the northeast corner of Mount Prospect and Verona Avenues, was Heller Brothers Company File & Rasp Works. Patriarch Elias G. Heller gradually acquired land along Verona Avenue and built more factories, including the Heller Brothers Steel Mill and the Cory and Heller Wallpaper Manufactory. The Hellers also constructed an airfield, where some of the earliest US Air Mail planes would land. But there were problems with worker turnover because North Newark was still remote from where their employees lived. So Elias Heller, together with John F. McLagan and James Dodge, formed the Woodside Improvement Company to purchase property and develop workers' housing. This venture eventually disintegrated, and McLagan continued on his own as a developer. Elias Heller and his sons proceeded to establish a series of real estate companies to acquire land and develop housing. In 1885, the North Newark Land Company was formed to focus on developing workers' housing in the Verona Avenue area. (NPL.)

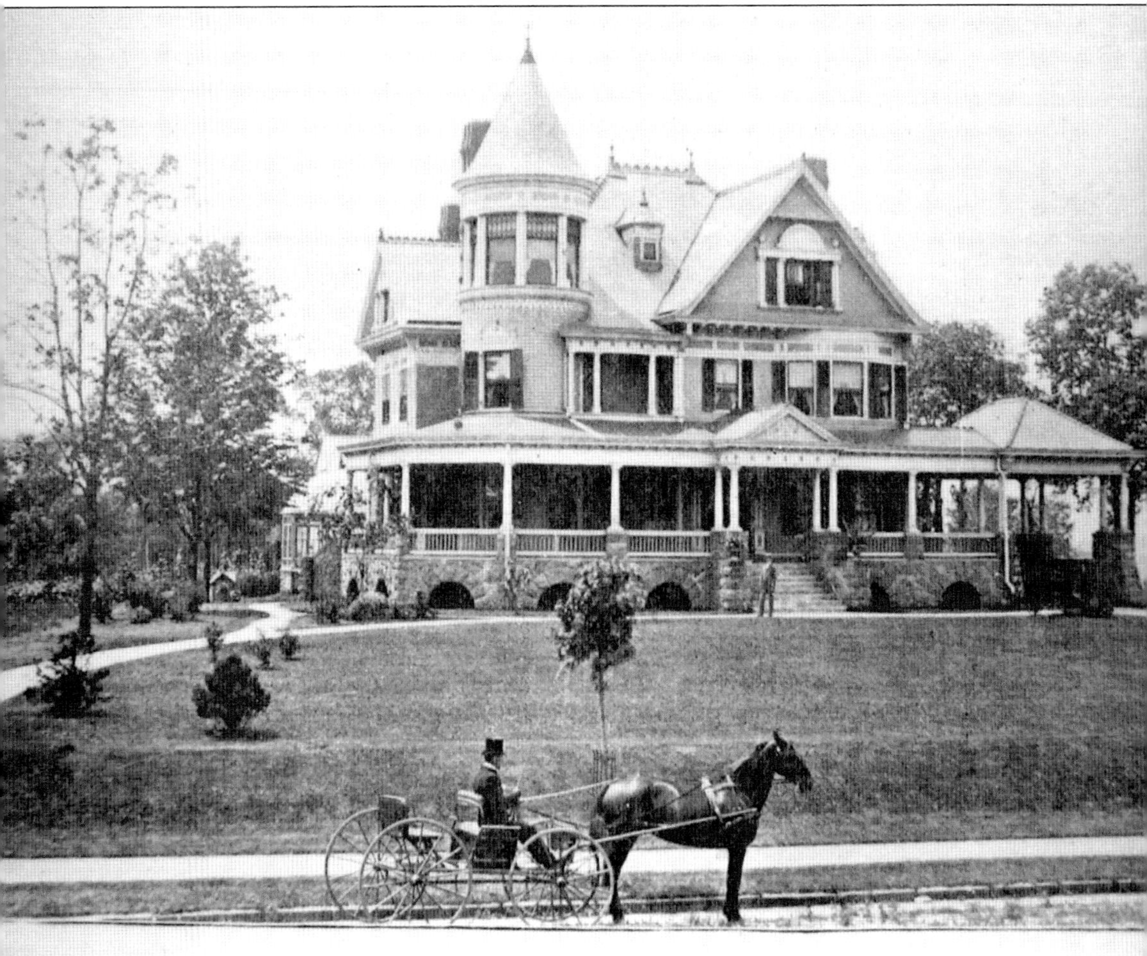

RESIDENCE OF ELIAS G. HELLER, ON ELWOOD AVENUE, FOREST HILL.

The Hellers were the first to employ the name *Forest Hill*, using it to market properties they had developed. In 1890, the Hellers formed the Forest Hill Association and, in 1894, the Forest Hill Land Company. Then, in 1909, they organized the Forest Hill Company and, in 1918, the Forest Hill Estates. In 1913, youngest son Arthur Heller formed Clark Estates to acquire a large parcel of the land held by the Estate of William Clark, subdividing it into lots and either selling the land or building homes to be sold. Arthur Heller kept the Clark Mansion for his own residence. The spectacular structure in the above photograph was the home of Paul Heller, who was the oldest of the Heller sons and who assumed leadership of the family businesses. Located on Elwood Avenue, the mansion was continuously occupied by Hellers until it was destroyed by fire in the 1940s. (CL.)

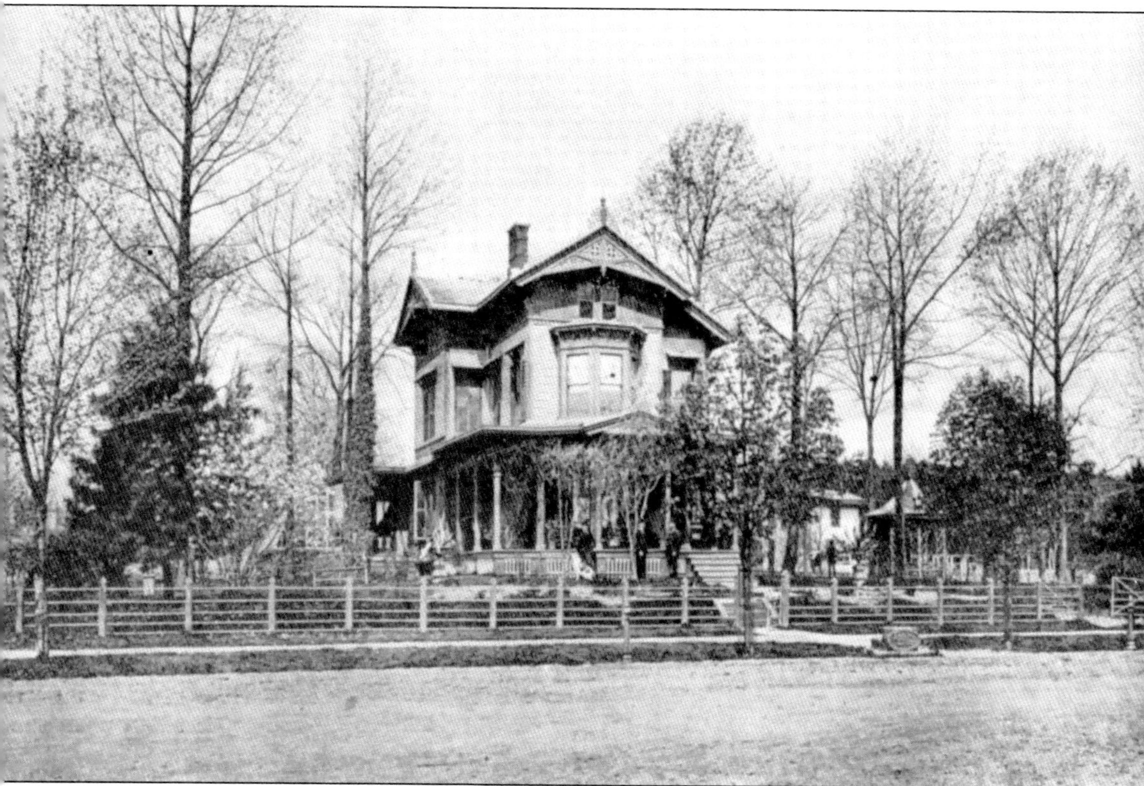

The residence shown in this c. 1913 photograph was the home of Elias G. Heller, father of Paul, Arnaud, and Arthur. This home was situated on Fredonia Avenue, the name of which was later changed to Heller Parkway. The Hellers prominently displayed these two homes in the promotional materials for their Forest Hill development businesses. Beginning in about 1895, the Forest Hill Association issued a series of marketing brochures containing photographs of homes already built in Forest Hill, presumably by the Hellers. The featured homes changed slightly in the three versions of the brochures, but they were all chosen to attract the type of investor, or homeowner, whom the Hellers wanted to bring into Forest Hill. Elias Heller was a prominent man in the Forest Hill community and took care to extend his efforts beyond his businesses. He was the major force behind the building of Forest Hill Presbyterian Church and Ridge Street School, where there is a plaque donated by the Heller family to commemorate the Gettysburg Address. (NPL.)

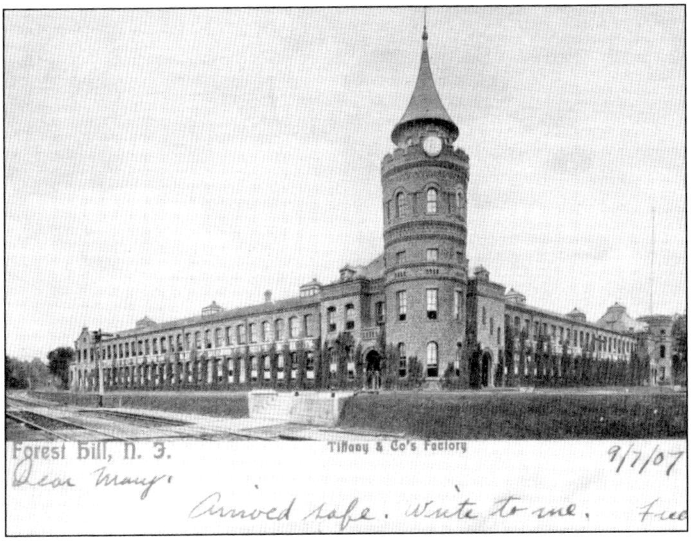

Featured on this 1907 postcard is the Tiffany & Co. silver factory, which was built in 1897 adjacent to Forest Hill, next to a station on the New York and Greenwood Lake Railway. Recognized for its iconic tower and often referred to as "the Castle," Tiffany's finest silverware was produced here until 1985, when the factory was relocated to a modern facility in Parsippany. Today, the building has been developed into condominiums. (CL.)

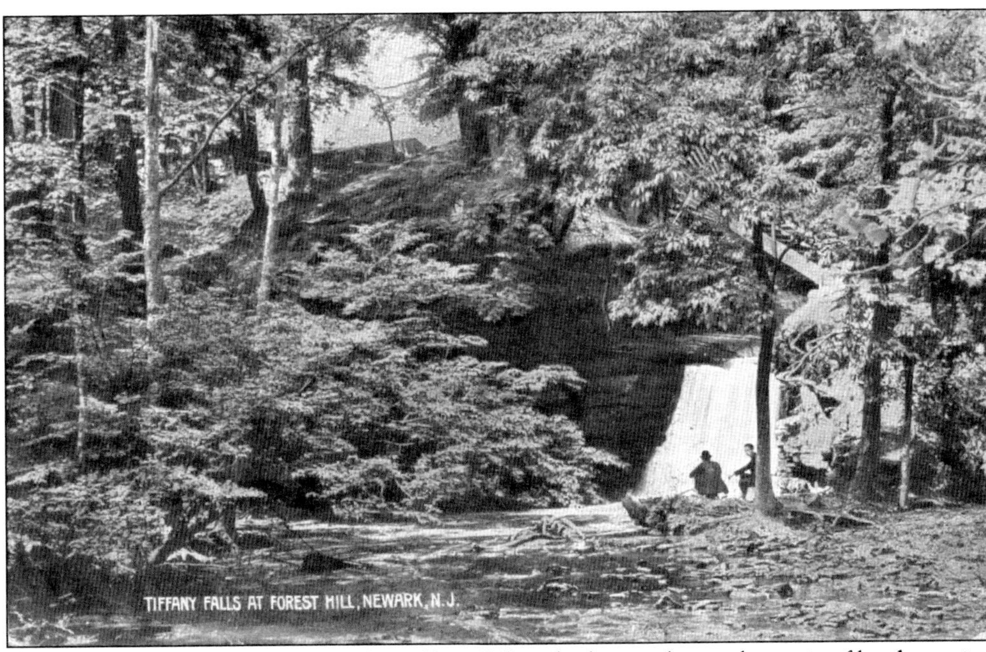

Adjacent to the silver factory was the Tiffany Falls, which, together with a strip of land running along the north side of Tiffany Boulevard, was donated to the Essex County Park Commission for the expansion of Branch Brook Park, enabling the landscape to showcase the donation of the flowering cherry blossom trees from Caroline Bamberger Fuld. (CL.)

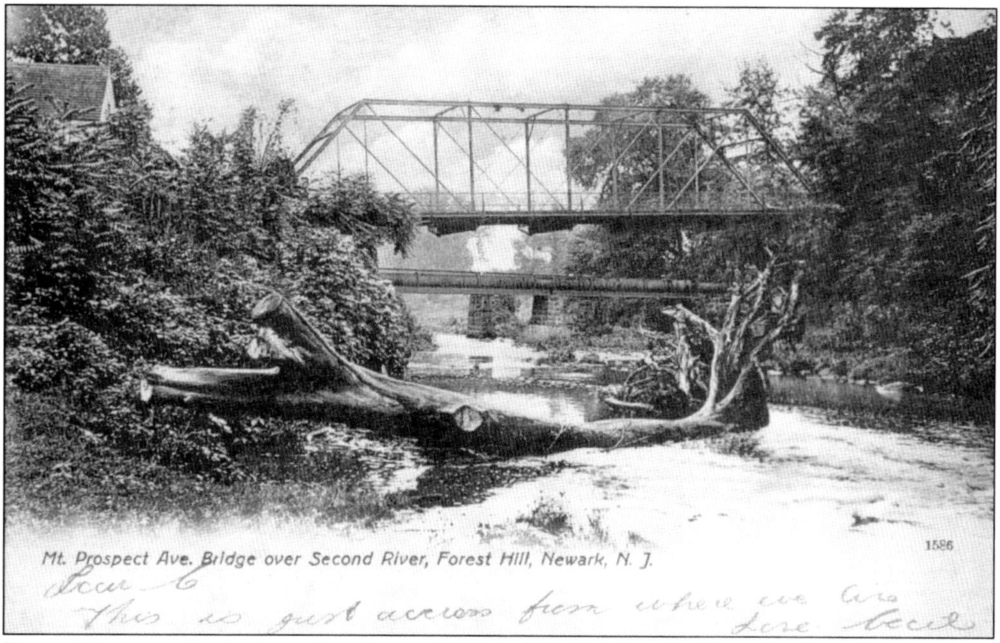

Second River marks the boundary between Newark and Belleville. References to it prominently appear on many of the early maps of Newark. At times, the land alongside the river was variously referred to as Bird's Woods and Woodside Park. Shown above is how the river appeared in the early 1900s before Branch Brook Park expanded into this part of the city. During the Great Depression, Works Progress Administration workers, engaged in projects in Branch Brook Park, undertook the task of channelizing the Second River and lining the riverbed with Belgian block. The WPA carved its initials in a block of one of the retaining walls to mark its contribution to this project. Below, the river is depicted in a most naturalistic setting. It was at this point that the river created the Tiffany Falls, which was included with the adjoining land as a grant from Tiffany & Co. for Branch Brook Park. Images of what the Second River looks like today can be found in the section of this book detailing Branch Brook Park. (Both, CL.)

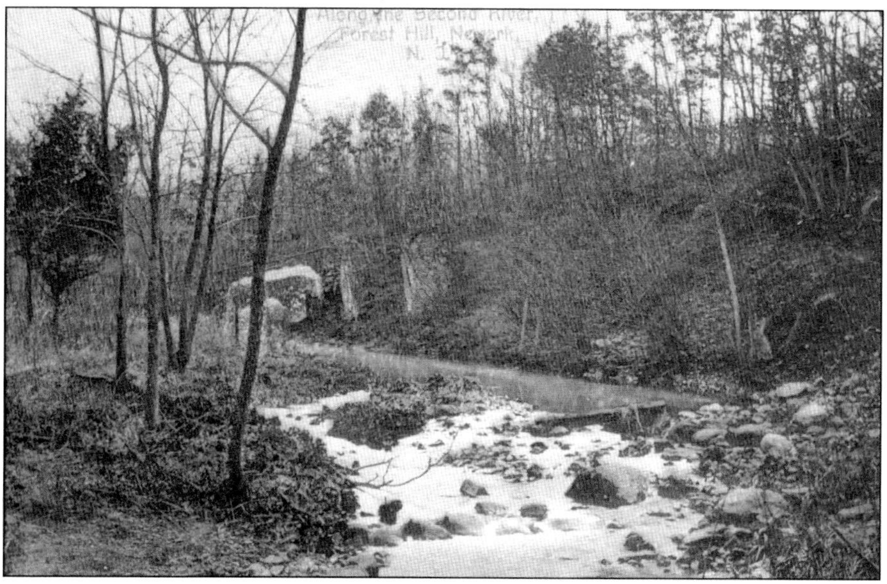

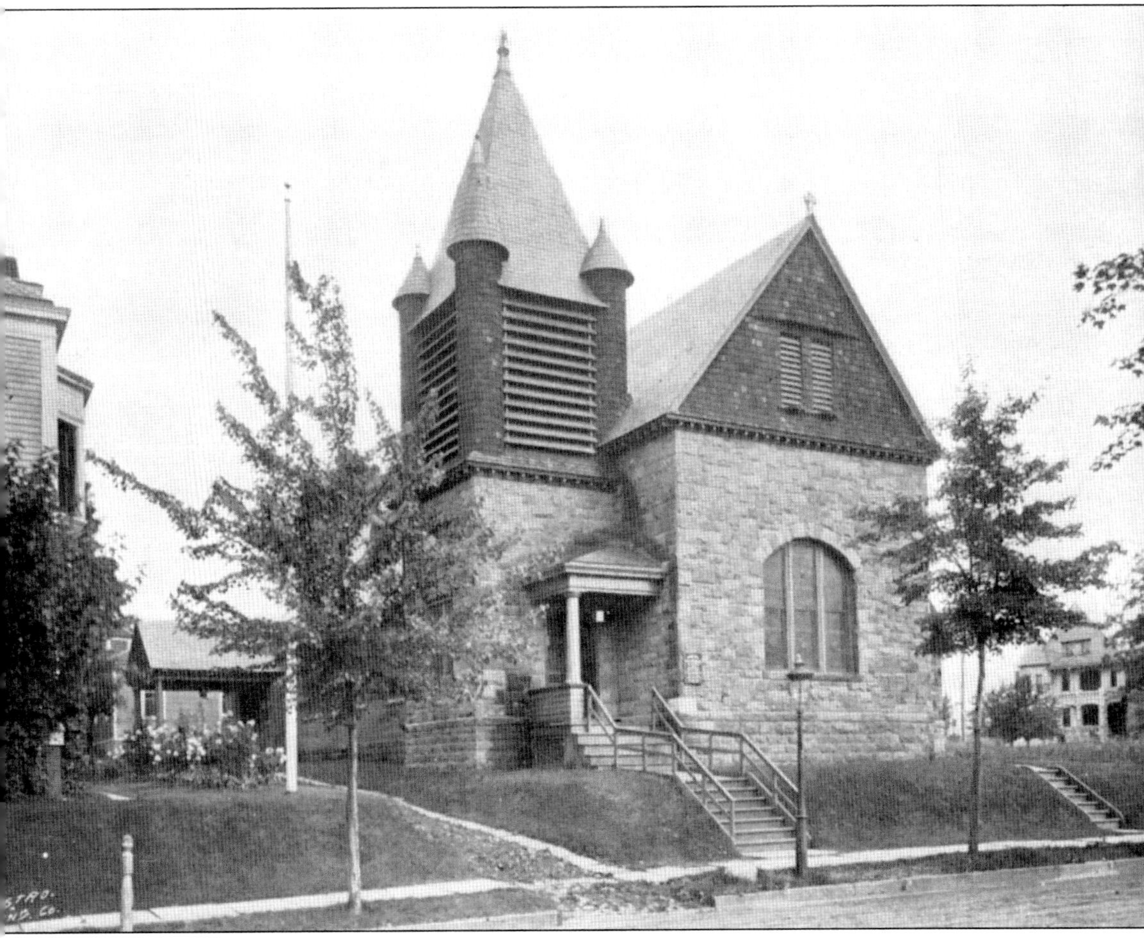

This photograph shows the original portion of the Forest Hill Presbyterian Church, built in 1891 with stones from the 1760 Crane farmhouse to replace Woodside Presbyterian Church. As soon as it was completed, the Woodside congregation abandoned their original church and moved up the hill to desirable Forest Hill, where many of them had likely already established new residences. In 1910, architect William S. Gregory designed an expansion for the church, more than doubling its size. As detailed in the *American Architect*, the exterior walls were Massachusetts granite, the roof was slate and copper, and all trim was oak. The cost was 18¢ per square foot, exclusive of the organ and other furnishings. In 1905, it was reported that Elias G. Heller donated $50,000 to Forest Hill Presbyterian Church. After the expansion, the original part of the church building was used as an auditorium and meeting hall. (CL.)

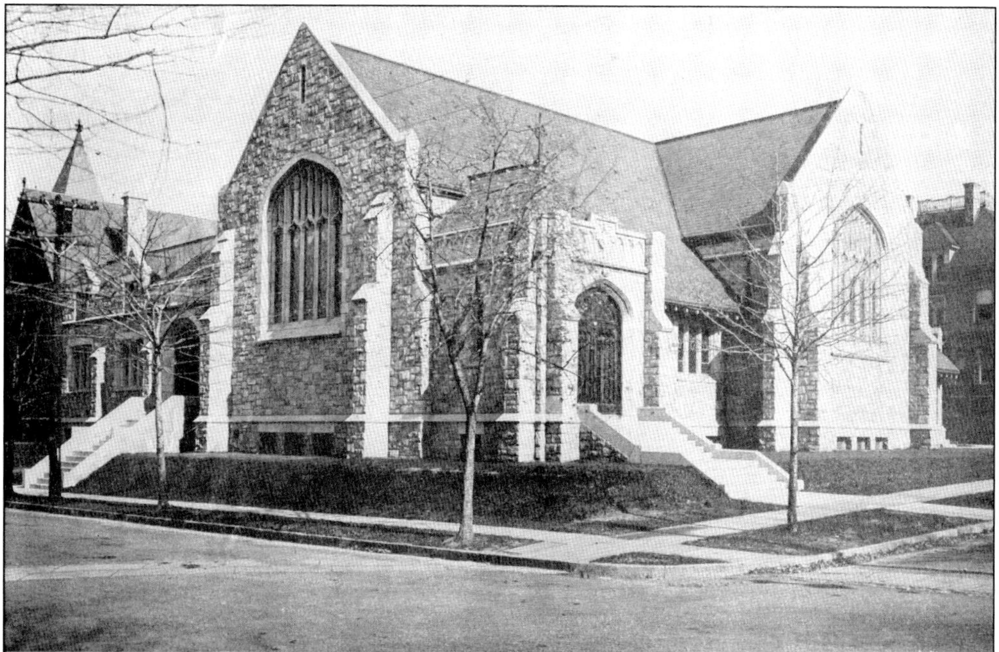

FOREST HILL PRESBYTERIAN CHURCH, NEWARK, N. J.

WILLIAM S. GREGORY, ARCHITECT

EXTERIOR WALLS, MASSACHUSETTS GRANITE. ROOF, SLATE AND COPPER. TRIM, OAK. STEAM HEAT. COST 18c PER CUBIC FOOT EXCLUSIVE OF ORGAN AND FURNISHINGS

The expanded Forest Hill Presbyterian Church is pictured above. In the National Register nomination, it is described as a "one story, five bay, cruciform plan, stone frame, Gothicizing Ecclesiastical building." It has a square, buttressed vestibule, and the impressive entryway boasts a pointed archway, cast-stone parapet, and double wooden doors. The nomination also highlights the arched stained-glass window and tripartite leaded-glass window groupings. Oddly, the entire description in the nomination relates to the newer part of the church structure and completely ignores the older, more historic part. Shown below is the interior of the main section of the church, with its incredible vaulted wooden ceiling. (Both, Robert Hartman.)

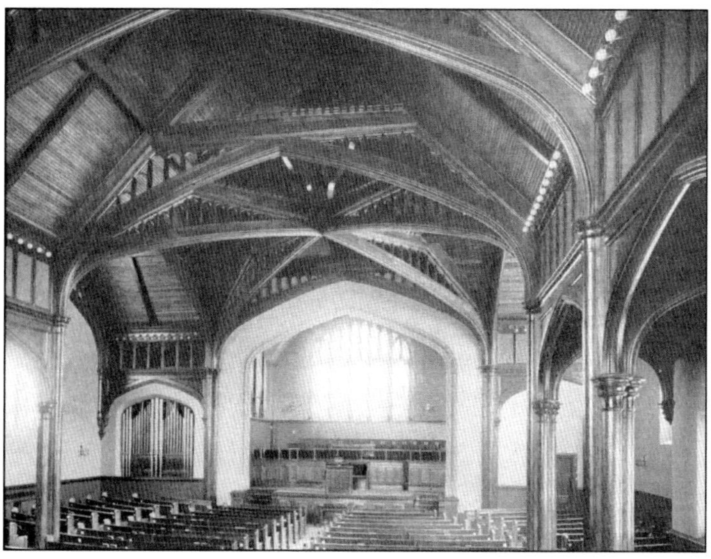

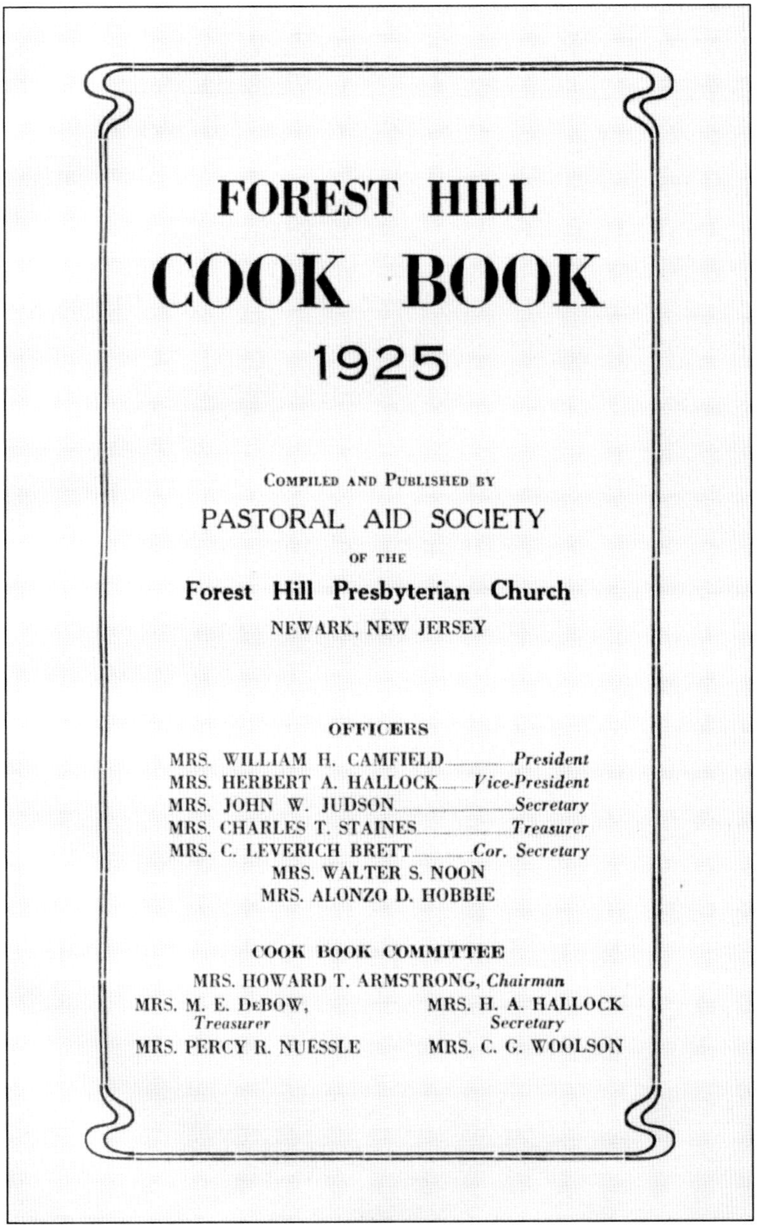

FOREST HILL

COOK BOOK

1925

COMPILED AND PUBLISHED BY

PASTORAL AID SOCIETY

OF THE

Forest Hill Presbyterian Church

NEWARK, NEW JERSEY

OFFICERS

MRS. WILLIAM H. CAMFIELD.............*President*
MRS. HERBERT A. HALLOCK.........*Vice-President*
MRS. JOHN W. JUDSON.................*Secretary*
MRS. CHARLES T. STAINES.............*Treasurer*
MRS. C. LEVERICH BRETT..........*Cor. Secretary*
MRS. WALTER S. NOON
MRS. ALONZO D. HOBBIE

COOK BOOK COMMITTEE

MRS. HOWARD T. ARMSTRONG, *Chairman*

MRS. M. E. DEBOW, *Treasurer*
MRS. H. A. HALLOCK, *Secretary*
MRS. PERCY R. NUESSLE
MRS. C. G. WOOLSON

Pictured here is the title page of the *Forest Hill Cook Book 1925*, compiled and published by the Pastoral Aid Society of the Forest Hill Presbyterian Church. A fundraiser project such as this was commonplace among church congregations at that time. The hardcover book was evenly divided between recipes (all on the right-hand pages) and advertisements from local businesses (all on the left-hand pages). Members of the congregation submitted the recipes. Most of the advertisers were providers of goods and services for the homemaker: stove manufacturers; prepared food makers, such as Mazola Oil and Royal Baking Powder; purveyors of eggs, dairy products, produce, and seafood; companies that delivered oil for heating and cooking; and repair services of every sort for the home, from roofers and electricians to paint and decorating specialists. Obviously, the ads more than paid for production of the cookbook, so proceeds from the sale of the book could raise a tidy sum for the church. (Michael Sheehan.)

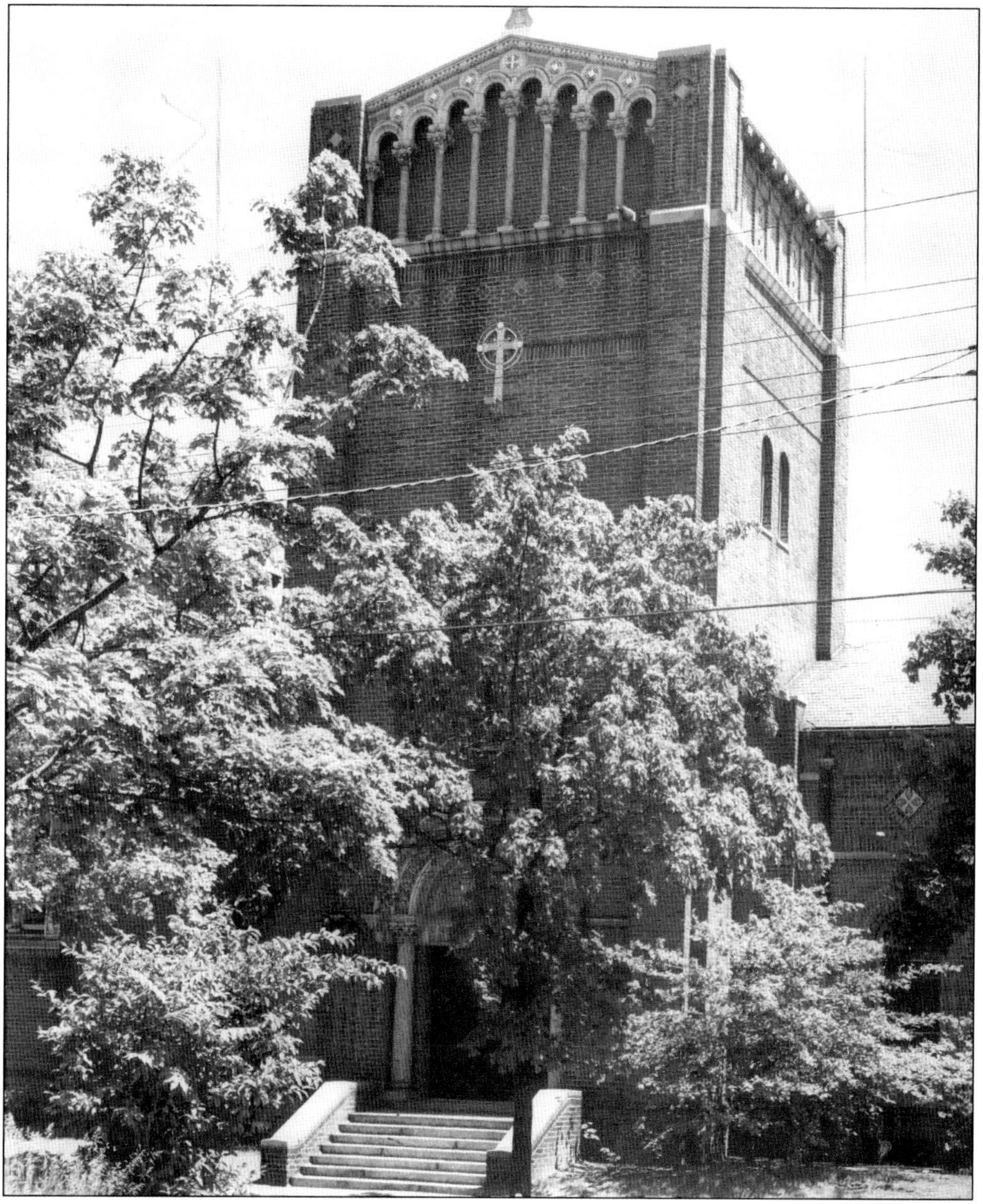

The Third Presbyterian Church was built in 1925 as a new home for its congregation, which had been formerly located in downtown Newark on Broad Street. The architect, William S. Gregory, had designed the earlier expansion of Forest Hill Presbyterian Church. The form of this church was very different from that of Forest Hill, with Third Presbyterian being described in the National Register nomination as a "one story, nine bay, irregular plan, brick, eclectic, ecclesiastical building." The decorative detail is also more elaborate. Another church within Forest Hill was the German Presbyterian Church, a wood-frame structure built around 1895. Located on the northern edge of Forest Hill, it was used primarily by the factory workers who resided in that area. There was also an Episcopal church within Forest Hill, but any Catholics who happened to live in Forest Hill would have to go down the hill, to the bottom of Heller Parkway, to attend Our Lady of Good Counsel Church, built in 1902. (NPL.)

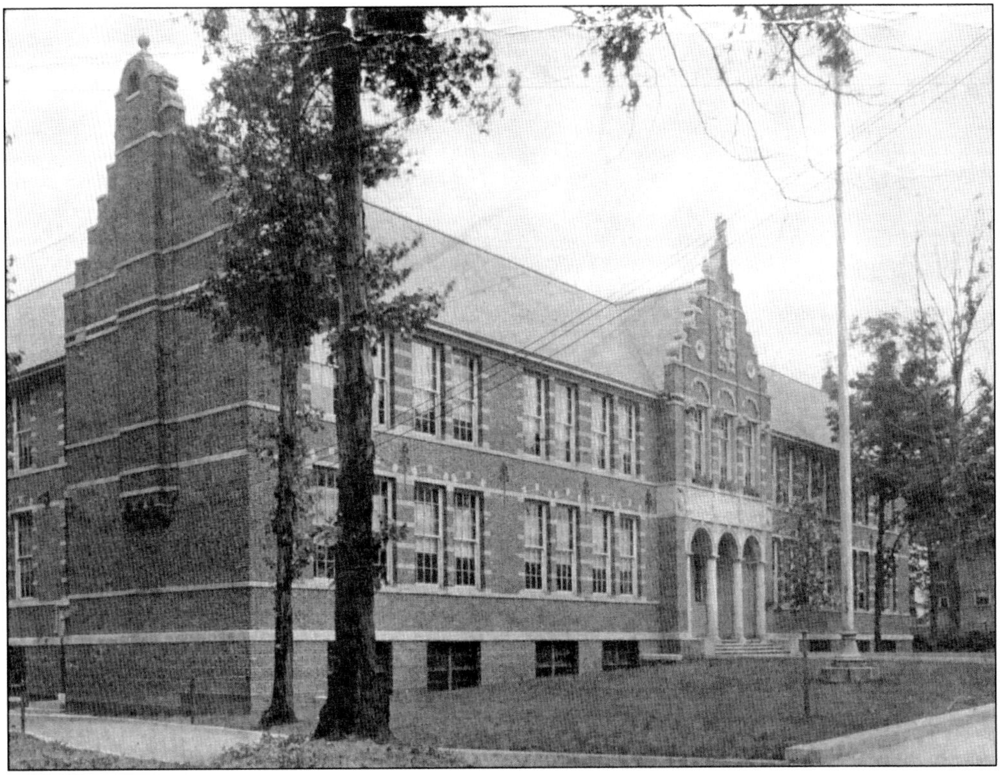

The Ridge Street School was built in 1910 to handle the increased demand for public school education that the Elliott Street School on Summer Avenue could not accommodate. Elias G. Heller funded, at least partially, the construction of this Flemish Revival school building. The school's architect, Ernest F. Guilberte, also designed and built himself a private residence on the northwest corner of the school block. Guilberte and his partner, James Betelle, were well-known architects, primarily for schools and civic buildings; in fact, they were the official architects for Newark schools for many years. Shown below is a 1903 class picture from the Ridge Street School. Some of the students' names are listed on the reverse of the photograph, but there is no indication of what grade these students were in at that time. (Both, NPL.)

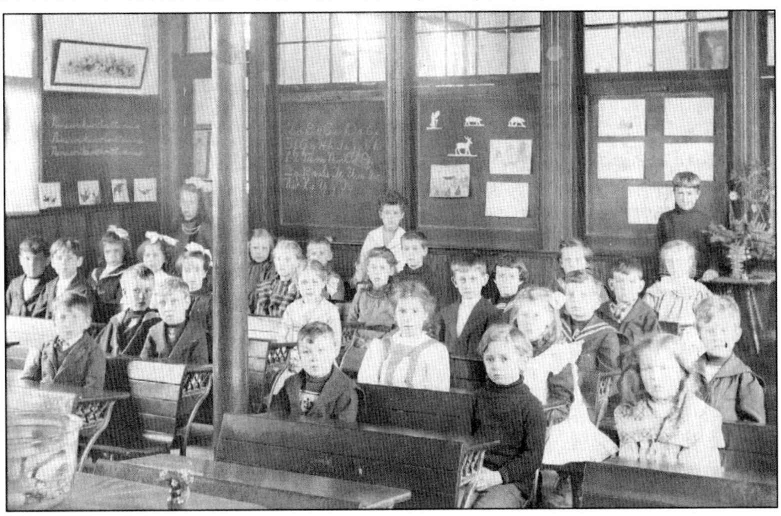

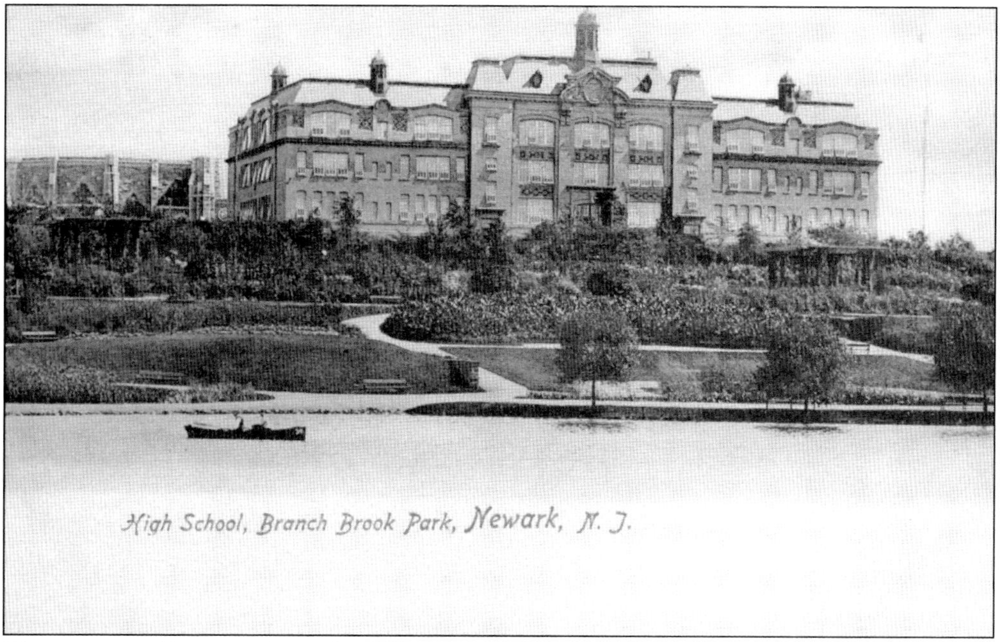

The nearest public secondary school for Forest Hill was Barringer High School, on Park Avenue at Branch Brook Park. The original building overlooked the elaborate gardens and peaceful lake of the park. Unfortunately, the original building was demolished to construct a modern 1950s school building. (CL.)

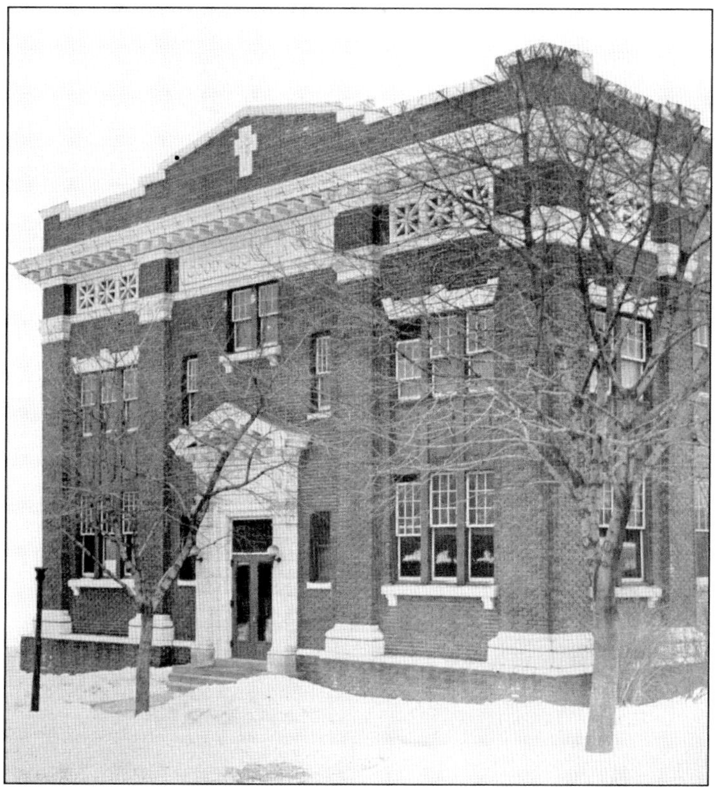

If Forest Hill residents wanted private education for their children, they had few nearby options. The Prospect Hill Country Day School (in the former Clark Mansion) had classes from kindergarten through high school. Located at the bottom of Heller Parkway, the Good Counsel Catholic Schools flourished, with a grammar school founded in 1913 and a high school in 1925 (which is the alma mater of the coauthors of this book). (CL.)

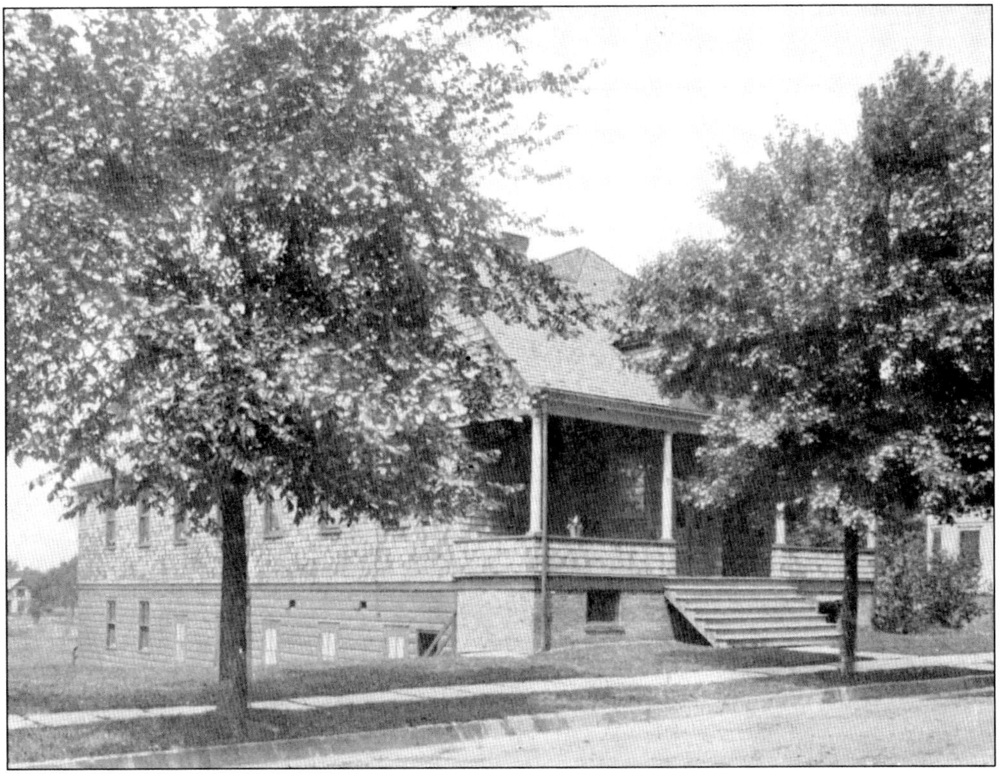

In 1891, the private Forest Hill Tennis Club was established at the intersection of DeGraw and Grafton Avenues for the purpose of providing lawn tennis facilities. As golf grew in popularity, the club secured land for a nine-hole course that opened in 1897. At the same time, a clubhouse was built on DeGraw Avenue, and the club changed its name to the Forest Hill Field Club. The club also had playing fields for baseball and football. The Hellers' Forest Hill Association exploited the location of this club within the Forest Hill district and touted its features in their brochures, including the photograph shown above as well as details of the clubhouse, such as slate bowling alleys, billiards, and a large assembly hall with a stage. Below is a postcard view of the clubhouse from the same era. (Above, CL; below, Samuel Rivera.)

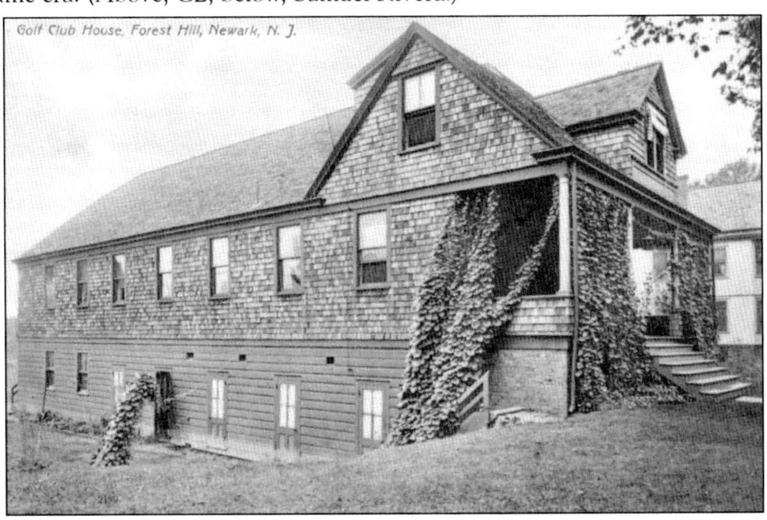

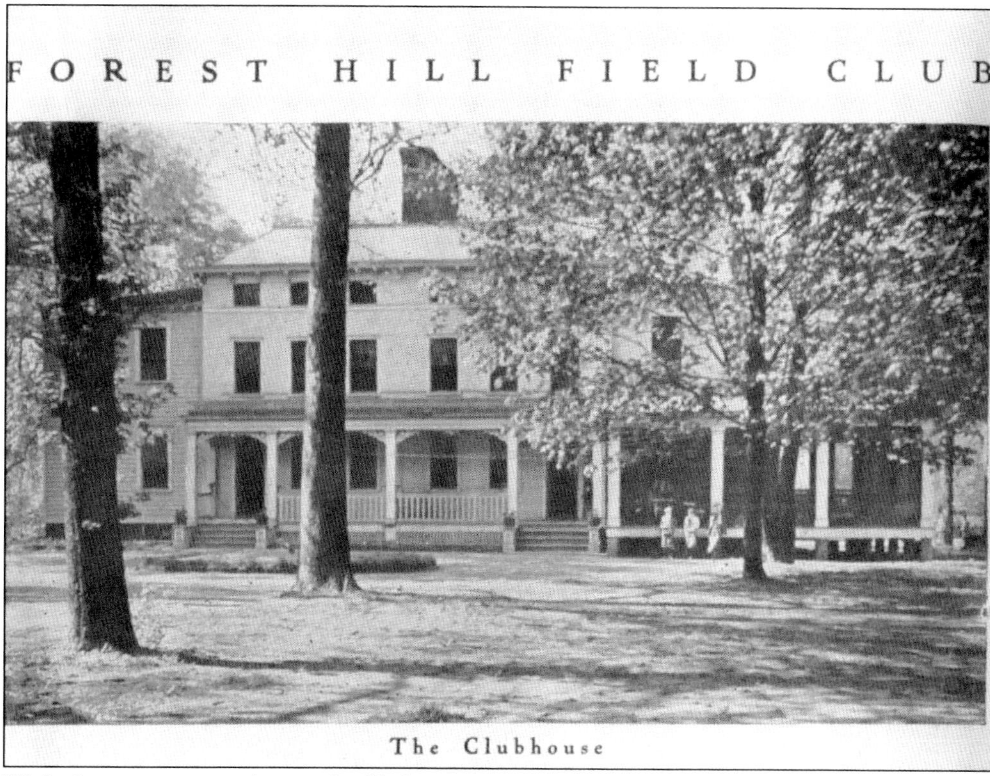

With the ongoing popularity of golf, the Forest Hill Field Club decided it had to expand to an 18-hole course, securing additional land in 1905. Meanwhile, the Newark Golf Club on Clinton Avenue had to cease operations due to increasing development in that area; thus many of its members joined the Forest Hill Field Club. This increase in membership made the development of the 18-hole course possible. The club also secured the right to use the old Hendricks homestead at Soho as a new clubhouse, and in 1909, the Forest Hill Field Club moved into its new home, pictured above. The 1909 postcard below shows the Forest Hill links, where the Eastern Professional Golfers Association held its championship tournament in September 1906. (Above, NPL; below, CL.)

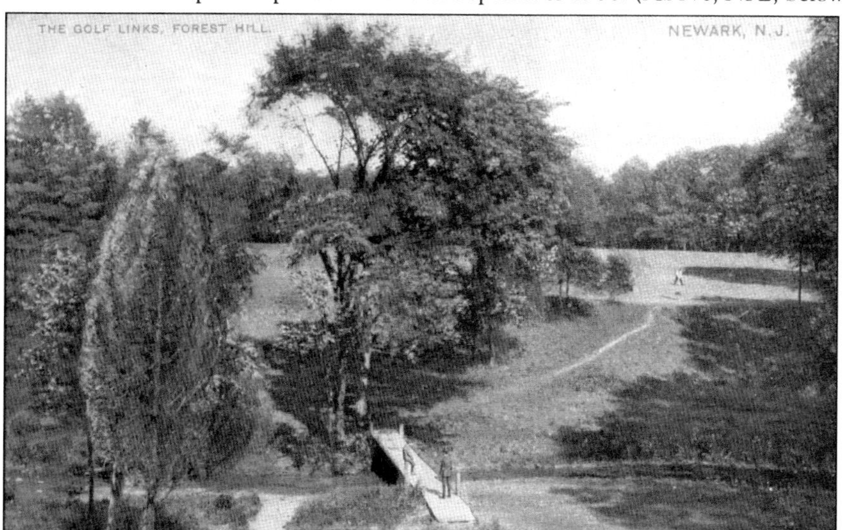

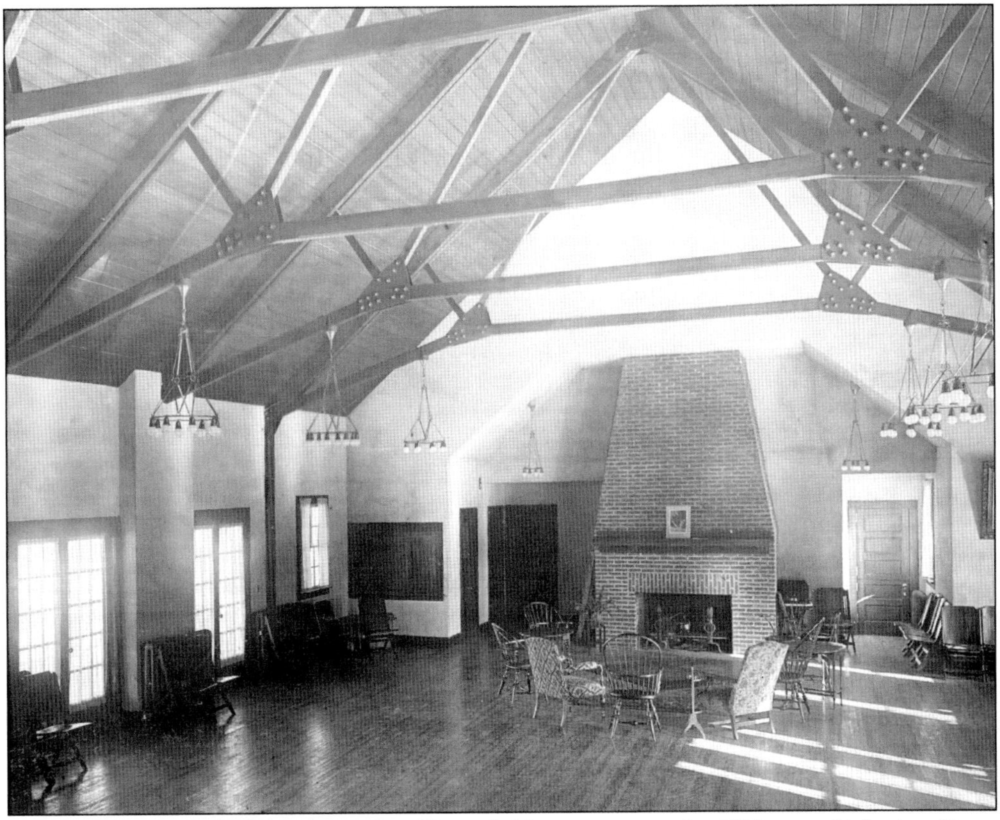

The Forest Hill Field Club relocated to Bloomfield sometime in the 1920s, at which time Essex County acquired its old 18-hole golf course and redeveloped it for a county golf course. The 1926 photograph above shows the assembly room on the second floor of the Forest Hill Field Club's new facility in Bloomfield, and the 1930 photograph below shows the men's lounge. (Both, NPL.)

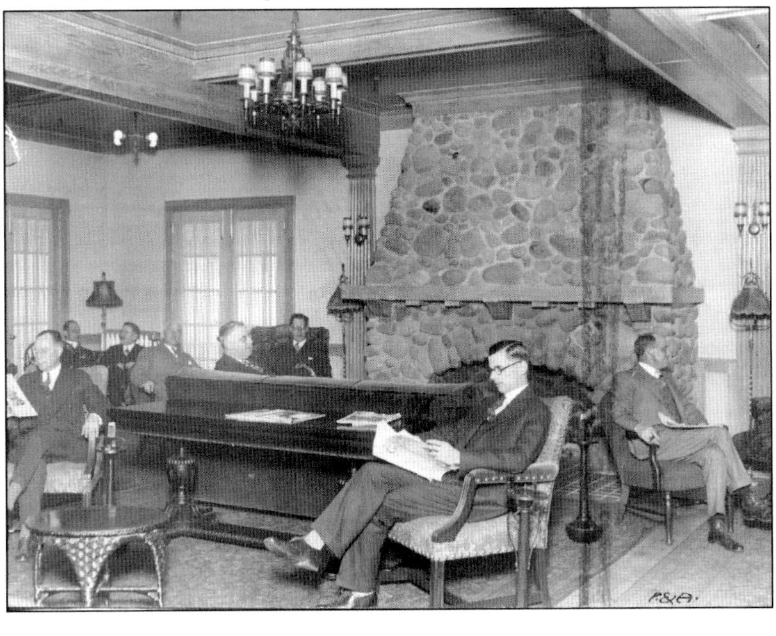

Three

Ghosts of Mansions Lost

Sadly, we do not always appreciate our own history. Particularly in urban areas with high-density populations, old buildings are too frequently torn down and replaced. Reasons given range from "progress," to "the greater good," to "too expensive to update," and most lamentable, to "old-fashioned."

The earliest mansions built in Forest Hill were concentrated in two areas. Many showcases were erected on Mount Prospect Avenue, from Second Avenue to approximately Ballantine Parkway and Delavan Avenue. At the same time, the Hellers were selling land and building grand residences above Mount Prospect Avenue, from Verona Avenue to Grafton Avenue. As business establishments began to spread west along Verona Avenue, affluent homeowners in that area moved south below Montclair and Grafton Avenues. The Hellers' Forest Hill Association began marketing homes in the area of Verona to Montclair Avenues. Their second promotional brochure featured homes from Montclair and Grafton Avenues to Heller Parkway and Elwood Avenue. Subsequent marketing efforts focused on properties south of Heller Parkway.

Another factor driving the shift further south in Forest Hill was the changing architectural styles. The older mansions had been built in the Queen Anne, Neoclassical, and Georgian Colonial style, among other classic designs. But beginning in 1900, Craftsman, Colonial Revival, and similar, less elaborate styles began to proliferate, as even wealthy families did not employ as much staff in residence and therefore could not maintain those huge Queen Anne homes.

Meanwhile, the earliest mansions on the northern edge of Forest Hill became housing for factory workers and began to suffer the neglect of remote landlords. Some homes were razed and replaced by small apartment buildings. Many were converted to multiple-family residences.

Proving that there is more than one way to lose an old building, this chapter features once magnificent residences that have been torn down, as well as some that have been altered beyond recognition.

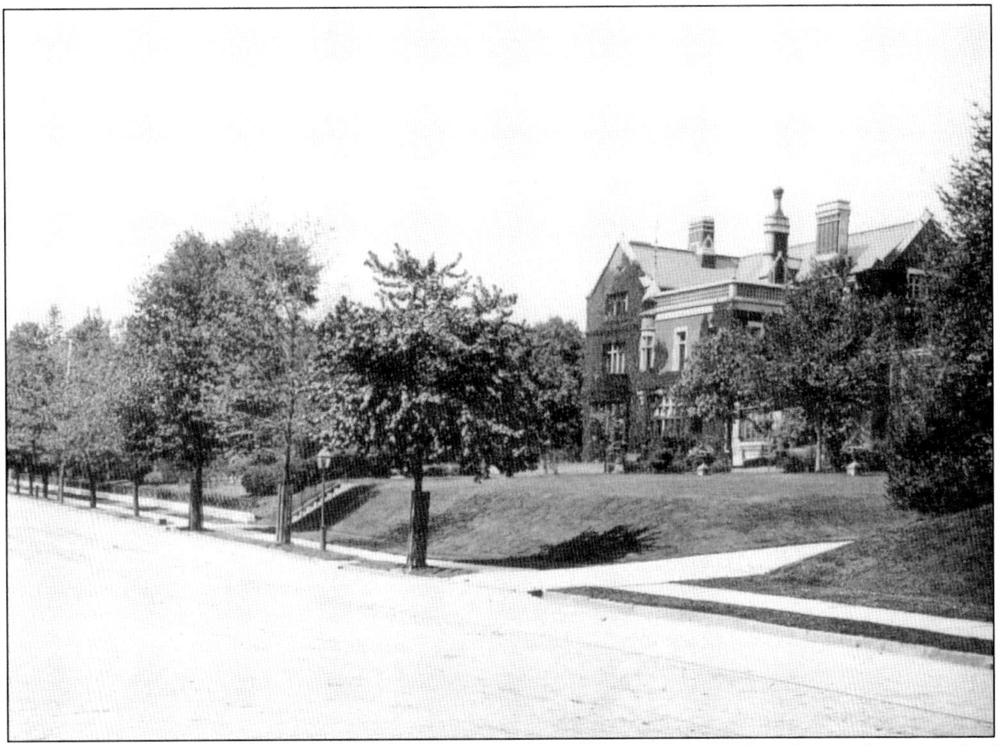

This 1892 scene shows a grand residence located at what appears to be the southern end of Mount Prospect Avenue, near the Clark Mansion. The road is not yet paved, and there is no sign of streetcar tracks. Since this was a major thoroughfare linking downtown Newark to this residential area, there may have been horse-drawn passenger wagons working this street. But it is more likely that, in 1892, the businessmen who lived in these homes would have had their own carriages. (NCC.)

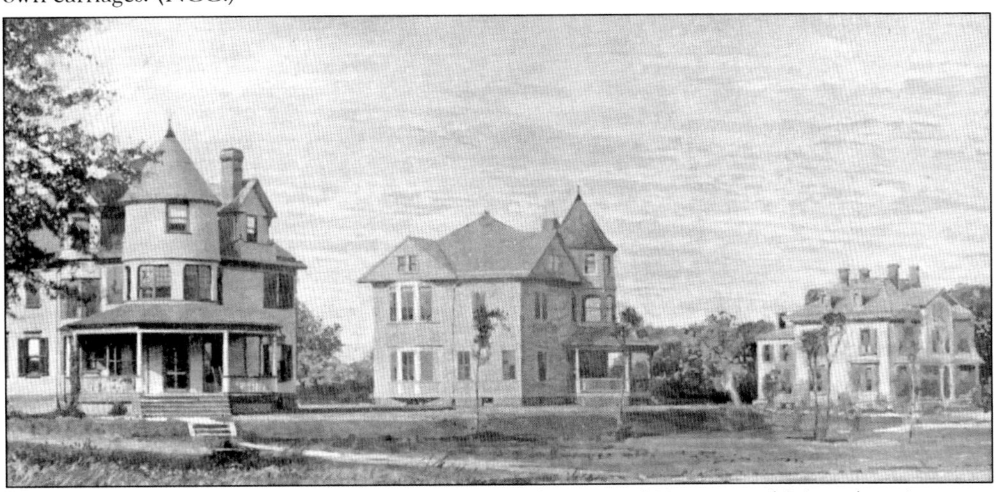

These homes were among the early ones built in the area of Verona and Montclair Avenues, probably between 1890 and 1900. Note the large lots with plenty of space between neighbors. In this photograph from a realtors' booklet, it appears as though the developers have deliberately chosen to feature wholly disparate architectural styles. Forest Hill was promoted as a residential suburb with a variety of home styles. (NPL.)

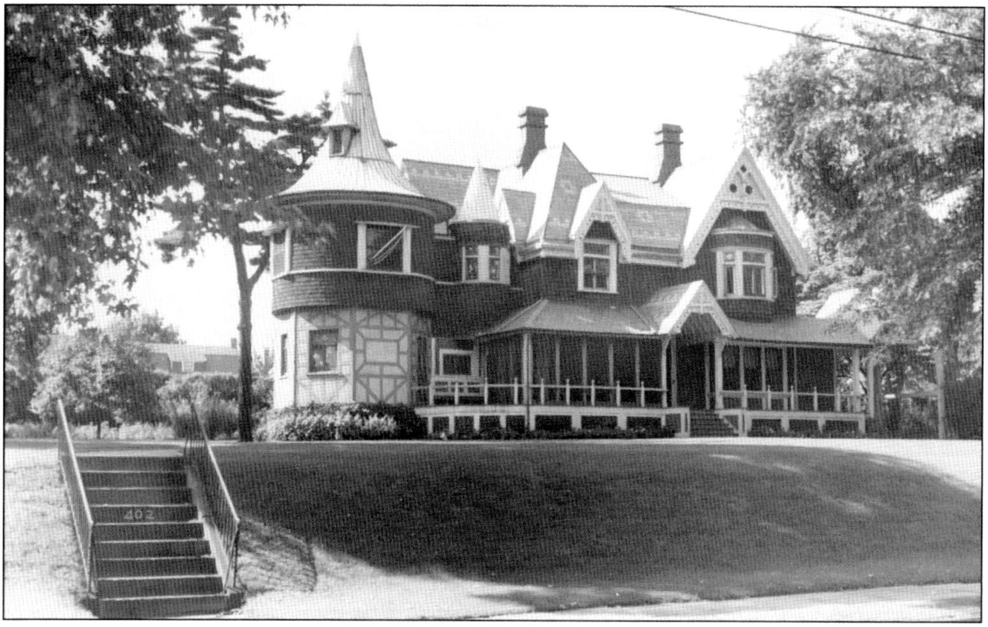

This lovely home at 402 Mount Prospect Avenue was probably the next-door neighbor heading north from the Turnbull residence pictured on the cover of this book. It would have stood out from its surroundings with its Tudor-style ground floor stucco and trim, fanciful gingerbread, elaborately tiled roof and witch's hat turret. It was probably built around the same time as the c. 1850 Turnbull home and is now the site of that same apartment complex. (NCC.)

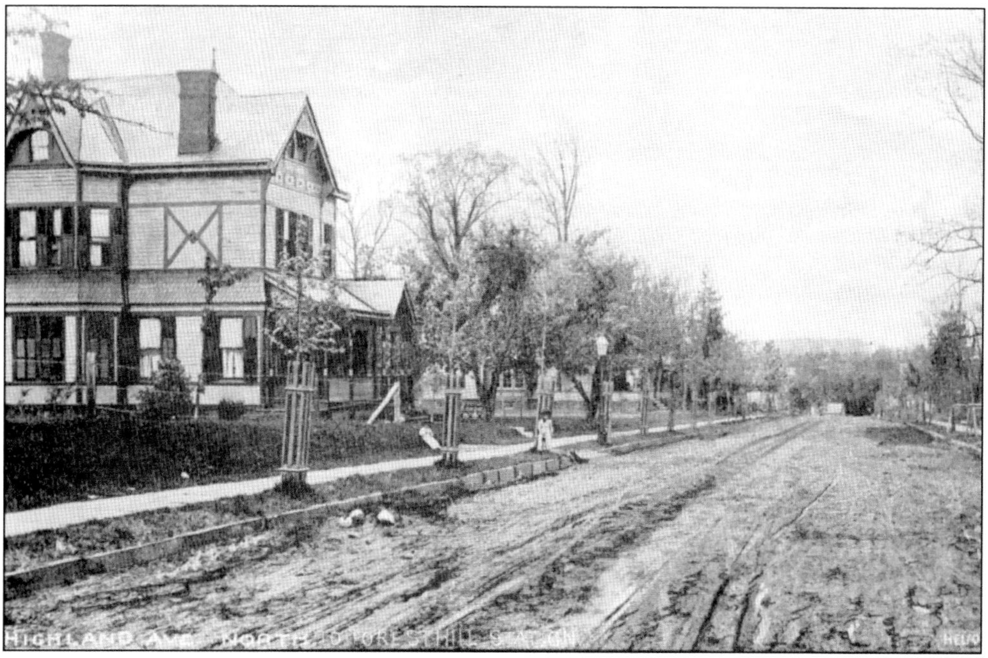

Looking north on Highland Avenue toward Verona Avenue, this section had evidently not come far beyond the farmland it replaced, with its residents eyeing the cameraman as they lounge in their front yard. Also visible are signs of construction, perhaps including excavations along the street to lay water, sewer, and gas lines. (NPL.)

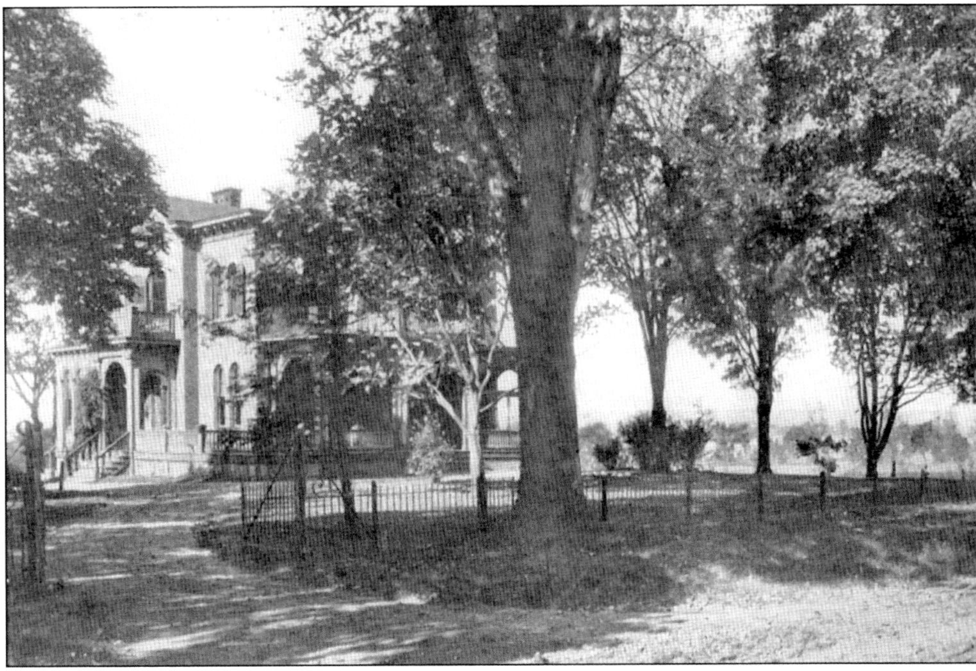

This home appears to have been built in the Italianate style. Not only is the home gone now, but so is the road. It was situated on the Old Road to Bloomfield, of which only a one-block stretch remains. When the Hellers and Clarks acquired the farmland in this area, the City laid out a neat housing grid that eliminated the Old Road to Bloomfield, which used to cut through Forest Hill on a diagonal line. (NPL.)

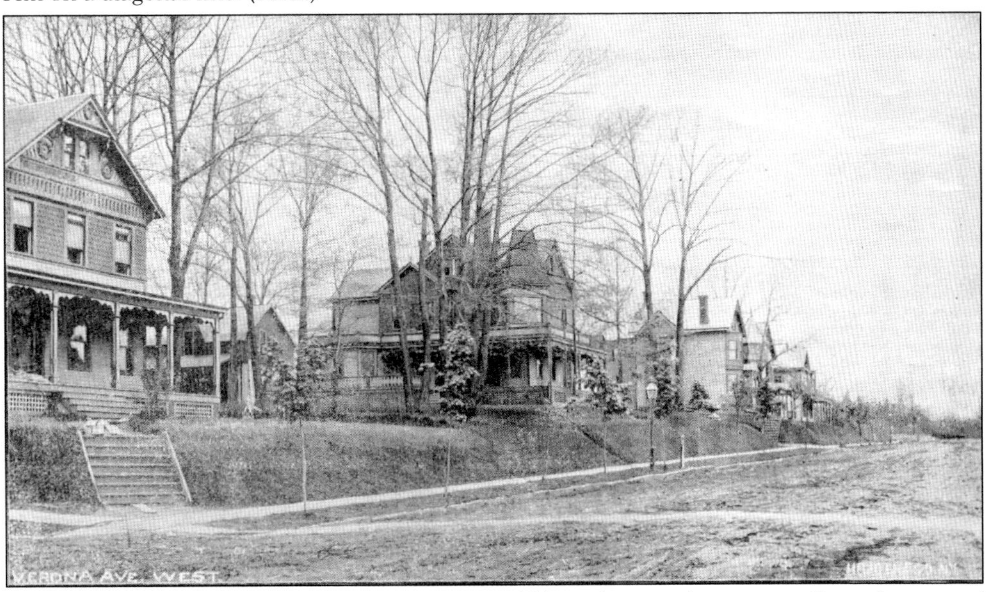

Residents of these homes on Verona Avenue would have been within easy walking distance of the Highland Avenue station of the Greenwood Lake Division of the Erie Railroad. At that time, there were over 20 trains daily to Chambers or 23rd Streets in New York City, and the monthly commuter fare was $5. Or if their offices were in Newark, they could walk down to Mount Prospect Avenue and catch the Forest Hill Trolley to Broad and Market Streets. (NPL.)

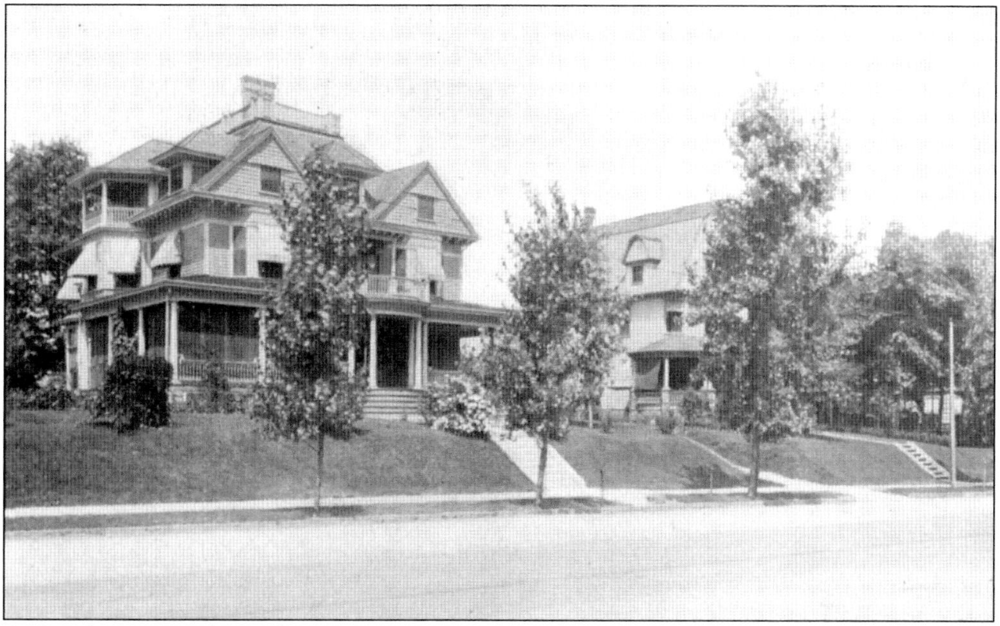

A church now stands on the site of this grand home shown on the left at the northwest corner of Mount Prospect and Delavan Avenues. When compared to the earlier 1892 scenes, the major thoroughfare in this c. 1910 photograph had been surfaced with trolley tracks installed. (CL.)

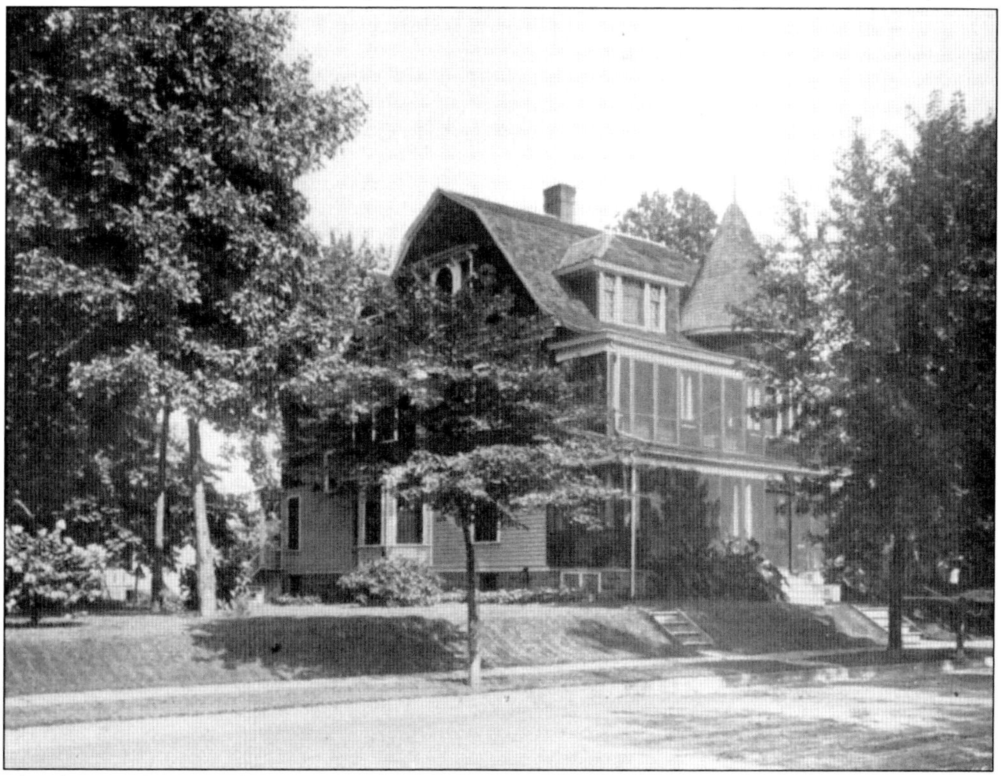

This large Lake Street home was built around 1900 in the Eclectic style, but it has been altered and updated so much that it is now classified as non-contributing. (CL.)

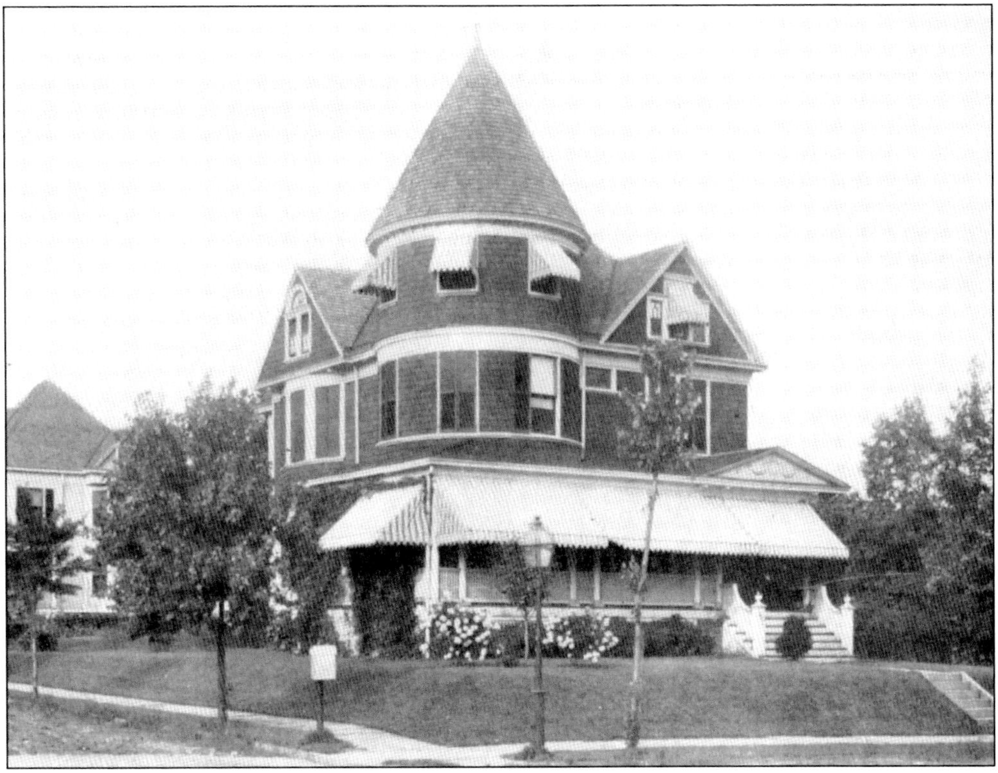

When built around 1900, this residence had all the classic features of the Queen Anne style: a three-story corner tower with conical roof, varying window groupings, and a wraparound porch sheltered by large canvas awnings. While these features are still visible, substantial modifications have made this house difficult to recognize today. (CL.)

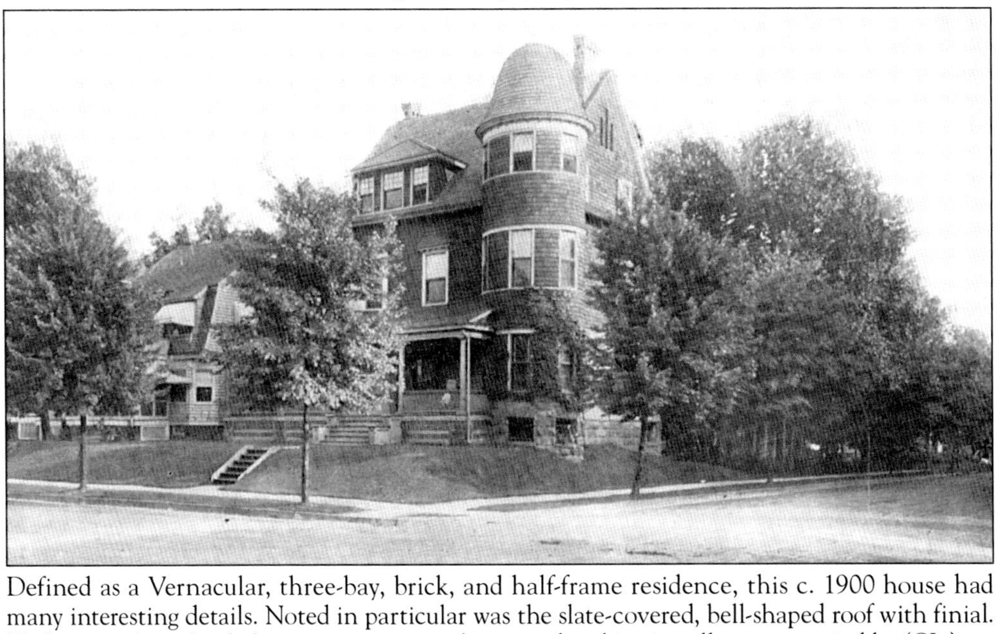

Defined as a Vernacular, three-bay, brick, and half-frame residence, this c. 1900 house had many interesting details. Noted in particular was the slate-covered, bell-shaped roof with finial. Unfortunately, radical alterations over time have rendered it virtually unrecognizable. (CL.)

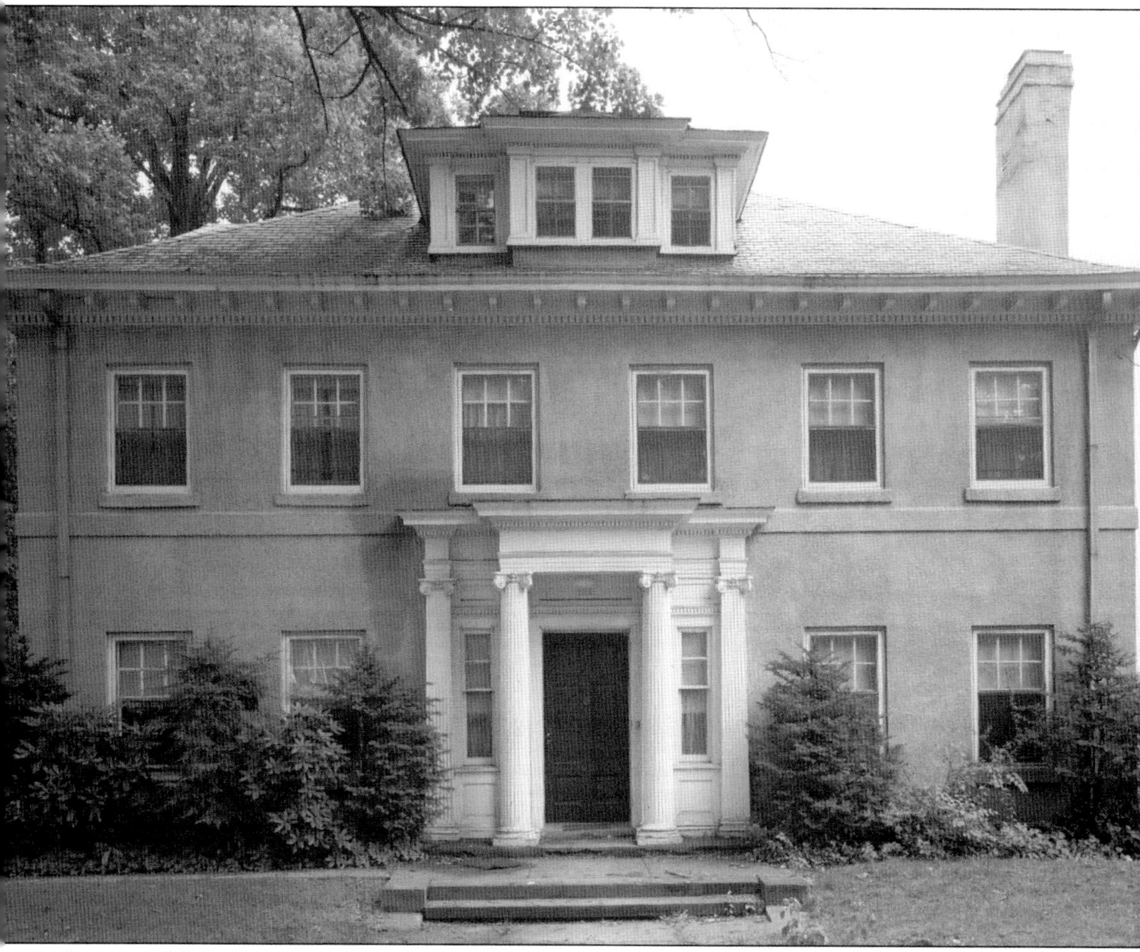

George S. Hobart, a Newark attorney, was probably the original owner of this classic structure located at 599 Mount Prospect Avenue. This Georgian Revival residence was built around 1900 and listed in the 1979 Historic American Buildings Survey (HABS), where it was described as "contributing to the general eclectic flow of the neighborhood" and determined eligible for the National Register of Historic Places. The design was well balanced, with bays, dormers, and an entrance portico all pleasingly symmetrical. On the north side of the house was a Venetian Palladian window. The interior appointments were correspondingly classic but not elaborate. Unfortunately, the HABS designation did not protect it, and an apartment complex replaced it shortly thereafter. (LC.)

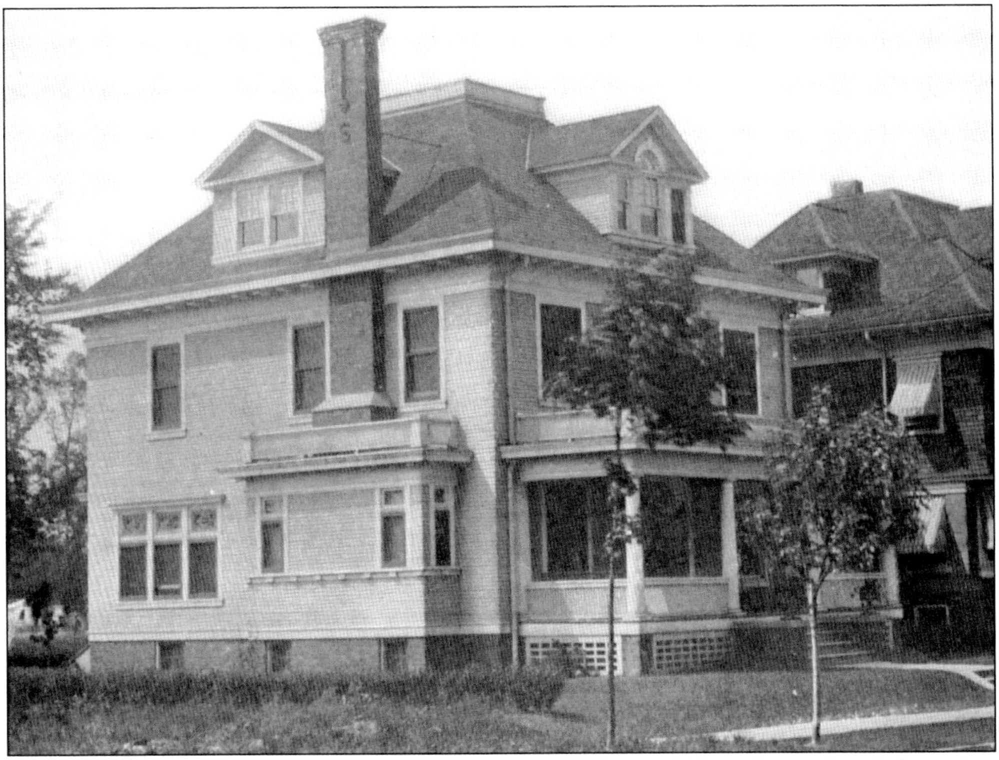

Built around 1905 in the Colonial Revival style, this house would have been classified as a key structure in the National Register nomination but for the unfortunate fact that it has been so heavily altered. Consequently, it is classified as a non-contributing former Colonial Revival structure. (CL.)

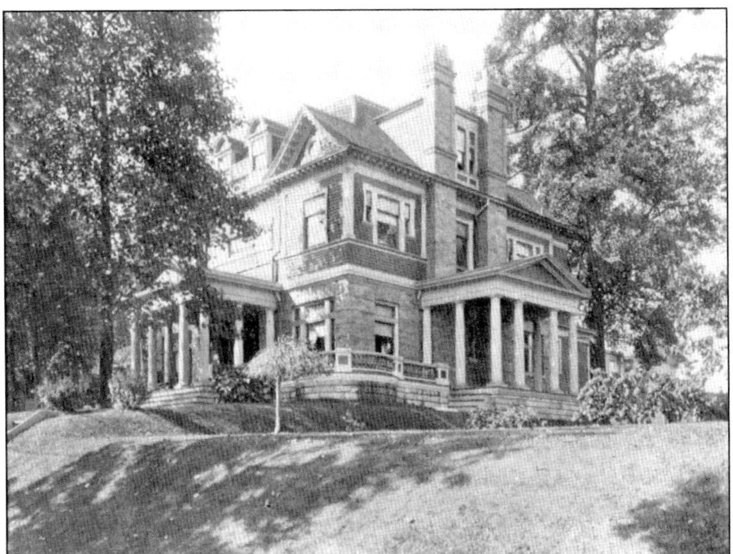

This imposing structure at 600 Mount Prospect Avenue was located between Elwood and Delavan Avenues. Note the two entrance porticoes connected by a wraparound stone balustrade, prominent chimneys, and various styles of dormers. (NPL.)

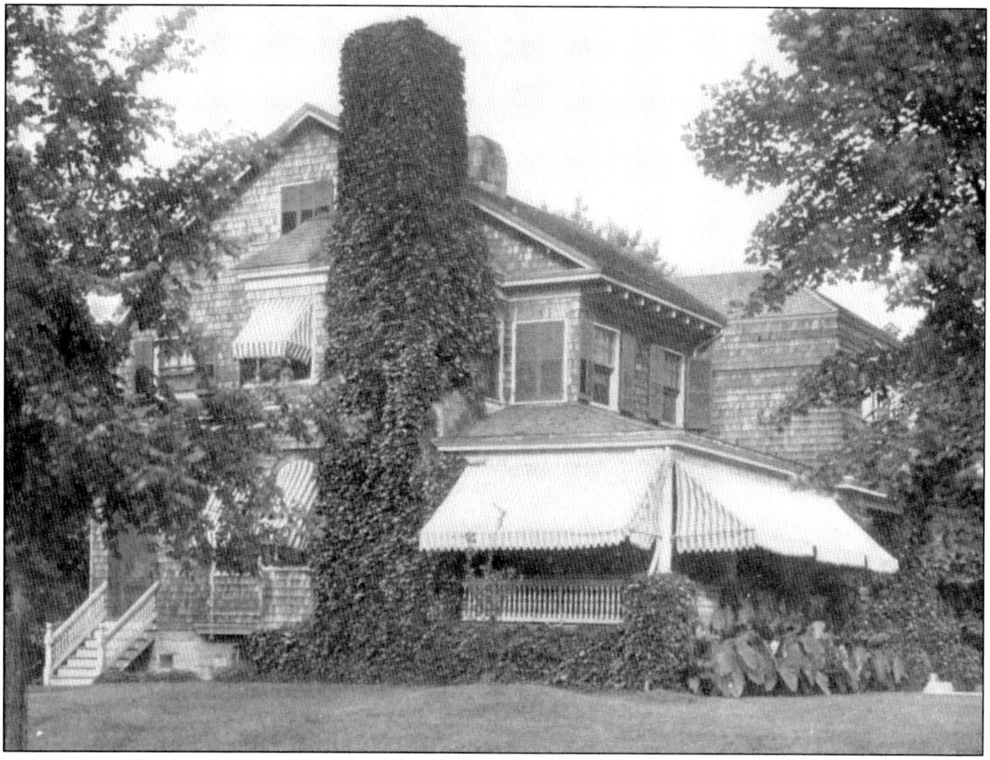

When it was built in the Vernacular style around 1900, this residence was the height of fashion. Note the extensive wraparound porch with luxurious awnings. It could be a vacation home in Newport or the Hamptons. Instead, it has become unrecognizable due to inappropriate alterations that have classified it as non-contributing. (CL.)

The c. 1890 Queen Anne residence on the left in this photograph is another severely altered residence now classified as non-contributing. By contrast, fate may have been kinder to the home on the right, which was demolished and replaced by a generic row house. (NPL.)

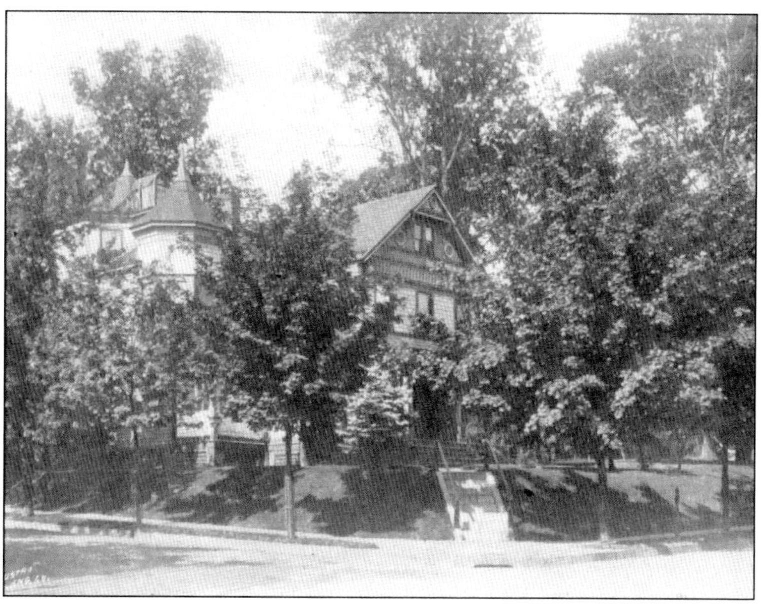

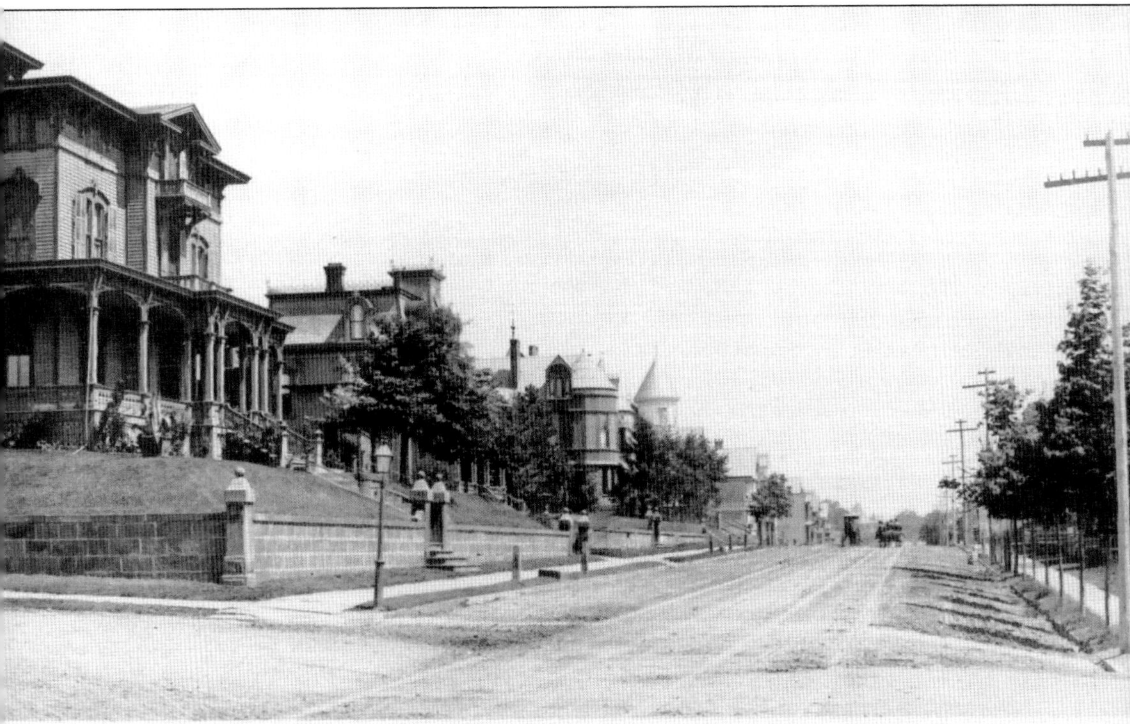

SCENE ON CLIFTON AVENUE.

In 1892, this stretch of Clifton Avenue would have been a desirable and exclusive residential area. Large, elaborate homes were well spaced and set back from the slate sidewalks, behind regal retaining walls and pillars. Note the gas streetlamps on the unpaved street and hitching posts for horse carriages. This is exactly how the developers of Forest Hill envisioned this exclusive suburb, and indeed, it was built to this plan throughout the neighborhood. But as time passed and fortunes dwindled, these homes disappeared. (NCC.)

Four

Notable Residences

Not every home in the Forest Hill Historic District is a mansion, although there are quite a few of them. Almost 60 percent of the structures in the district qualify as key or contributing to the historic character of Forest Hill. The authors attempted to present a mix of architectural styles and interesting stories in order to portray the neighborhood's overall character and appearance.

Some of the most noteworthy residences, however, are covered in other chapters, like the Sydenham House in chapter 2 and the Karr-Milburn home in chapter 7.

The property descriptions rely to some extent on how they were classified in the nomination to the National Register, although with the large number of structures surveyed for that document, there are some differences of opinion. Also, it was impossible to research actual construction dates for every structure, so the qualifier *c.* (circa) was used in some cases.

Most of the images found in this chapter are period or vintage photographs, so the homes pictured may not be easily recognizable. But look carefully; you may recognize several from episodes of *The Sopranos*.

During the course of research for this project, a particular detail of note was discovered. If a home was built by one of the Heller development companies, the letter *H* was engraved in one of the slate sidewalk slabs in front of that house. Unfortunately, many of the old slate sidewalks have been replaced over the past 100 years, but look for the *H* anyway. Happy hunting!

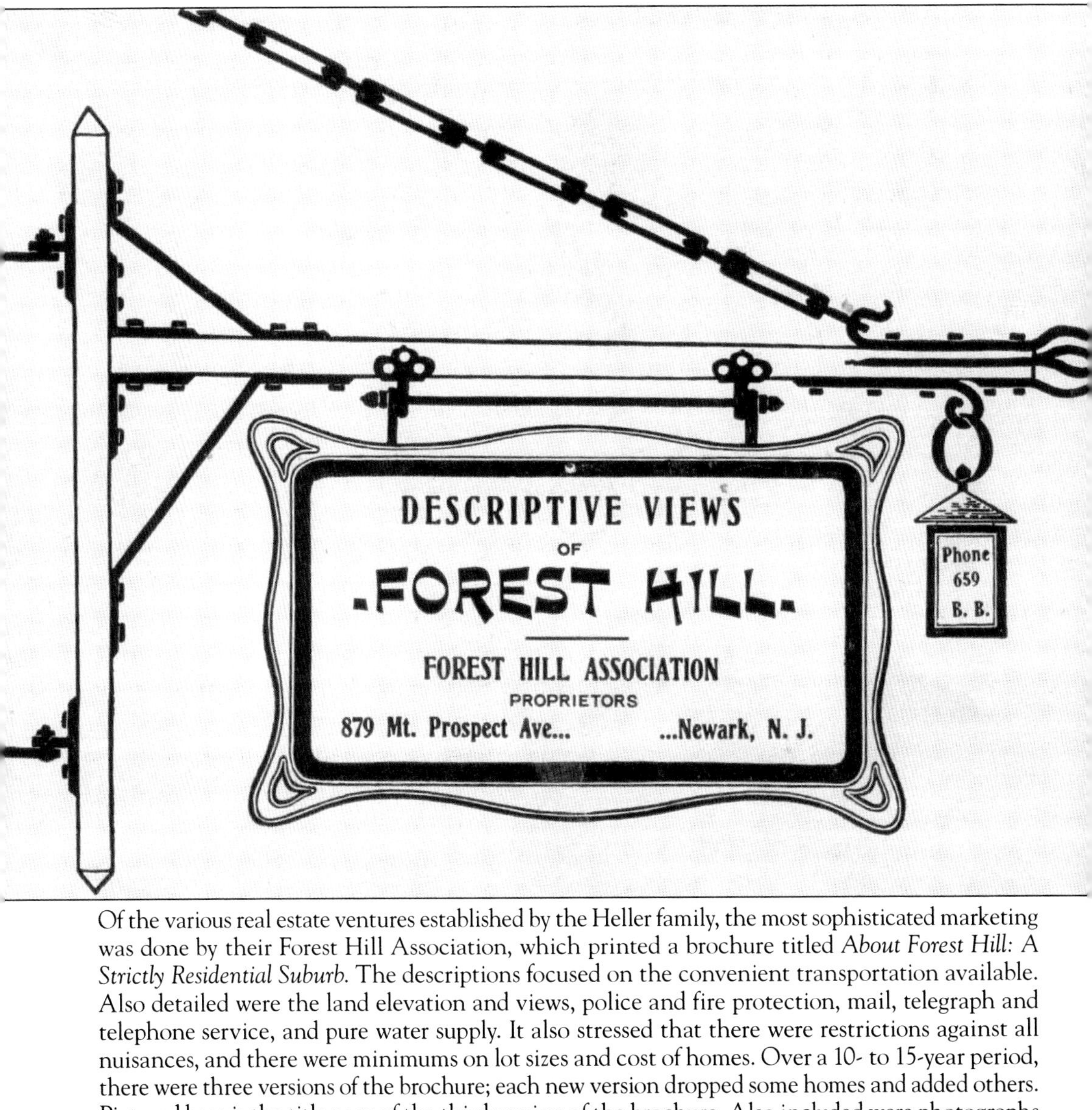

Of the various real estate ventures established by the Heller family, the most sophisticated marketing was done by their Forest Hill Association, which printed a brochure titled *About Forest Hill: A Strictly Residential Suburb.* The descriptions focused on the convenient transportation available. Also detailed were the land elevation and views, police and fire protection, mail, telegraph and telephone service, and pure water supply. It also stressed that there were restrictions against all nuisances, and there were minimums on lot sizes and cost of homes. Over a 10- to 15-year period, there were three versions of the brochure; each new version dropped some homes and added others. Pictured here is the title page of the third version of the brochure. Also included were photographs of church, school, and recreational facilities (including Branch Brook Park), specifically chosen to convince potential investors of the desirability of Forest Hill for their new homes. Many of the images contained in this chapter, as well as the previous chapter, were reproduced from these marketing materials. (CL.)

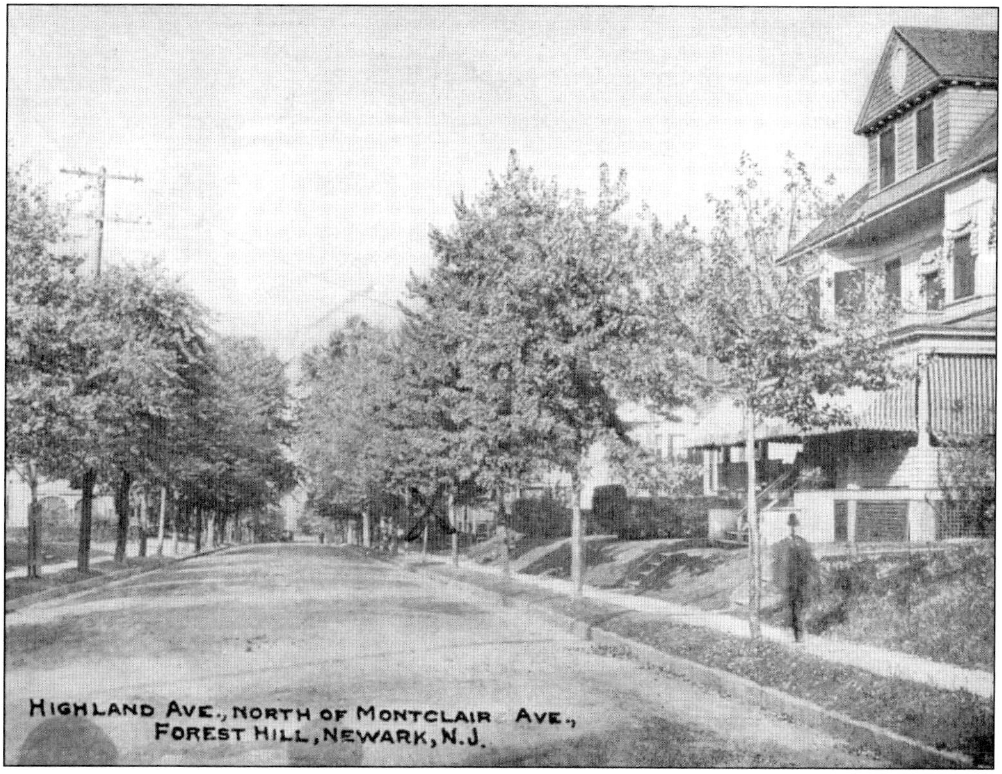

This early-1900s postcard view of Highland Avenue north of Montclair Avenue shows a typical street scene in Forest Hill, with a broad, unpaved road, fairly young shade trees, and large homes with porches protected by expansive awnings. Judging from the direction he is walking, this gentleman may be coming from the nearby train station or perhaps returning from his New York City office. (CL.)

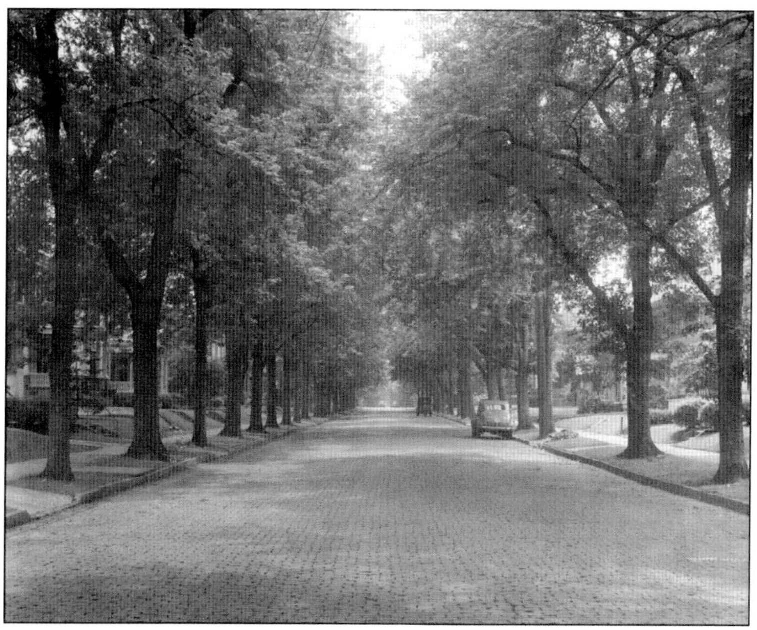

Another view of a Forest Hill street, this one a section of Clifton Avenue dated 1947, clearly shows the changes over those 50 years. Note the cobblestone paving of the street. The trees have matured and would provide much more shade as well as wind protection. (NCC.)

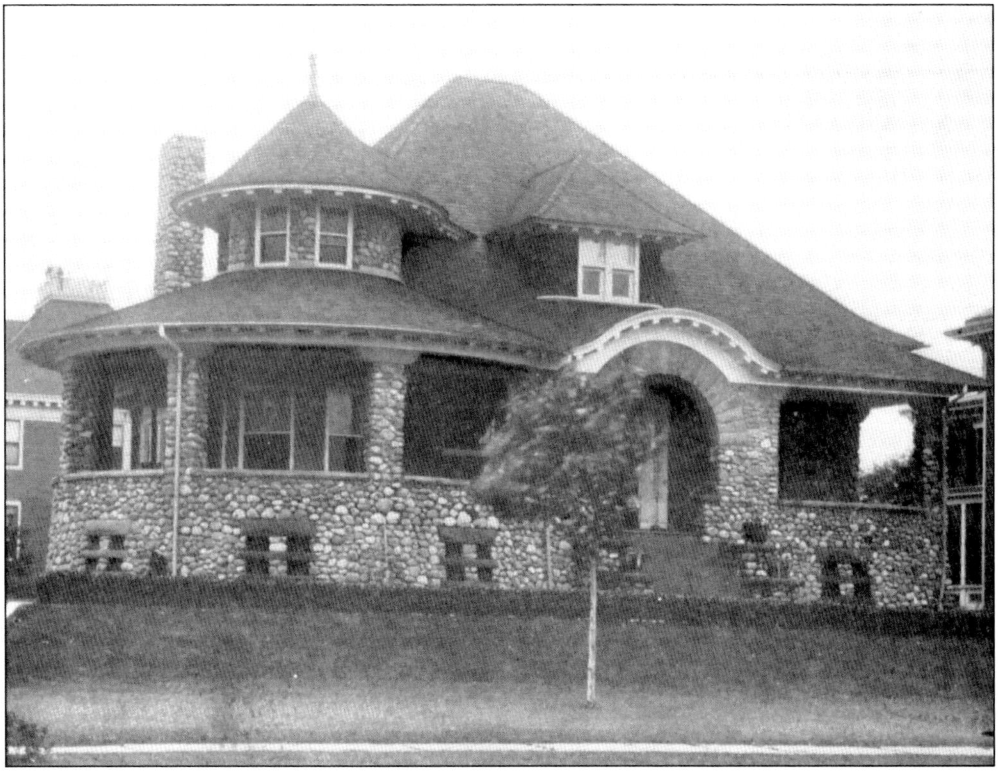

One of two examples of Richardsonian Romanesque architecture in Forest Hill, this c. 1900 house was built for Jacques Hohl, a silk manufacturer. The stonework is very distinctive, featuring a wraparound semicircular porch with river rock piers and brownstone stylized capitals. The structure is not very large, only one and a half stories, but has a two-story round tower with a conical roof. (CL.)

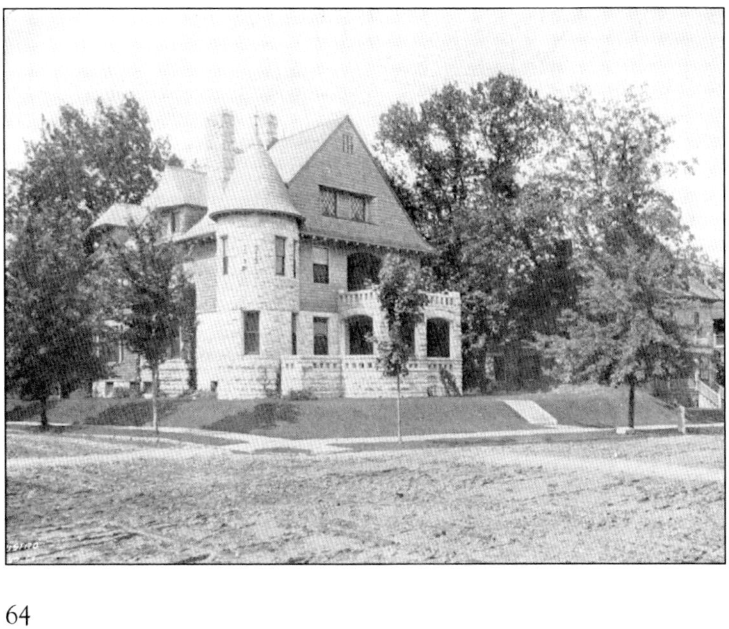

This is the other Forest Hill residence designed in the Richardsonian Romanesque style, which was built around 1900 for James M. Hunt. Appropriately, the Hunt brothers sold marble and stone in Newark. This home is larger than the one pictured above, although it has a more modest entrance bay built of stone with a pair of segmented arches. (CL.)

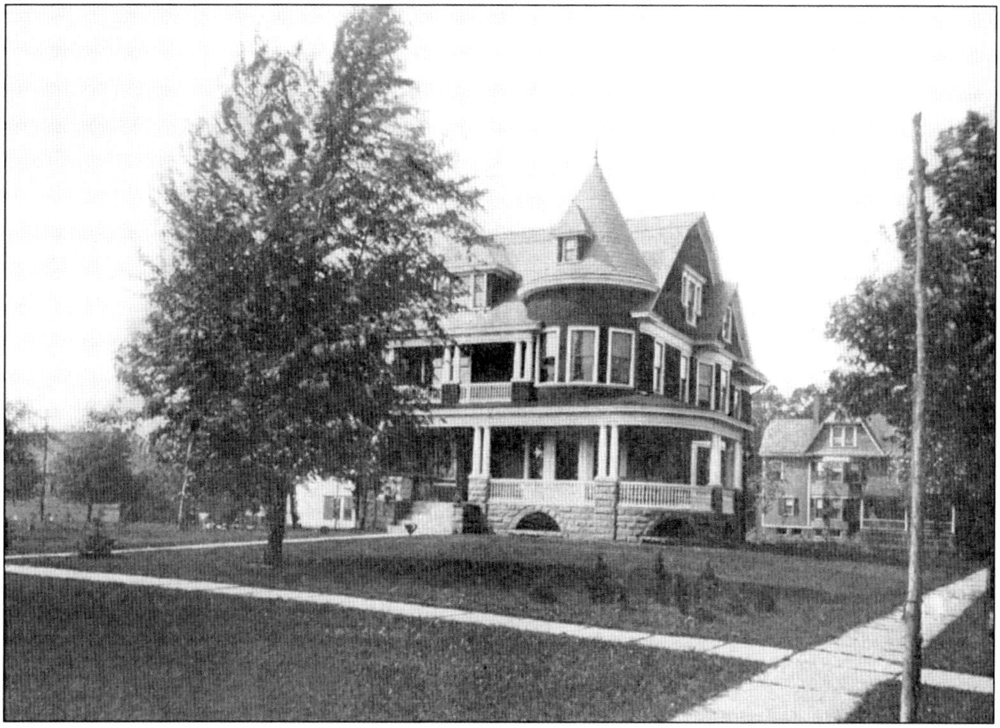

These two homes sit directly opposite each other. Although one has had extensive surface alterations in the intervening years, they remain almost mirror images as far as their structure. Built around 1895 in the Queen Anne style, both have wraparound porches and three-story corner towers with conical roofs. (Both, CL.)

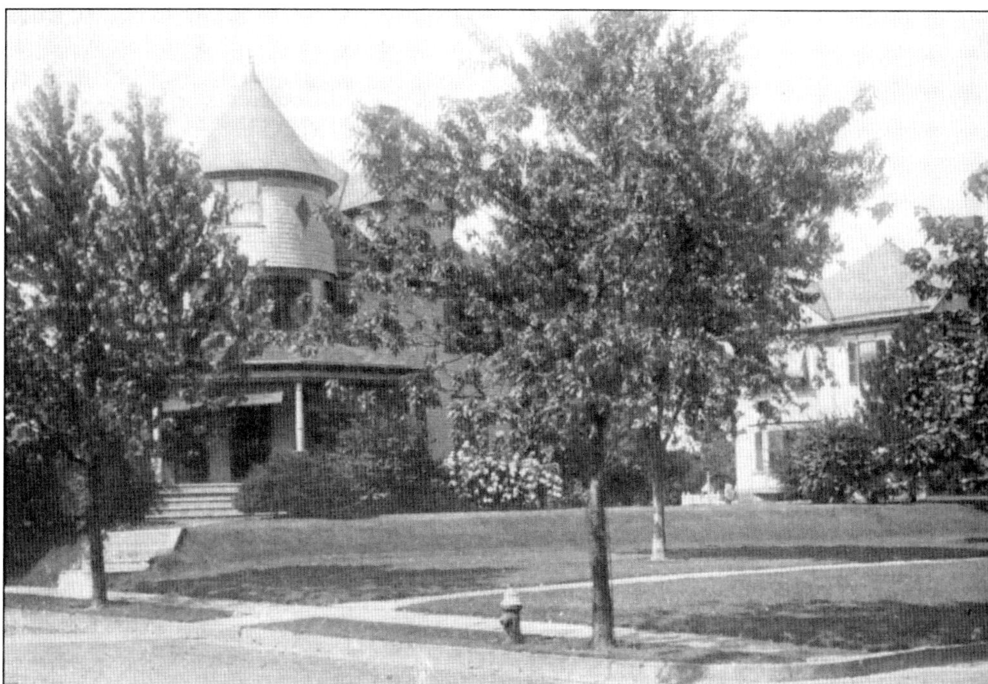

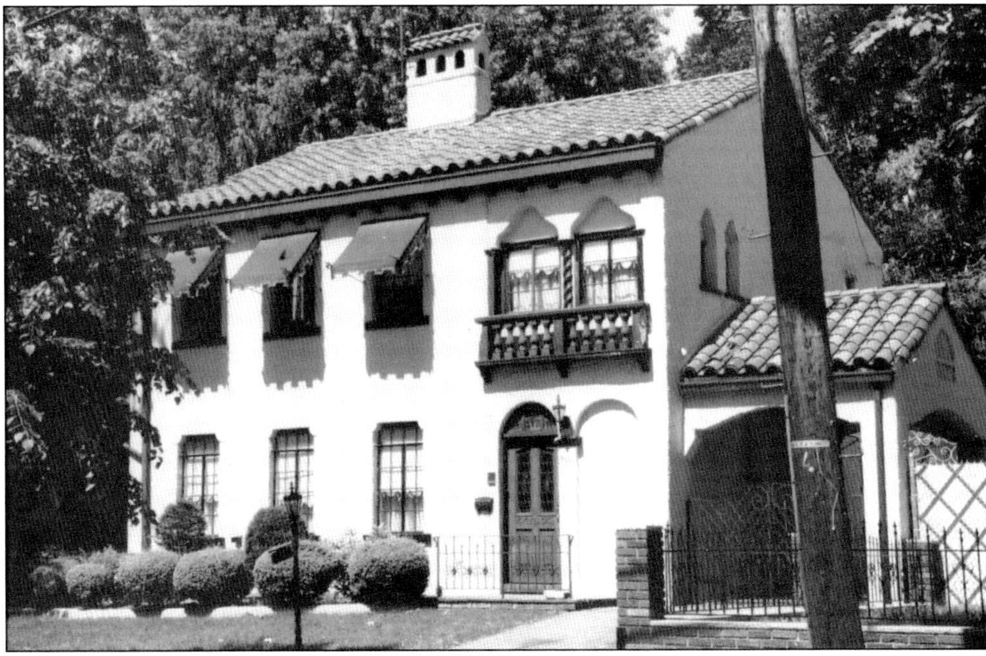

There are a number of Forest Hill residences built in the Spanish Eclectic style. This c. 1920 stucco structure with a red clay-tile roof and chimney cap has a paired arched entry and arched porte cochere. (NR, photograph by Ulana Zakalak.)

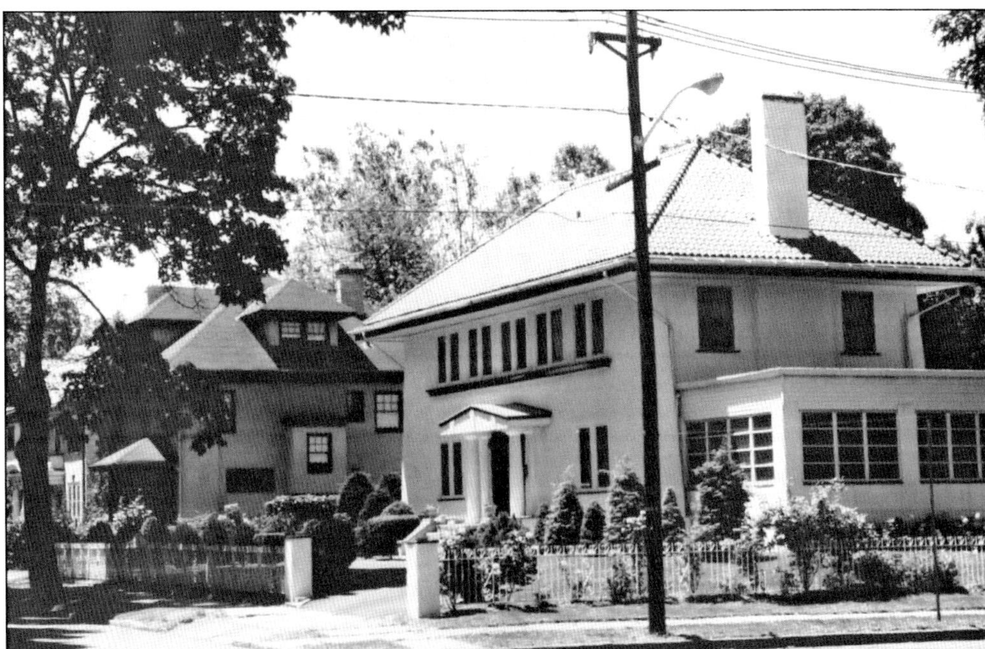

Another distinctive style is Mediterranean Revival. This c. 1910 stucco house features a Greek Doric pedimented portico, but the facade's dominant feature is a horizontal band of leaded casement windows, along with its green clay-tile barrel roof. (NR, photograph by Ulana Zakalak.)

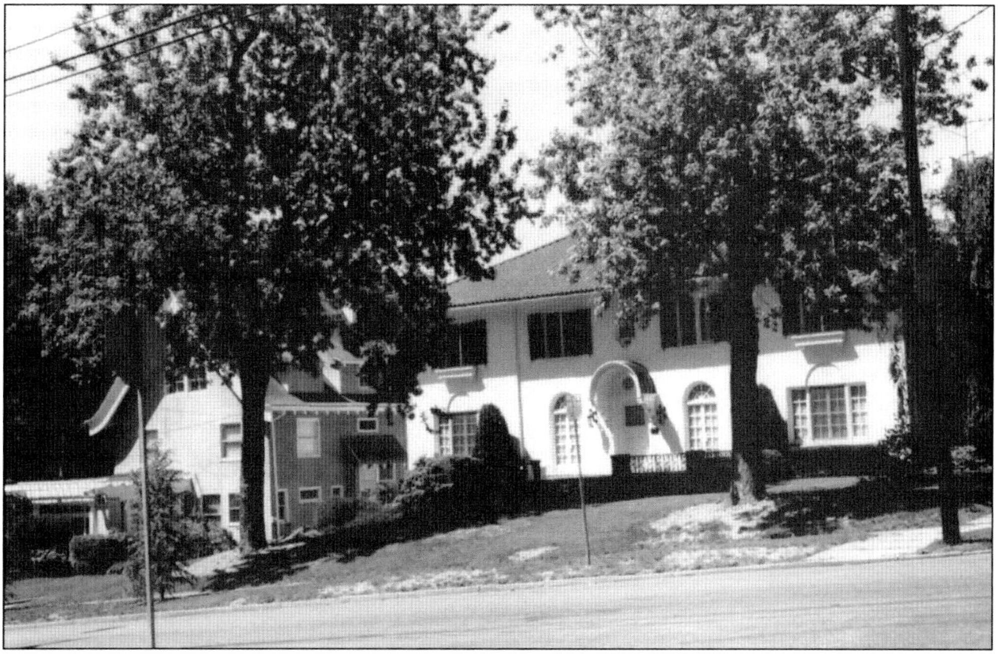

This c. 1920 Mediterranean villa also features stucco walls and a clay-tile roof. Note the round-headed French doors to either side of the entrance, which features a bracket-supported semicircular door hood. (NR, photograph by Ulana Zakalak.)

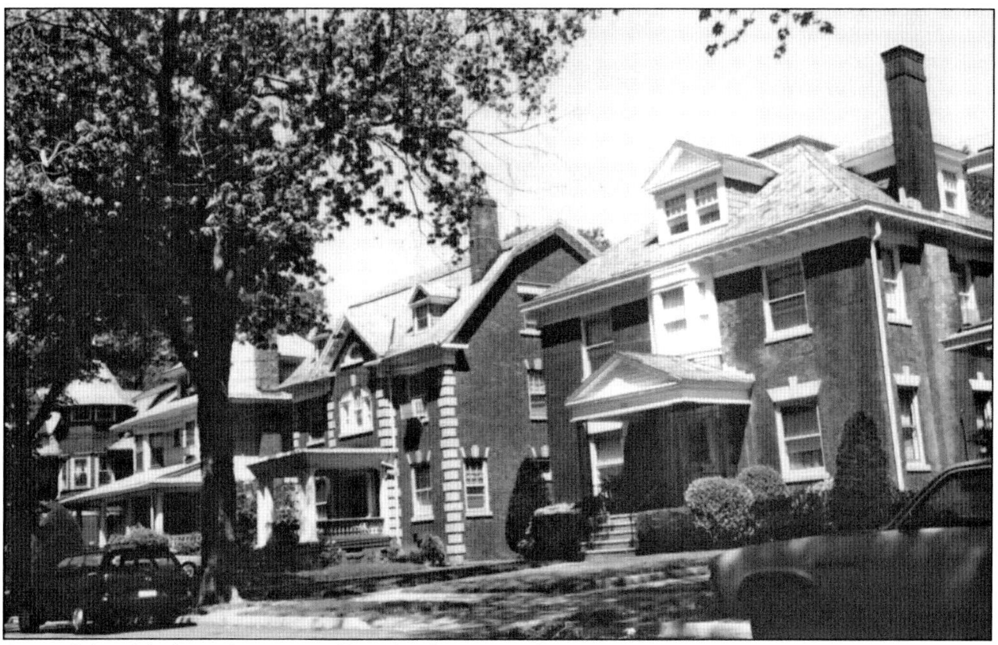

One of the delights of Forest Hill is the diverse architecture. Here, the Colonial Revival house in the center coexists with the Prairie home on the right, both of which were built around 1905. The brick Colonial Revival has a Palladian window above the front entrance, and the corners have contrasting brick quoins. The clapboard-clad Prairie has semi-hexagonal bay windows and a stained-glass oriel window on the north facade. (NR, photograph by Ulana Zakalak.)

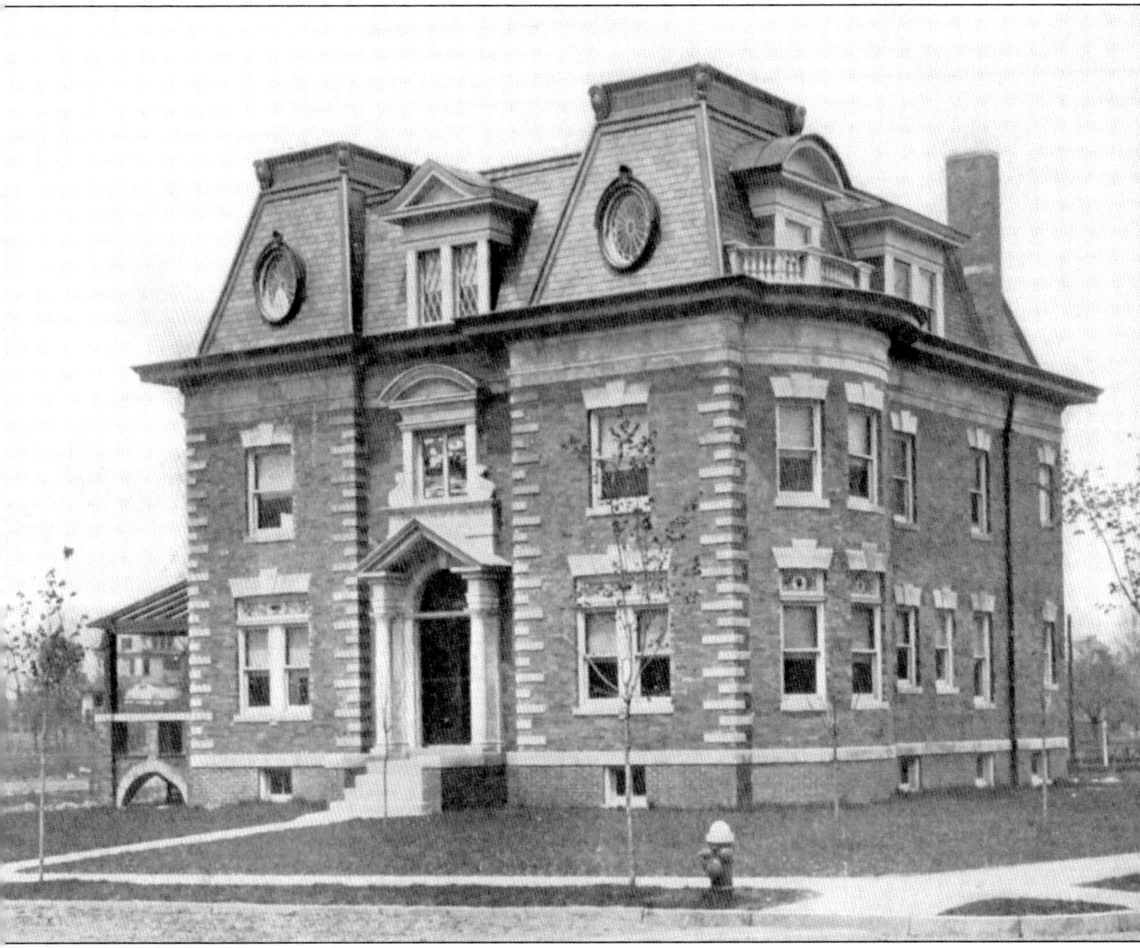

One of the earliest residences still standing in Forest Hill has long been referred to as the Tiffany Mansion, yet this home's history remains a mystery. Research does not disclose whether anyone affiliated with Tiffany & Co. ever resided here, though the nomination of the Forest Hill Historic District to the National Register states that the house was built in 1890 for Louis Comfort Tiffany. Research does show, however, that Hugo L. Kleinhans, president of Charles Cooper & Co., Inc., and the Kerotal Company located at 348 Van Buren Avenue in Newark, resided in the house in 1920. Situated on a corner property, the home's address has been listed with house numbers on both streets. The Tiffany Mansion was featured in the September/October 2011 issue of *Preservation* magazine, a publication of the National Trust for Historic Preservation, under the title "Tiffany Setting." The architectural style has been variously described as Chateauesque influenced or Second Empire. In addition to its mansard roof and stone quoins, it features oval leaded-glass windows on the upper level. (CL.)

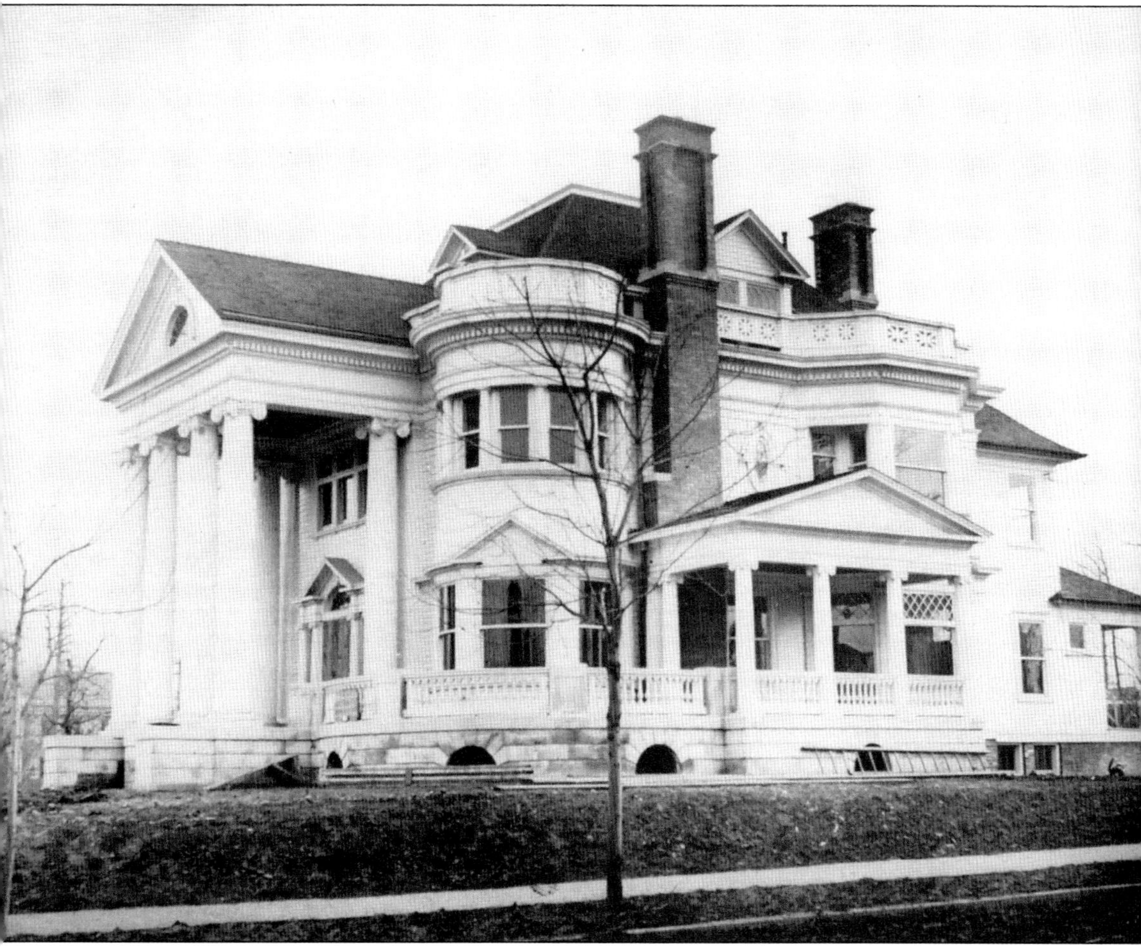

This Neoclassical gem designed by William Davenport Jones of New York City dominates the intersection of the large corner lot on which it sits. Built in 1902 for Edward Maher, a partner in the Maher-Flockhart Foundry in Newark, it is one of only a few Neoclassical-style residences in Forest Hill, none of which are as grand as this one. The dominant feature of this wood-frame, clapboard-clad structure is the pedimented portico, with its colossal Ionic columns. Note also the two-story circular bays flanking the front portico, as well as the side porticoes. This photograph was taken shortly after primary construction had been completed. The ladder resting against the side foundation indicates there is still work to be finished on the rear entrance. Not visible in this image is the carriage house built in a style similar to the main house. (William R. Mikesell.)

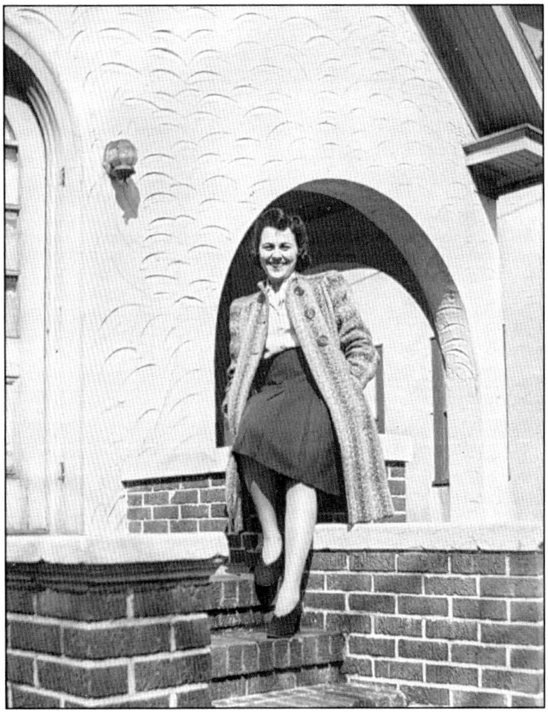

During the 1940s, the Nittoli family lived on Highland Avenue, moving from one house to another just two doors away. In the photograph on the left, Irma Nittoli (Morgese) poses on the front stoop of the family's second Highland Avenue home, modeling her new fur coat from, of course, Flemington Fur Company. Pictured below on graduation day 1941 in front of the family's first home on Highland Avenue, Michael Nittoli (St. Benedict's Prep) and Irma Nittoli (Morgese) (Newark State Teachers College) flank their father, James Nittoli. Older sister Lena Nittoli (Lecky) is on the steps. (Both, James P. Lecky.)

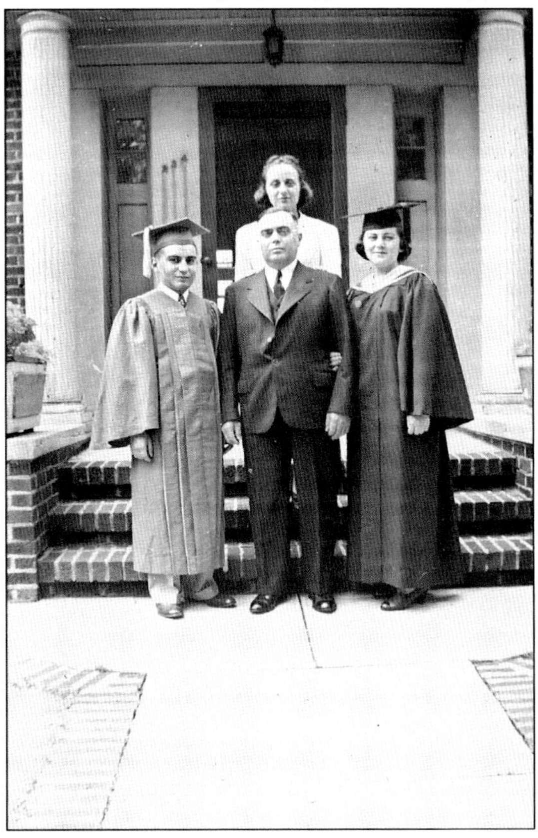

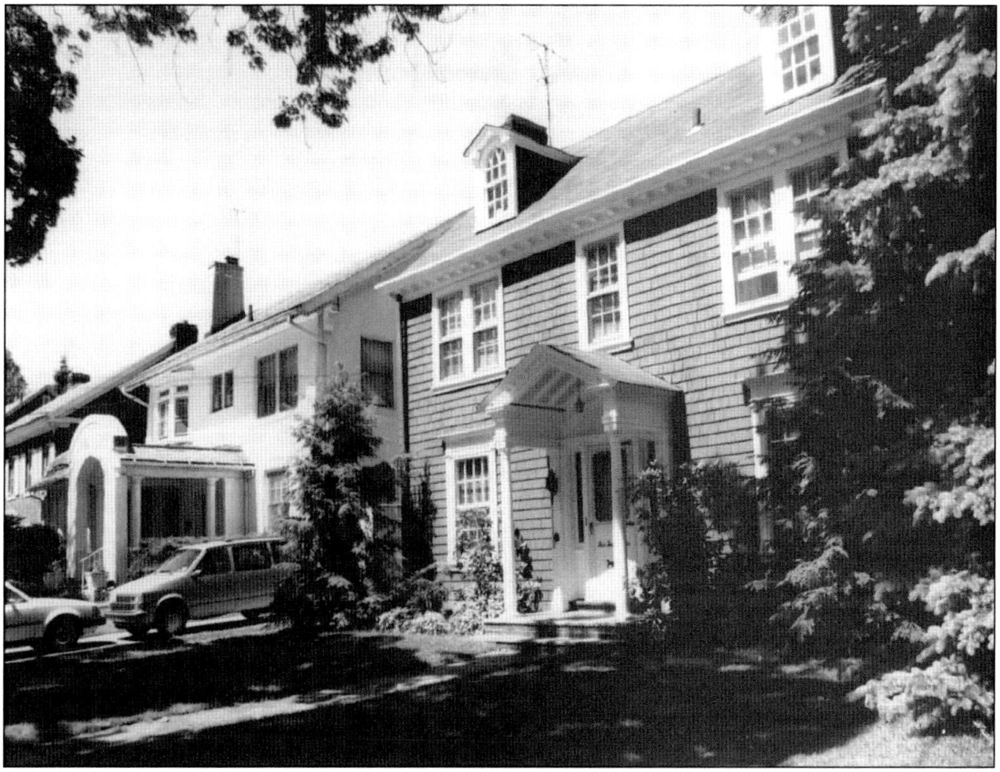

This Colonial Revival home was built in 1917 by Emma Gahviller. It was purchased in 1958 by John and Lena Lecky, and their son James still lives here. In the photograph on the right, a young James, dressed in his favorite Hopalong Cassidy outfit, is shown with his dog Lucky in front of a neighbor's house. In the 1950s and 1960s, neighborhood children thought nothing of riding their bicycles (or horse, in the case of this young cowboy) all over the neighborhood to play with their cousins and schoolmates, who almost always lived within a few blocks. (Both, James P. Lecky.)

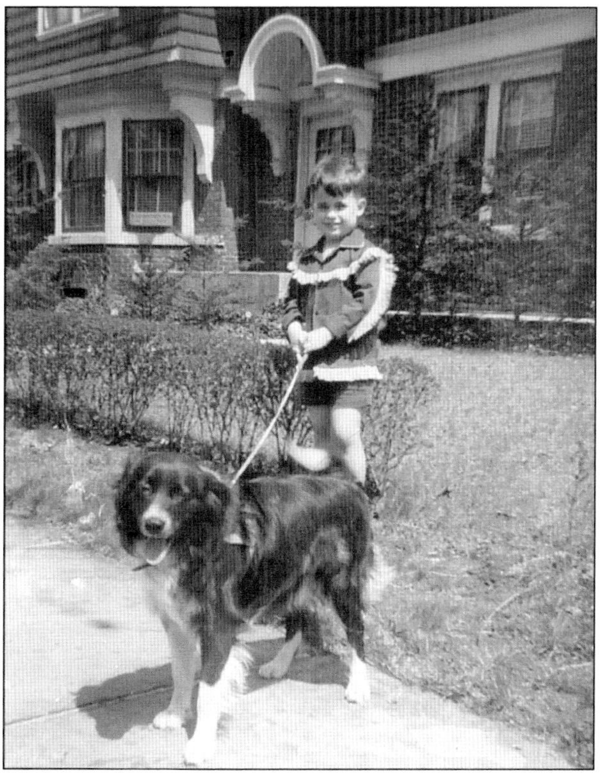

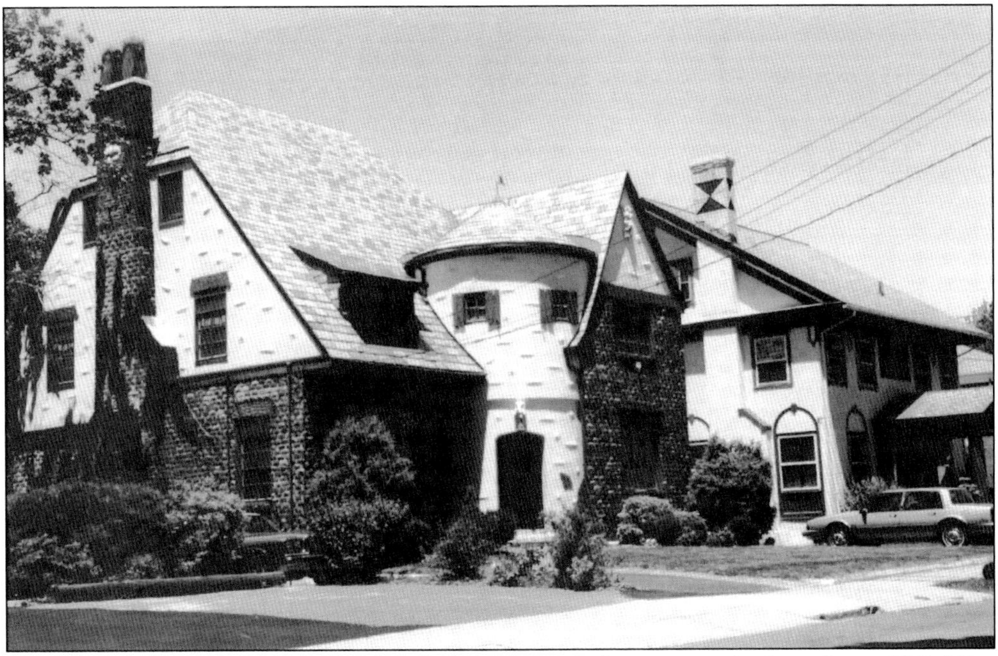

The Tudor style was very popular during the time most homes were built in Forest Hill. This c. 1920 residence has rough-textured brick and stucco walls with a multicolored slate roof. Its irregular massing makes an immediate impact, as well as the two-story circular turret that serves as the entry. Note the grotesque mask set into the upper portion of the massive chimney. (NR, photograph by Ulana Zakalak.)

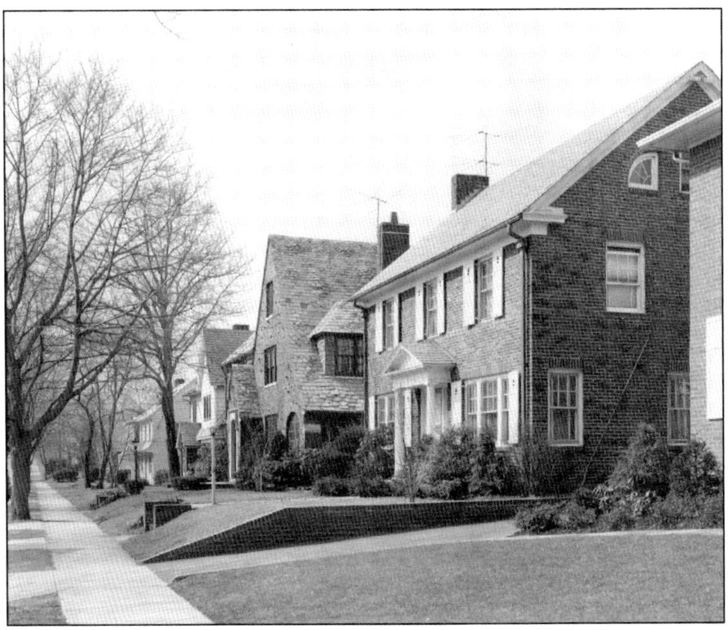

Here is another example of varying styles situated side by side for an appealing dichotomy. The house on the extreme right is a c. 1920 Colonial Revival with a Doric pedimented portico; note the quarter-round windows on the attic bays of the side facade. Next to it is a charming Tudor, also built in about 1920, which has a stone ogee arched surround on the entrance gable and a segmentally arched enclosed porch. (NCC.)

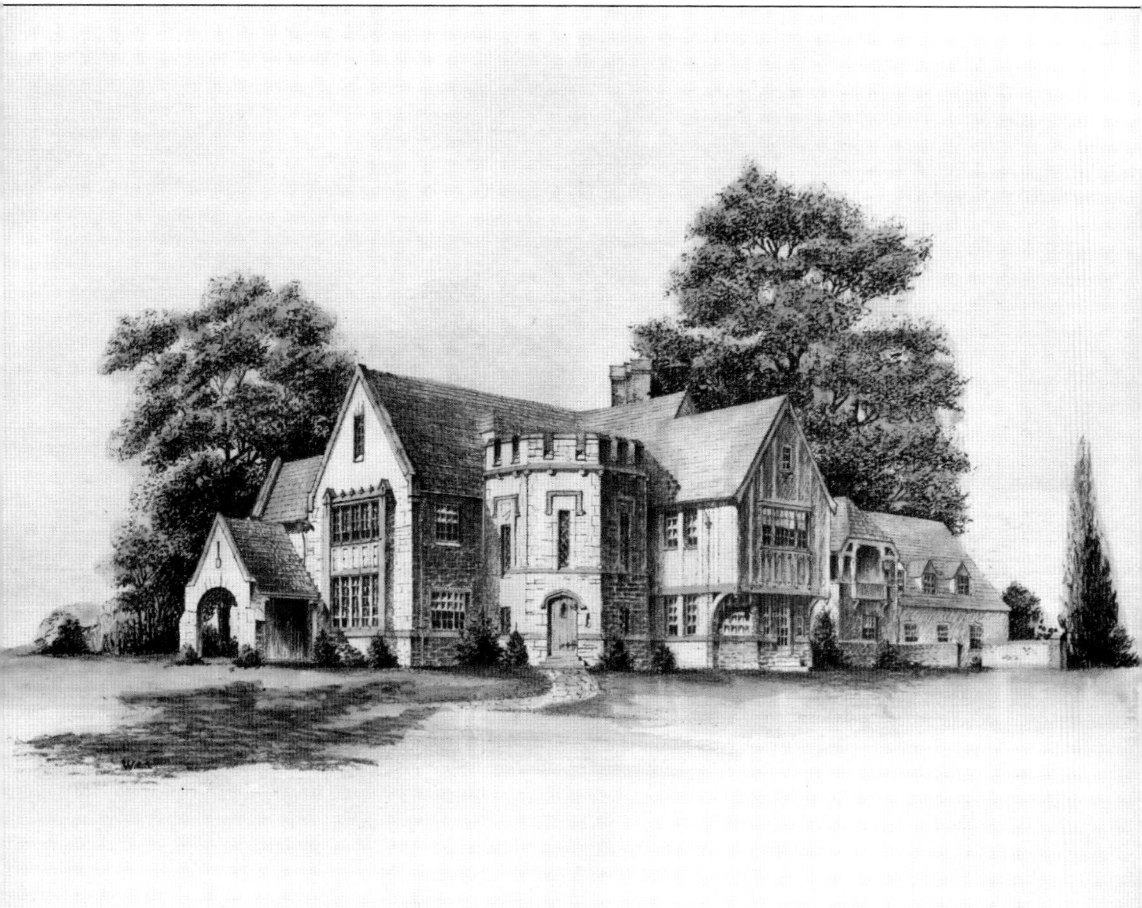

This is the original hand-drawn depiction of the residence of Dr. Earl LeRoy Wood. The nomination identifies it as Tudor style, but it is commonly referred to as "the Castle" because of its hexagonal, crenellated tower and turrets, semi-hexagonal bays, and irregular masonry and fenestration. William Clark built it for his daughter in 1928 when she married Dr. Wood, and included a private tennis court for the couple. Dr. Wood liked to tell about the retaining wall he later had built during the Depression, when Italians from the First Ward planted "weekend gardens" nearby. They walled off each garden space, and as Dr. Wood was strolling along and admiring the gardens, he was enamored with these improvised walls. He picked the one he liked best and asked the builder to create one for him. With materials scarce, the man gathered whatever stones he could find. He then began working the stones into a uniform facade, but Dr. Wood stopped him, explaining that he wanted an irregular surface. And as a result, the wall at the foot of this incredible home contains odd pieces of broken pottery and statuary. (Mark A. Covey.)

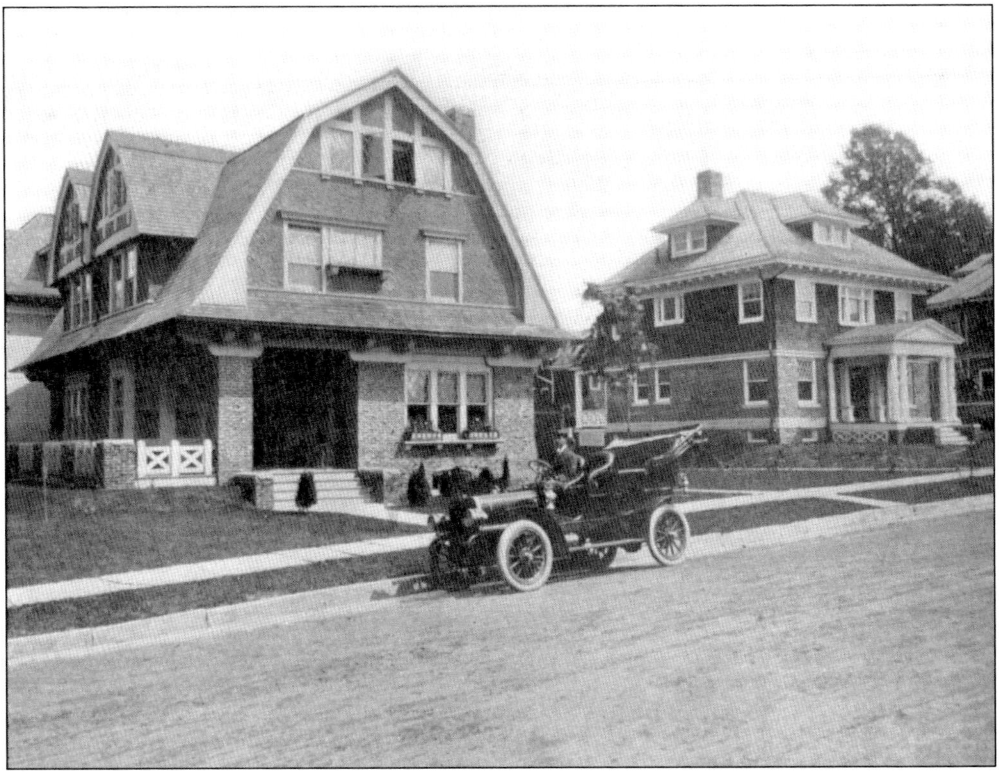

In 1913, Edwin C. Feigenspan, of the famous brewing family, built this Colonial Revival residence. The house has a segmentally arched portico, central double dormer, and Doric-order supported porte cochere. Note the unpaved street with brick-lined gutters. There is no record of whether that is Feigenspan or his chauffeur seen behind the wheel. (CL.)

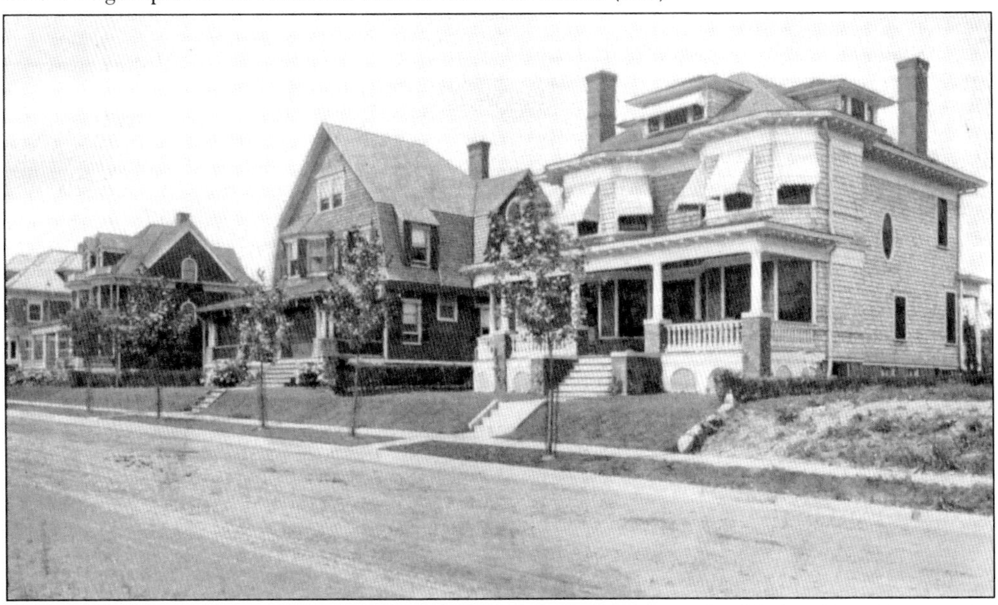

This c. 1900 Colonial Revival is a clapboard-clad, three-bay structure highlighted by a Doric-order supported porch. The young trees mark this street scene as newly developed at that time. (CL.)

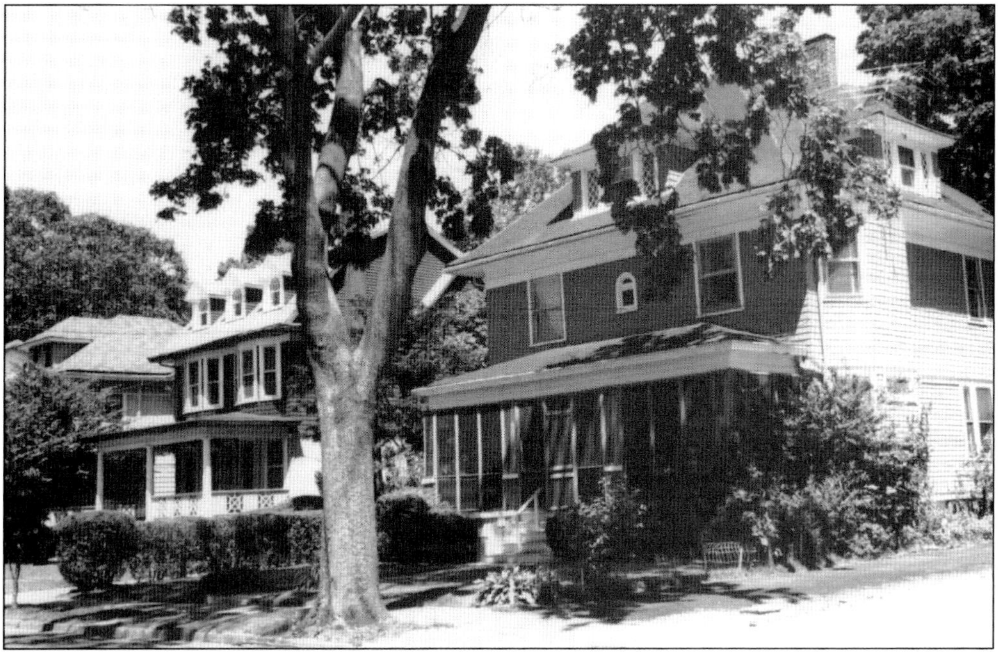

The nomination identifies the above house on the left as Eclectic, but its Craftsman heritage is apparent. The house has a Doric column-supported full front porch, stuccoed first floor, and shingled second floor. There are two hexagonal bay windows and three gabled dormers. The interior woodwork has survived in its original finish, and the inlaid hardwood floors are intact. Shown here are the front entry hall and its classic paneling, along with the original staircase and window and door surrounds. While many homes in the historic district have not survived this well, many others still retain the original detailing that identifies them with their particular architectural style. (Above, NR, photograph by Ulana Zakalak; below, photograph by Catharine Longendyck.)

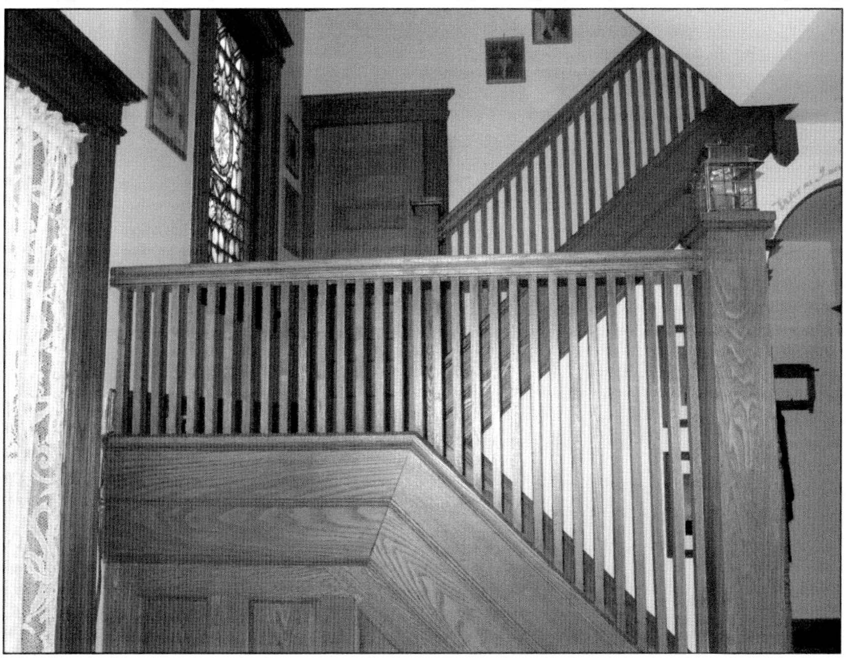

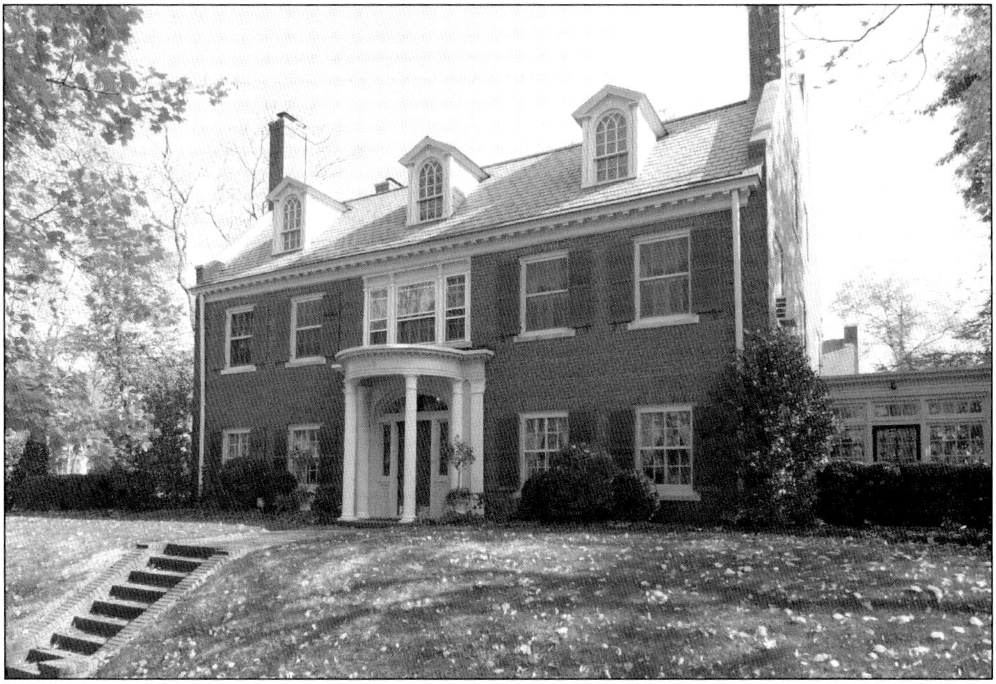

Meadow View is a 1920 Georgian Colonial Revival with a semicircular portico supported by fluted columns with stylized papyri capitals. The door surround has sidelights and an elliptical fanlight. A tripartite window grouping with Doric columnettes surmounts the entrance portico. The slate-covered roof has stone-coped brick parapets and three pedimented, gabled dormers. (Photograph by Greg Martz, In House Photography.)

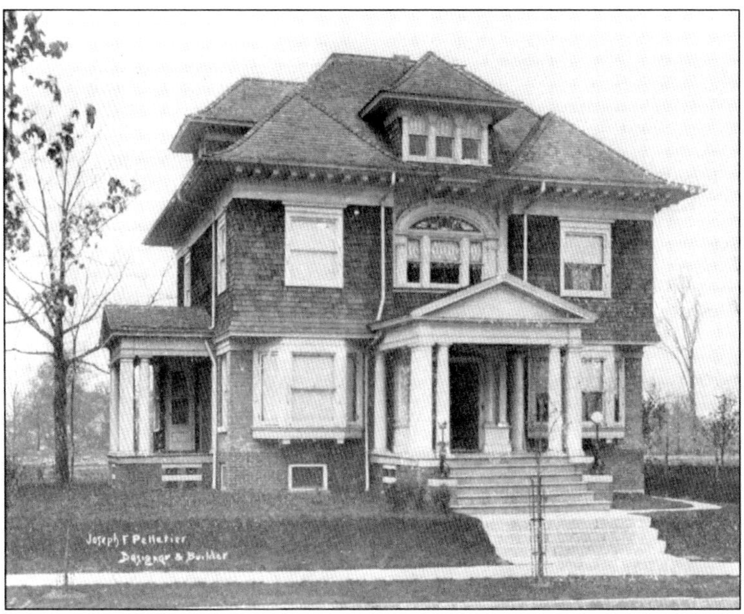

Architect Joseph F. Pelletier designed and built this Colonial Revival house in 1905 for Willard Hamilton. This brick and half-frame residence has front and side pedimented Doric porticoes and a pedimented oriel window on the second story. The second-floor central bay features a segmentally arched window grouping with a stained-glass fanlight. (NPL.)

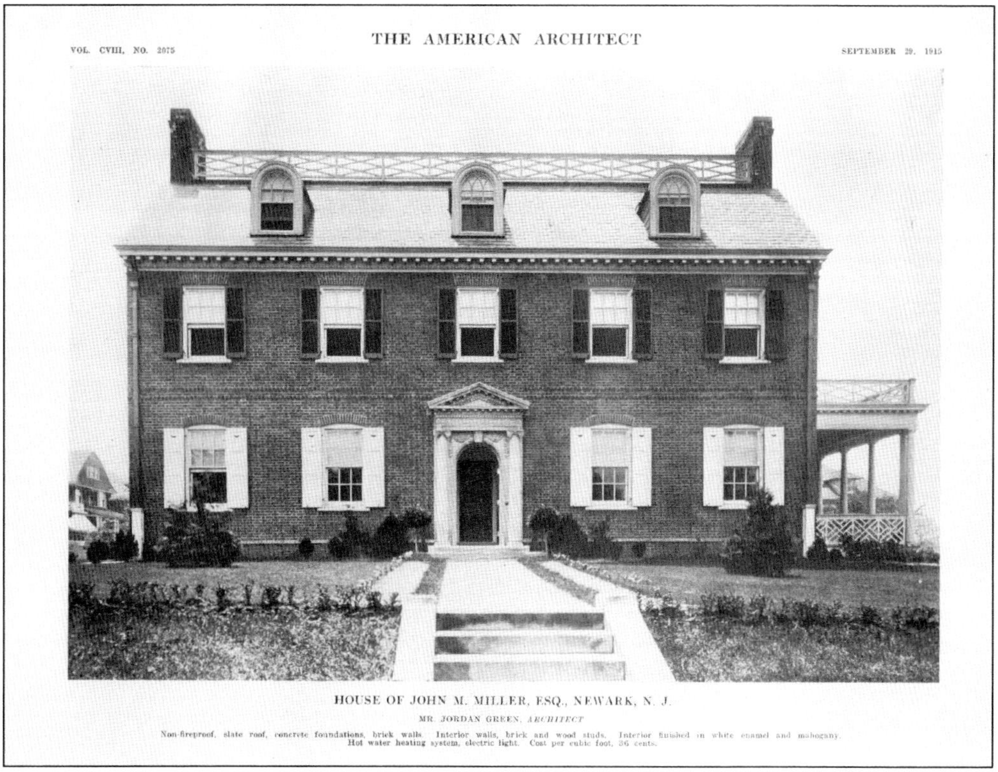

The John Miller house was designed by Newark architect Jordan Green and built in 1910. Not visible in this image is the adjacent carriage house, which is a miniature version of this Georgian Colonial Revival. An elaborate pedimented stone door surround frames the front entrance. Note also the side portico with roofline cresting, which matches that on the slate roof connecting the paired end-wall chimneys. This photograph originally appeared in the *American Architect*, published September 29, 1915. (Mark A. Covey.)

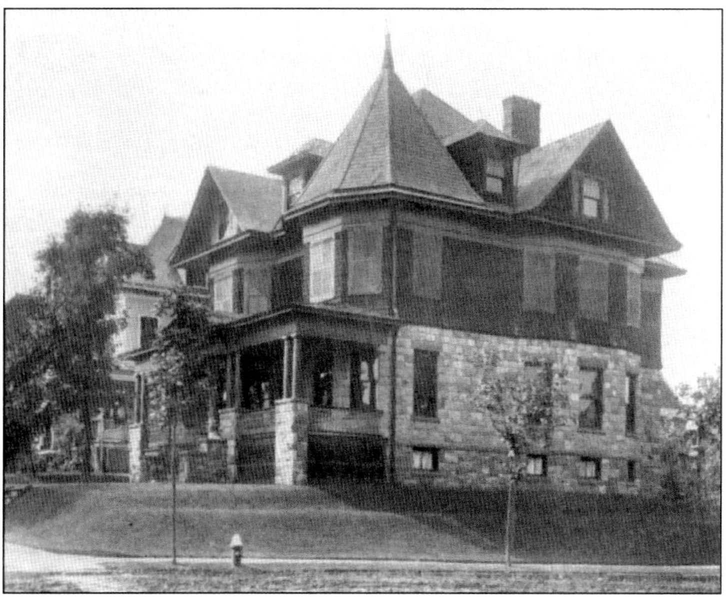

This c. 1900 Queen Anne residence was built on an irregular plan with three semi-hexagonal bay windows and an octagonal tower. Among the many elaborate features of this classic style are a full front porch with center gable and paired columns supported by stone piers. The brownstone first floor and shingled second story horizontally divide the facade of this imposing structure. (CL.)

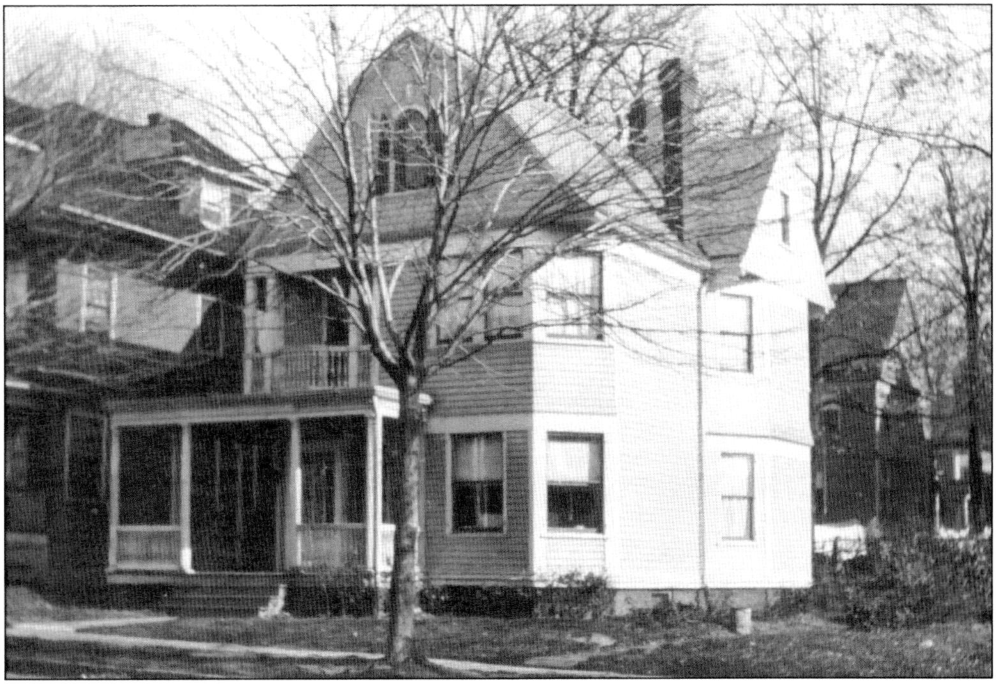

The term *Eclectic* is applied to structures that do not fit neatly into any of the strictly defined architectural styles. This c. 1910 Eclectic residence has clapboard siding, a column-supported porch with spindled balustrade, and a second-story porch. The door surround is embellished with a swag-motif frieze, and there are Palladian windows in the front-facing apex, which is adorned with interesting fish-scale and diamond shingles to offset the beautifully variegated colors of the slate roof. (Samuel Rivera.)

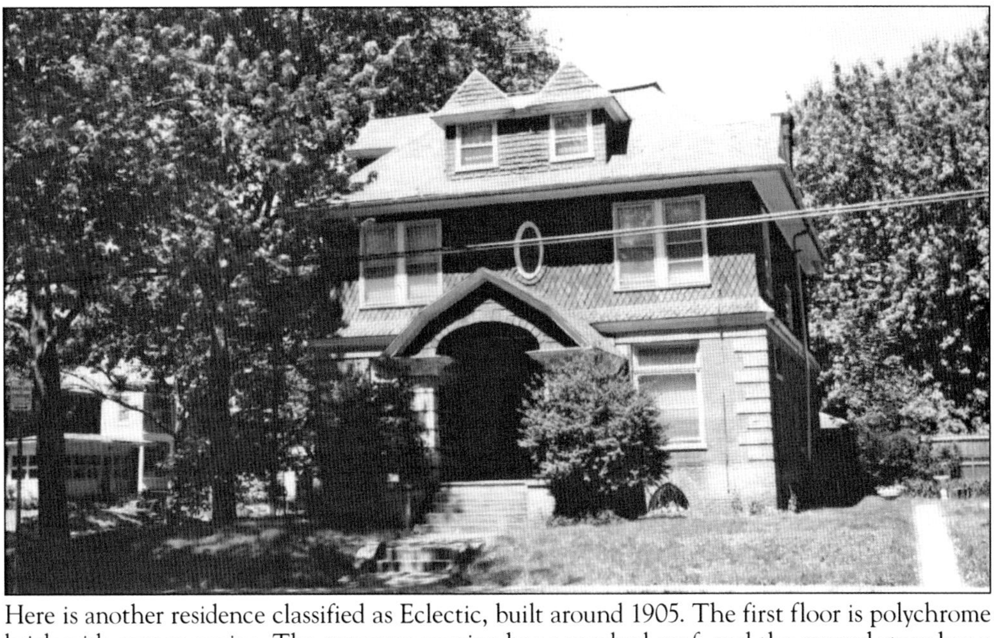

Here is another residence classified as Eclectic, built around 1905. The first floor is polychrome brick with corner quoins. The entrance portico has a gambrel roof, and the second story has a distinctive shingle pattern, with a centered oval window. (NR, photograph by Ulana Zakalak.)

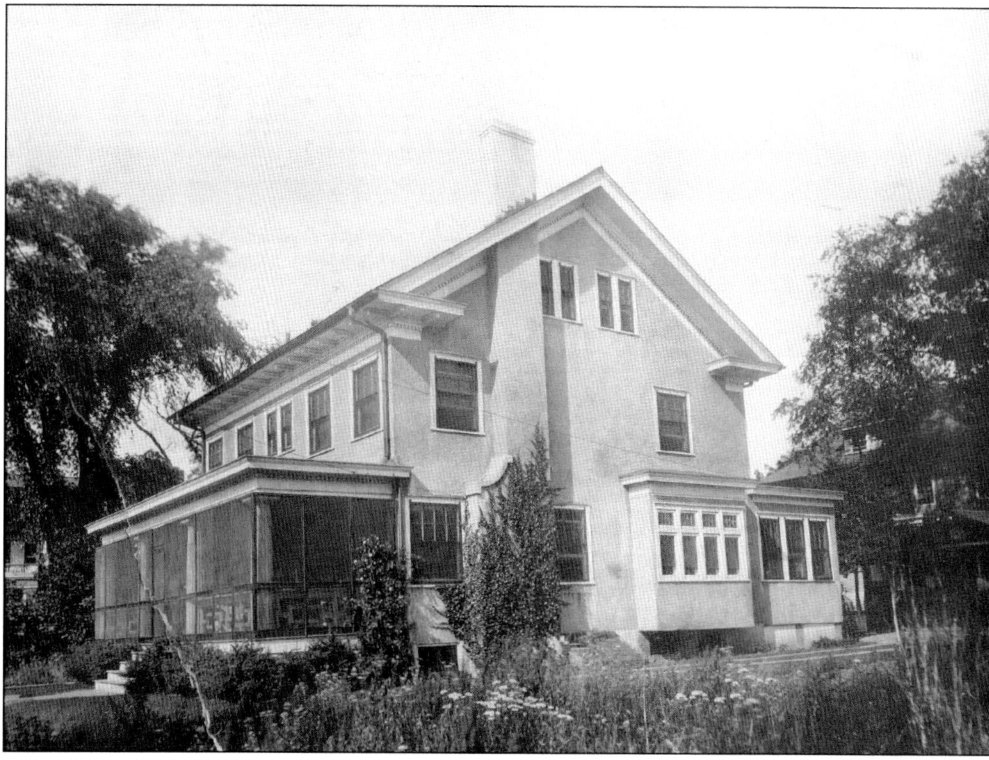

Judge Samuel Bigelow, a descendant of Newark mayor Moses Bigelow, was the original owner of the c. 1920 Colonial Revival home above. It has a full front porch supported by fluted columns, a double-door entry, and multipaned windows. The photograph to the right shows the judge's study. His daughter, on a visit to Newark, stopped by and told the current homeowners about growing up here and about her wedding, held on the grounds of this house. (Both, Joseph Oliverie and Linda Oliverie.)

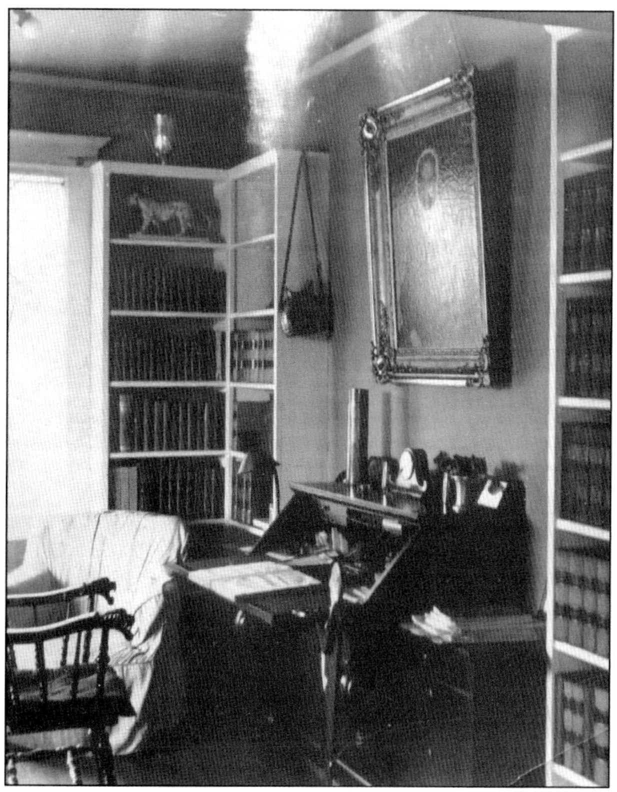

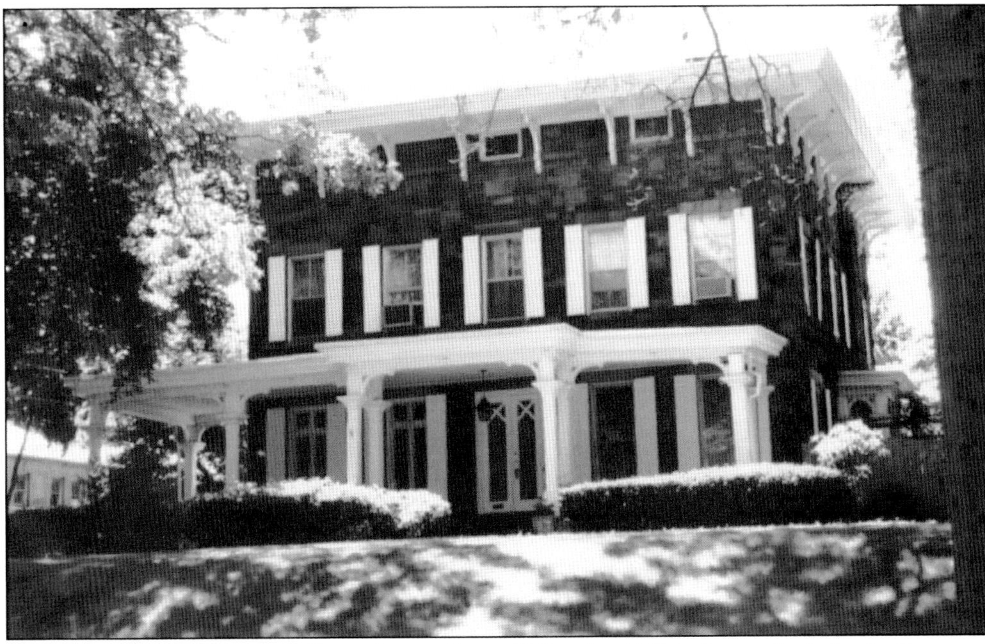

Another of the older homes still standing in Forest Hill is this 1875 Italianate built for the Reverend William Hayes Ward. This large home has a brownstone foundation and walls, a wooden porch, and large overhanging bracket-supported eaves. Reverend Ward was a prominent church figure and champion of minority groups, as well as editor of the *New York Independent*. (NR, photograph by Ulana Zakalak.)

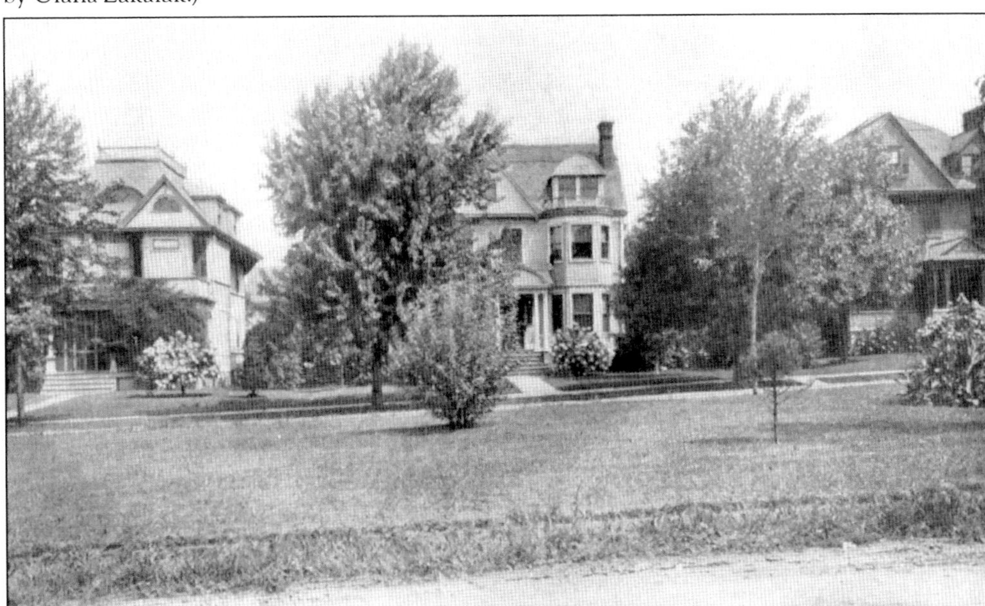

From Highland Avenue to Branch Brook Park Drive, Heller Parkway is divided by a wide, landscaped median. This photograph shows one block of the parkway with varying styles of homes and the large lots on which they were built. The c. 1915 house in the center is Queen Anne influenced, with a wraparound porch, an enclosed side porch, an arched pediment entryway, two-story semi-hexagonal bays, and fish-scale shingles. (NPL.)

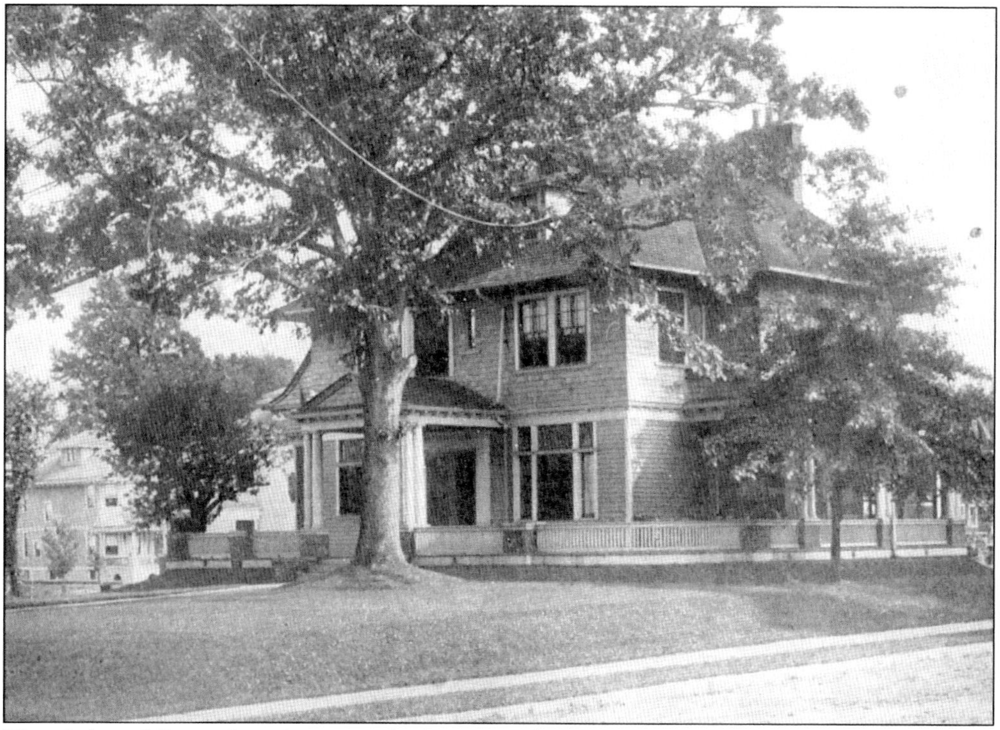

This Colonial Revival residence was built in 1913 for noted surgeon Dr. Wells Phillips Eagleton and his wife, a women's suffrage activist. The clapboard house has a paired Doric column-supported portico and side porch. It later became part of the estate acquired by Newark businessman Irving Seery and his wife, opera singer Maria Jeritza, who resided in another house within the gated compound of five structures, including carriage houses. (CL.)

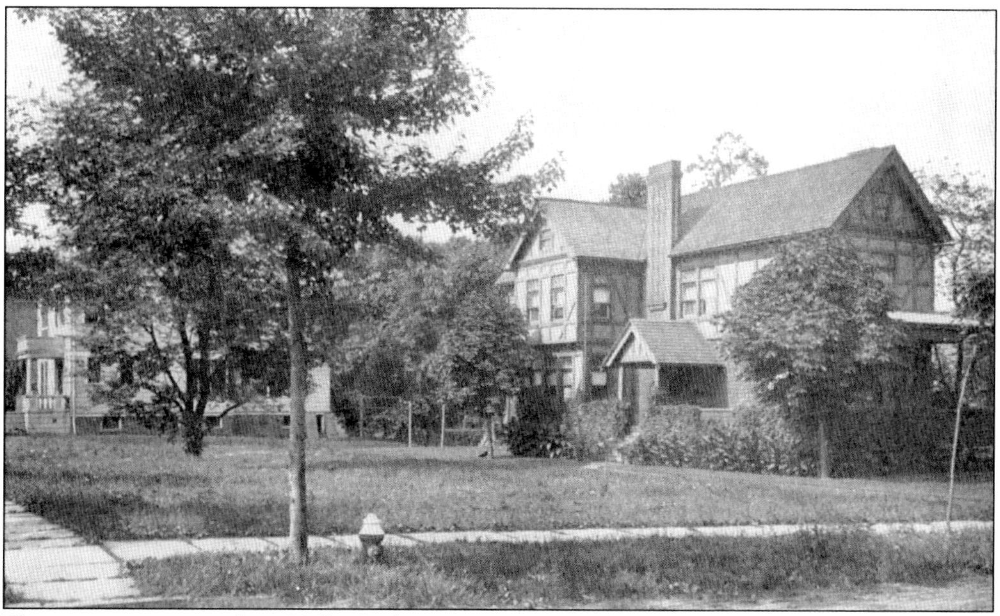

The spacious scenery along Heller Parkway is apparent in this view of a c. 1905 Tudor home. The empty lot on the left is now the site of a Colonial Revivial–style home built in 1911. (CL.)

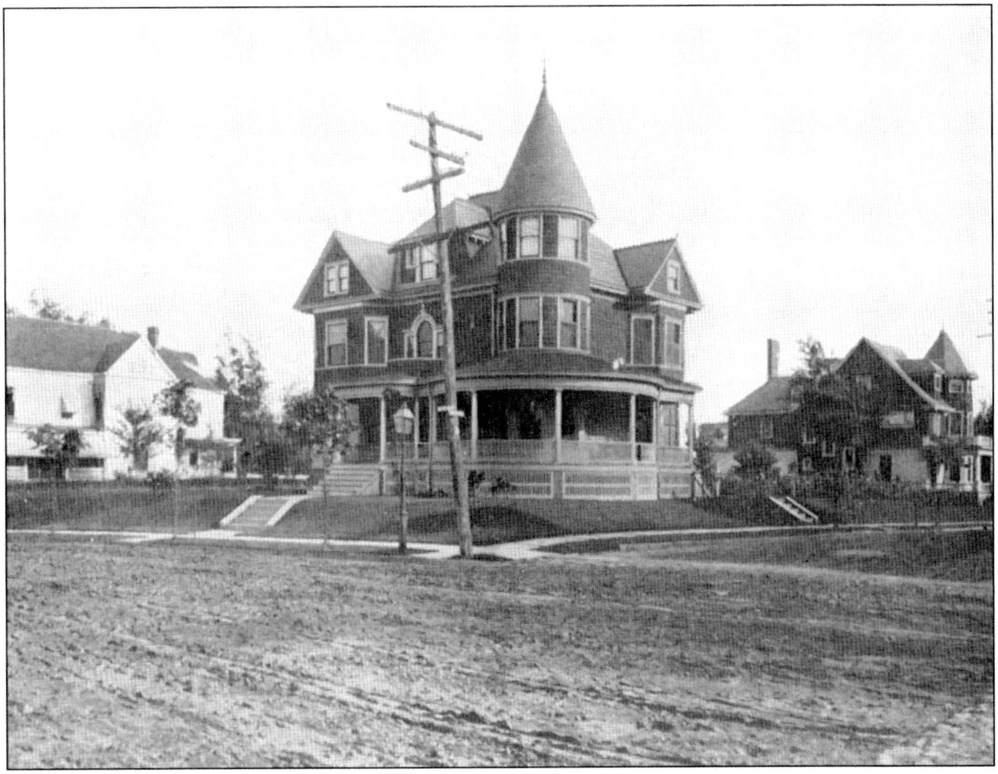

This Queen Anne was built by the Forest Hill Association in 1897 for William and Viola Sinnock. It remains remarkably intact, with its semi-hexagonal bays and three-story circular corner tower. It has a wraparound porch and a Palladian window on the shingled second story, which is topped with a roof of fish-scale slate shingles. (Samuel Rivera.)

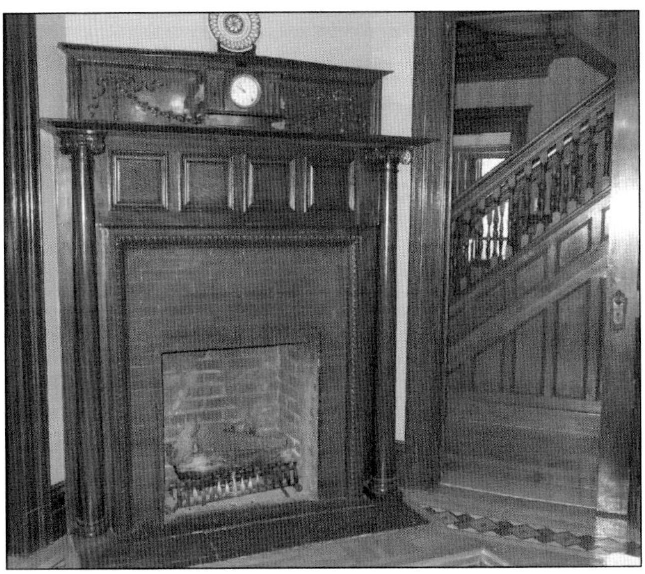

This photograph and those on the next page show interior design features typical of a Queen Anne residence. This particular house was once owned by a doctor whose patients would enter through a separate entrance off the wraparound porch. The fireplace shown here in the back parlor on the main floor backs up to a contrasting one in the front parlor. Note the ornate fireplace surround, the patterned inlay of the floorboards, and the coffered hallway paneling. (Photograph by Catharine Longendyck.)

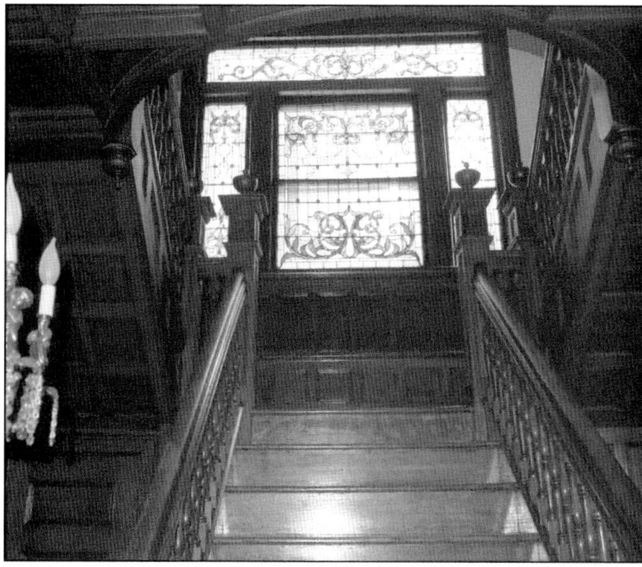

The finely detailed balustrades of this elegant winged staircase, the underside of which is adorned with more elaborate paneling, draw the eye to the focal point of the landing. On a sunny afternoon, this staircase, first-floor entrance hall, and second-floor hall are all bathed in a wash of colored light from this intricately designed stained-glass window and surround. The front door opposite this staircase also features a stained-glass transom and sidelights. (Photograph by Catharine Longendyck.)

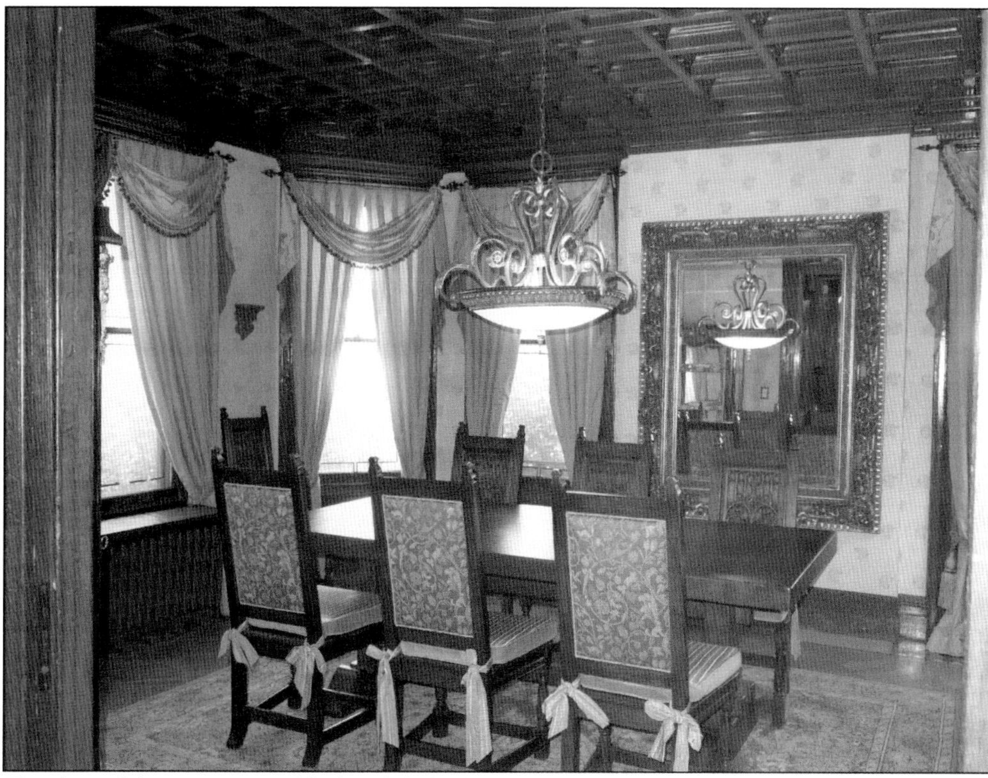

This formal dining room is filled with light from its four windows, including the three-part bay. The wooden coffered ceiling reinforces the classic design esthetic found throughout the home, with its pocket doors, tall windows, inlaid hardwood floors, and magnificent paneling and woodwork. (Photograph by Catharine Longendyck.)

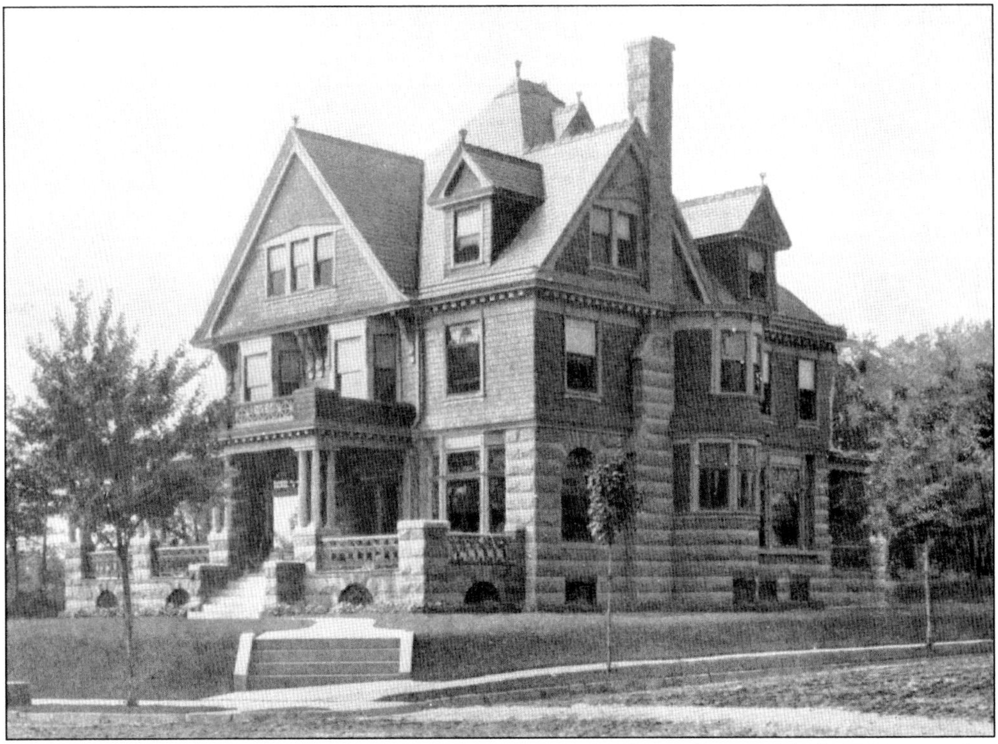

Built in 1898 by the Cory brothers of the Newark jewelry firm of Cory, Clark & Noone, this imposing Eclectic residence is characterized by rusticated stone on the first story with alternating rough and smooth courses of brownstone. There is a wraparound porch and paired fluted columns supported by brownstone piers. The house also features semi-hexagonal bays, multiple window groupings, and gabled dormers. (CL.)

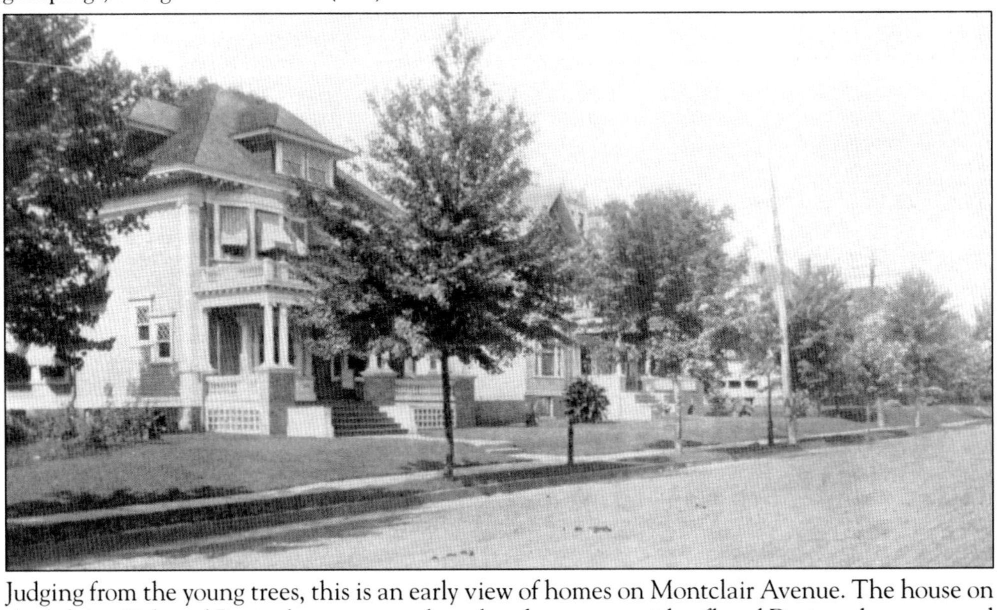

Judging from the young trees, this is an early view of homes on Montclair Avenue. The house on the left is a Colonial Revival structure, a three-bay foursquare with a fluted Doric order-supported wraparound porch set on brick piers. (CL.)

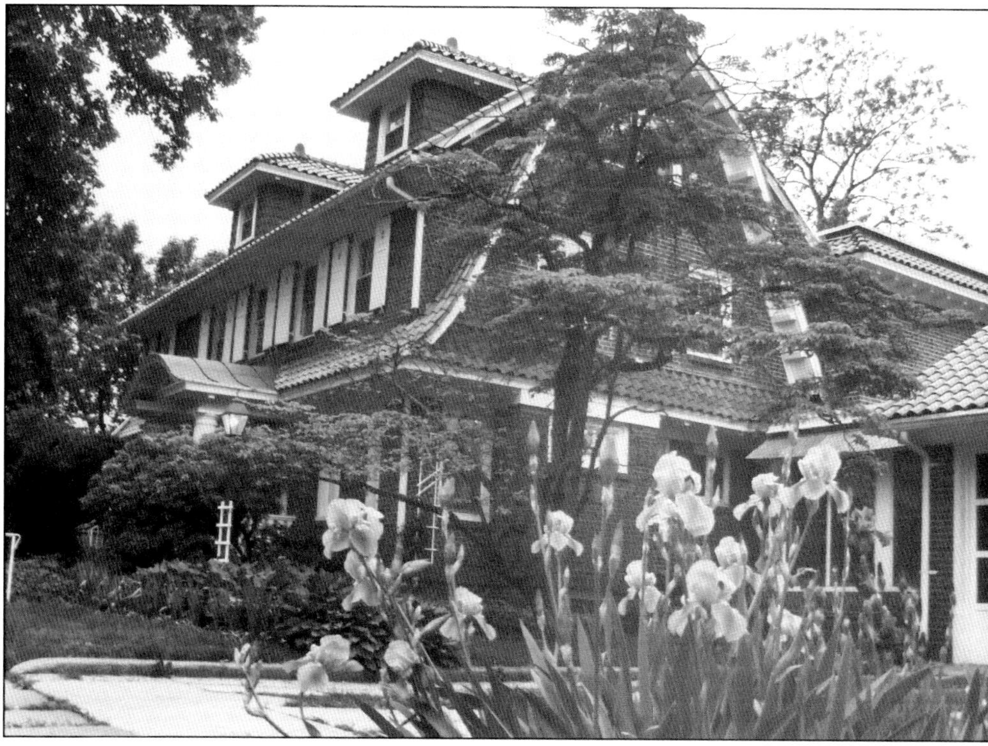

While there are many, many Colonial Revival homes in Forest Hill, the c. 1925 Dutch Colonial Revival style seen here is less common. The house has a segmentally arched fluted Doric order-supported portico and a tripartite door surround with beveled and leaded-glass door and sidelights. Both the house and its adjacent garage have barrel roofs of green clay tile. (Photograph by Dan Karslake.)

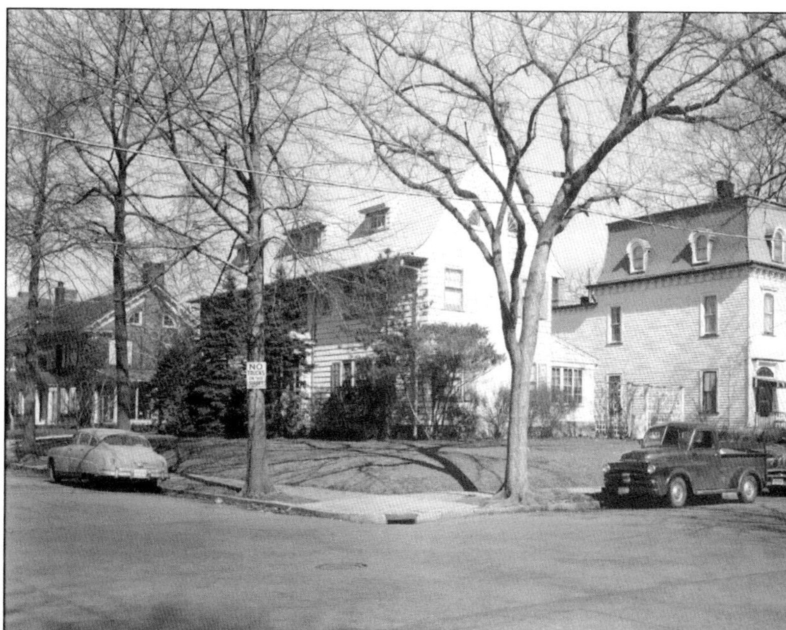

Photographed in 1961, this Colonial Revival dates to 1920. This weatherboard-sided house has a tripartite entry with leaded-glass sidelights, an elliptical fanlight, and a post-supported portico. (NCC.)

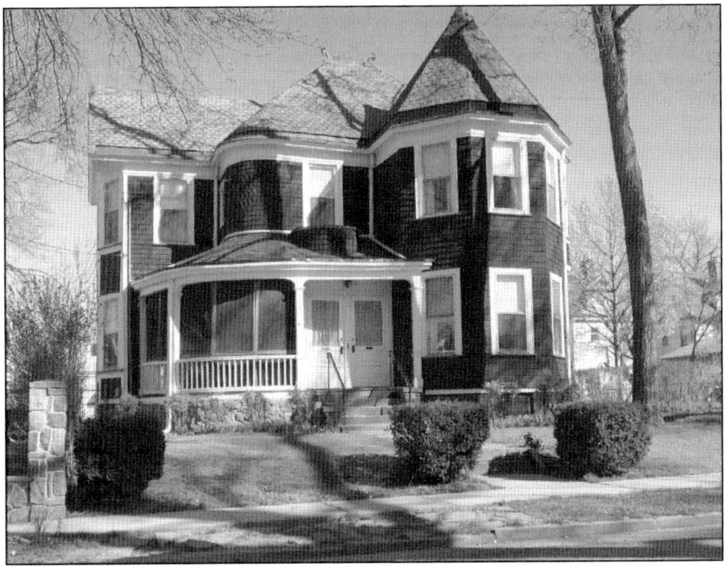

This c. 1900 residence built in the Shingle style with Queen Anne influences has a semicircular column-supported porch, an octagonal two-story tower with conical roof, and semi-hexagonal bay. The rounded wall surface above the porch is adorned with a diamond-shaped shingle detail. Note the special cresting along the roofline as well. (Photograph by Catharine Longendyck.)

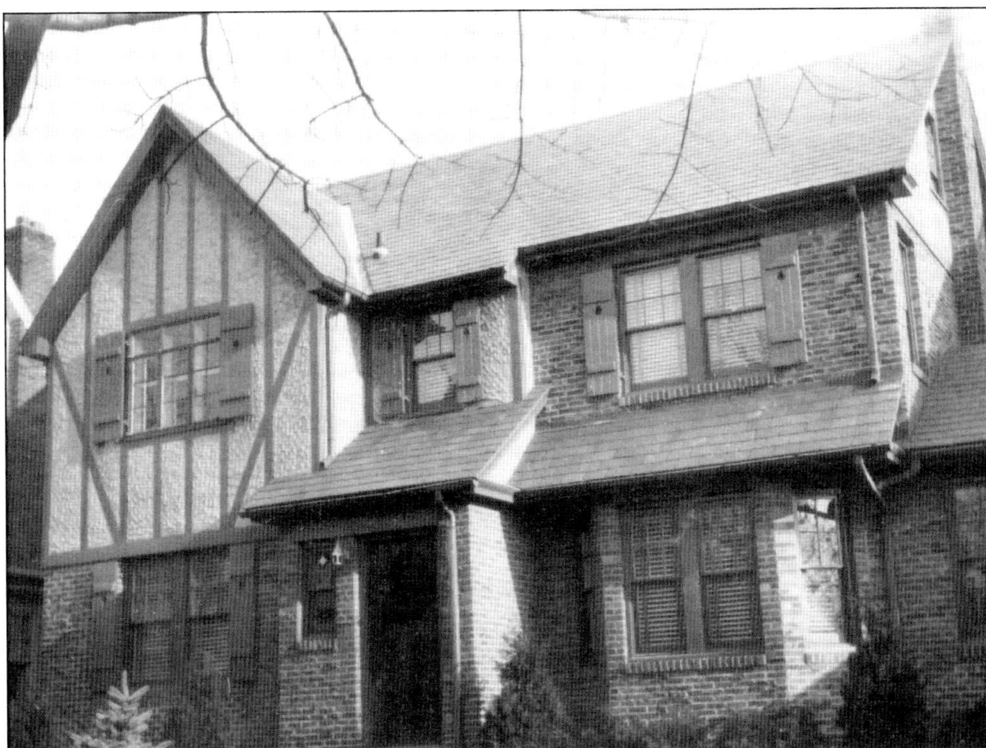

A c. 1920 Tudor residence, this mostly brick home features a section of stucco and false half-timbering on the second-floor facade, which is topped by a slate roof with an intersecting-gable roofline. There are two- and three-part window groupings and a shed roof enclosing an entrance porch, in addition to its enclosed side porch. (Joyce Fernicola.)

Five

NEIGHBORING LANDMARKS

Not surprisingly, walking a few blocks in any direction from Forest Hill will reveal a wealth of historic landmarks and properties. Part of the attraction of living in Forest Hill extends well beyond its borders.

Unquestionably, one of Forest Hill's greatest assets is its proximity to Branch Brook Park—America's first county park, developed by the Essex County Park Commission. Envisioned by Frederick Law Olmsted and Calvert Vaux in 1867 in response to a request from the Newark city park commissioners, the park was not developed until 1895 because specific legislation was needed. Branch Brook Park serves as the western border of Forest Hill, and many residents claim the park as their own.

The resting place for some of Newark's most influential citizens is just a few blocks to the east of Forest Hill, on Broadway, at Mount Pleasant Cemetery. Barely 36 acres in size, this site embodies the Rural Cemetery Movement and is a profusion of flowering trees every spring. Also on Broadway is the Greek temple-like structure that was home to the Mutual Benefit Life Insurance Company before its headquarters were relocated to downtown Newark, opposite Washington Park.

At the south end of Branch Brook Park and a few blocks from Forest Hill is the seat of the Roman Catholic Archdiocese of Newark, the Cathedral Basilica of the Sacred Heart. This French Gothic Revival masterpiece is the sixth-largest cathedral in the United States, its front towers surpassing Paris's Notre Dame by 28 feet and rising 7 feet higher than Westminster Abbey. Its great copper spire soars to 260 feet. Built on one of the city's highest elevations, the cathedral overlooks the Newark horizon in a manner reminiscent of the Cathedral of Chartres' dramatic rise over the French countryside.

Just a few blocks from the cathedral is the surviving parish of St. Lucy's Roman Catholic Church—an anchor in Newark's Old First Ward and all that remains of Newark's Little Italy.

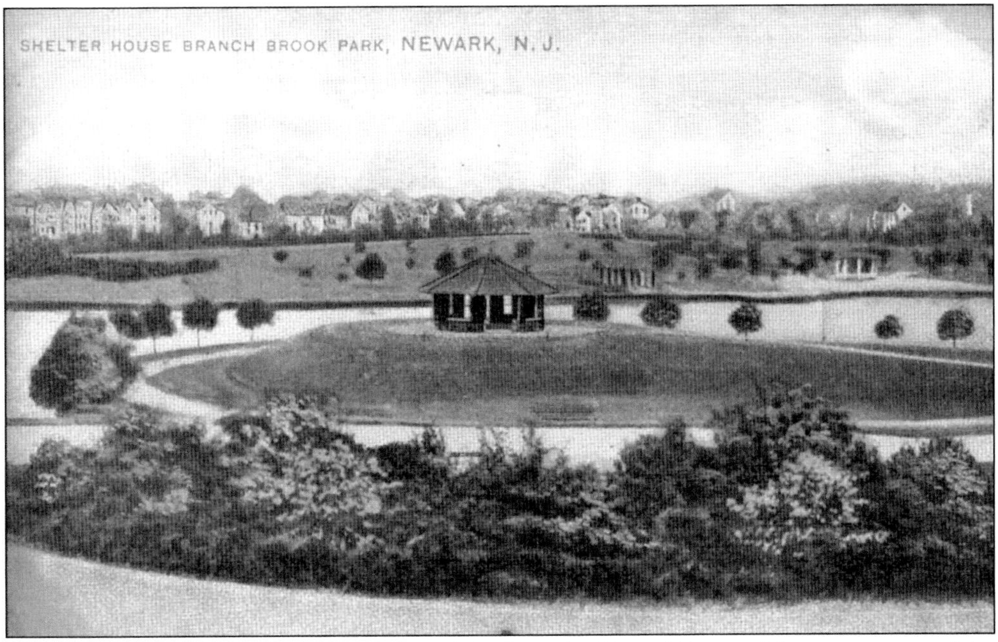

Branch Brook Park was the first county park built in the United States. After enactment of the County Park Act in March 1895, the development of Branch Brook Park commenced on June 15, 1895. A land grant of 60 acres from the City of Newark, including the site of the former city reservoir, enabled work on the Southern Division to begin. Construction moved from its southern boundary northward as Nathan Bogart and John Barrett were hired to create the initial landscape design. Featured in their design was the Carrere and Hastings–designed Octagon Shelter shown above. The Southern Division was bordered on its northern edge by the elegant Park Avenue bridge shown below. Unhappy with the formality of the Bogart & Barrett design, the park commission hired the Olmsted Brothers firm in 1898 to design the rest of Branch Brook Park. (CL.)

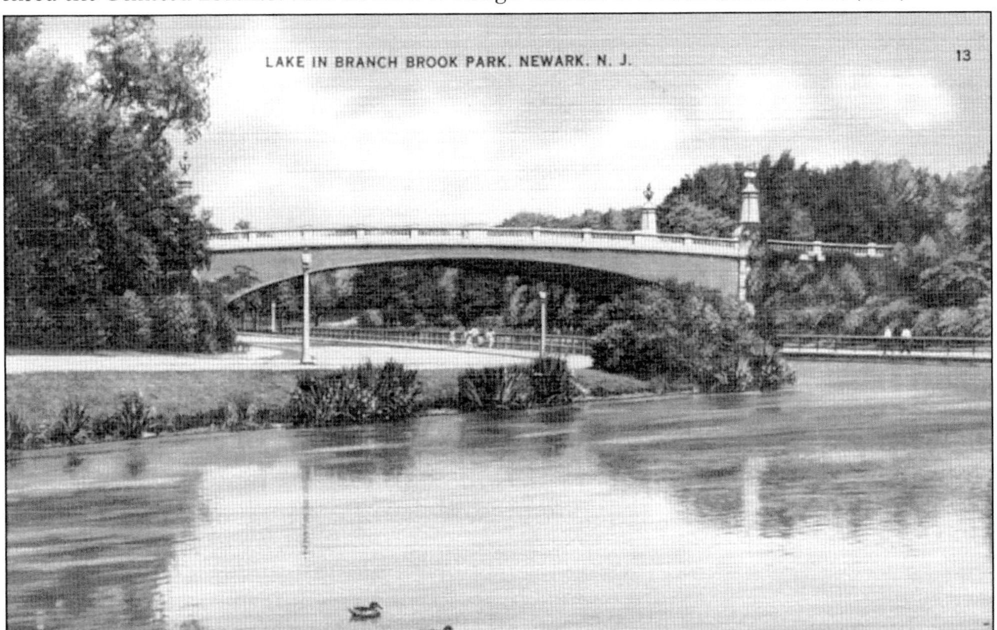

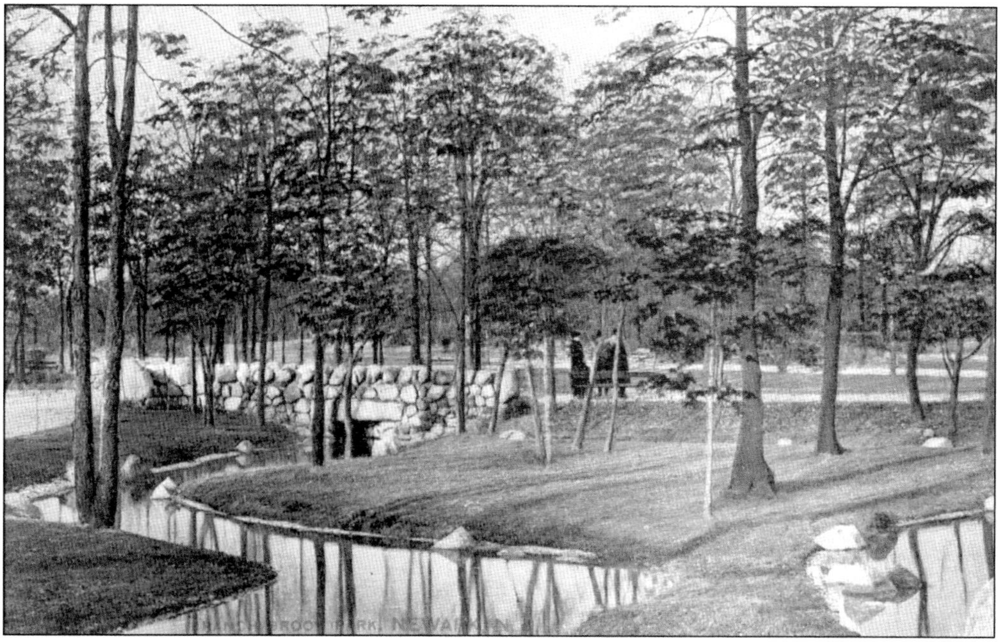

Noted features in the Olmsted Brothers design for the park, including the Northern Division, are represented in the historic postcard above, depicting a meandering stream with the fieldstone bridge in the background. Curvilinear paths, stands of century-old oaks, and open meadows exude the naturalistic setting as the park moves northward. The predominant feature of the Northern Division must be the Carrere and Hastings–designed Ballantine Gates, serving as the grand entrance into the park from the Forest Hill neighborhood. The design of this massive entrance gate is based on Scottish castles from the homeland of the Ballantine family, who funded this structure. The photograph to the right was submitted for the park's nomination to the New Jersey and National Registers of Historic Places, on which the park was included in 1980 and 1981, respectively. (Above, CL; right, NR, photograph by Joseph Calaminici.)

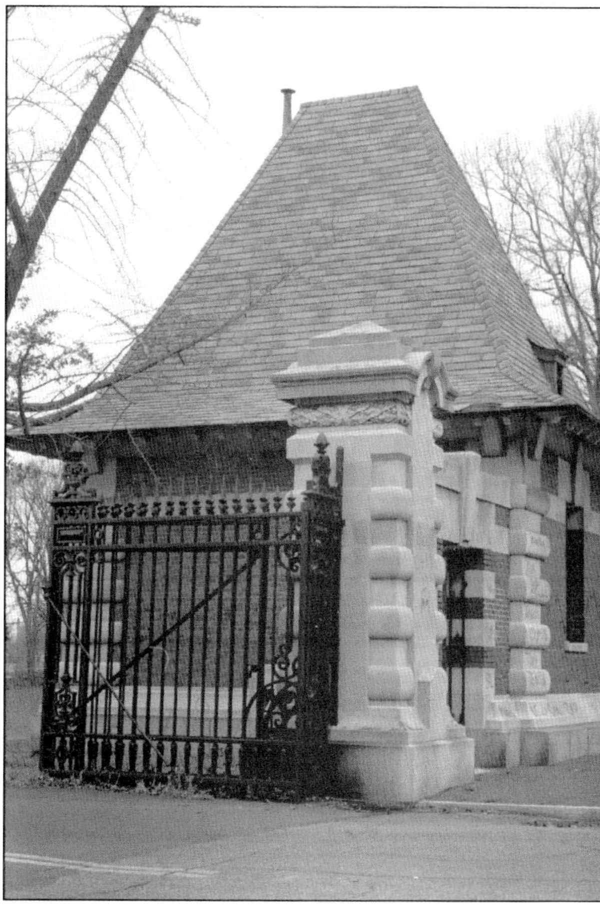

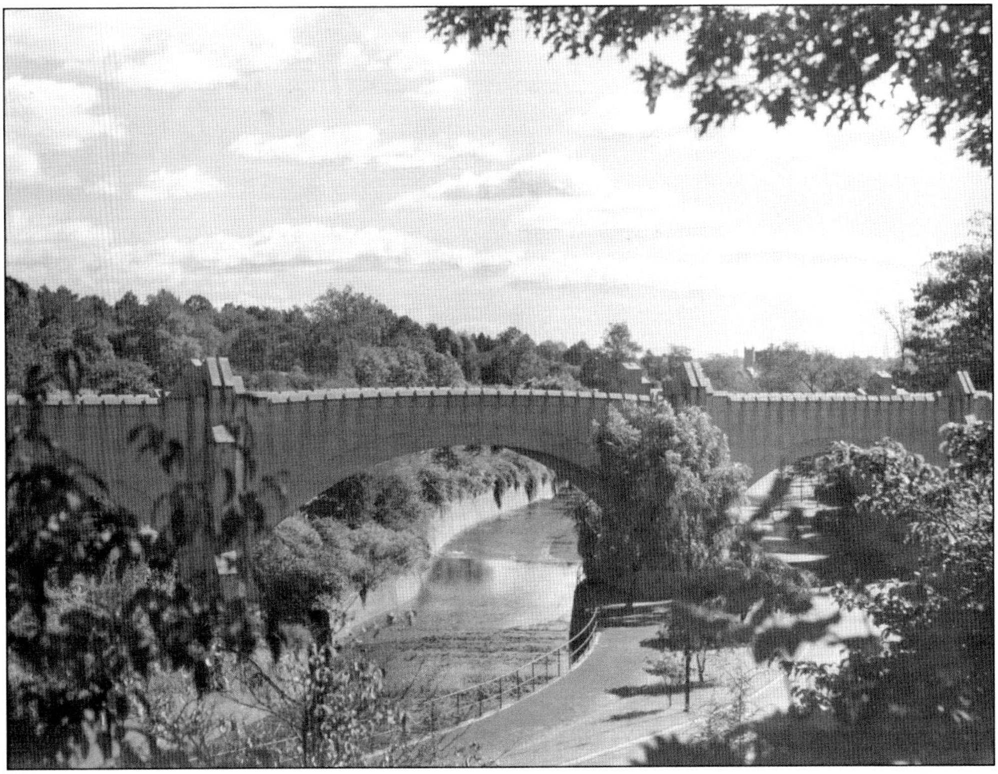

Branch Brook Park's beauty is unparalleled. Seen here is the architectural appeal of a pedestrian bridge extending over the Second River, enabling visitors to move easily between the Newark and Belleville sections of the park. The Second River was reconfigured by the Works Progress Administration during the Depression and channelized over a Belgian-block riverbed into the calm waterway that it is today. The river is bordered on both sides by yellow forsythia spilling over the walls and one of most magnificent displays of flowering cherry blossom trees, closely resembling a Japanese landscape in springtime. The photograph below, titled *Petals on the Water*, displays the quiet beauty of the flowering trees as their fallen petals float gently along the Second River. (Above, CL; below, photograph by Kathleen P. Galop.)

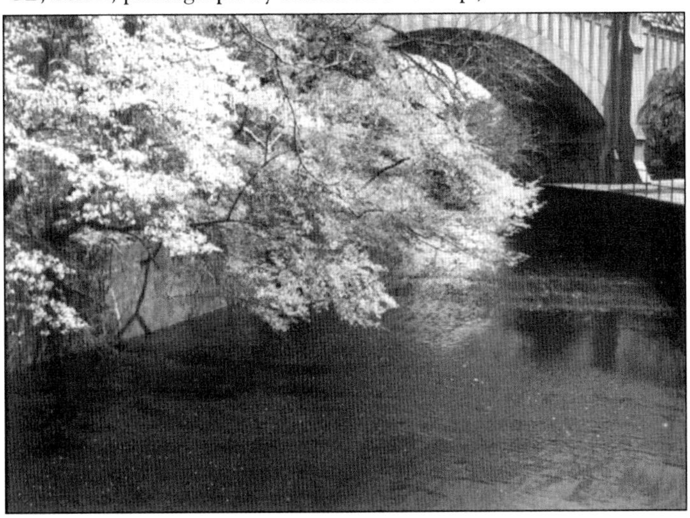

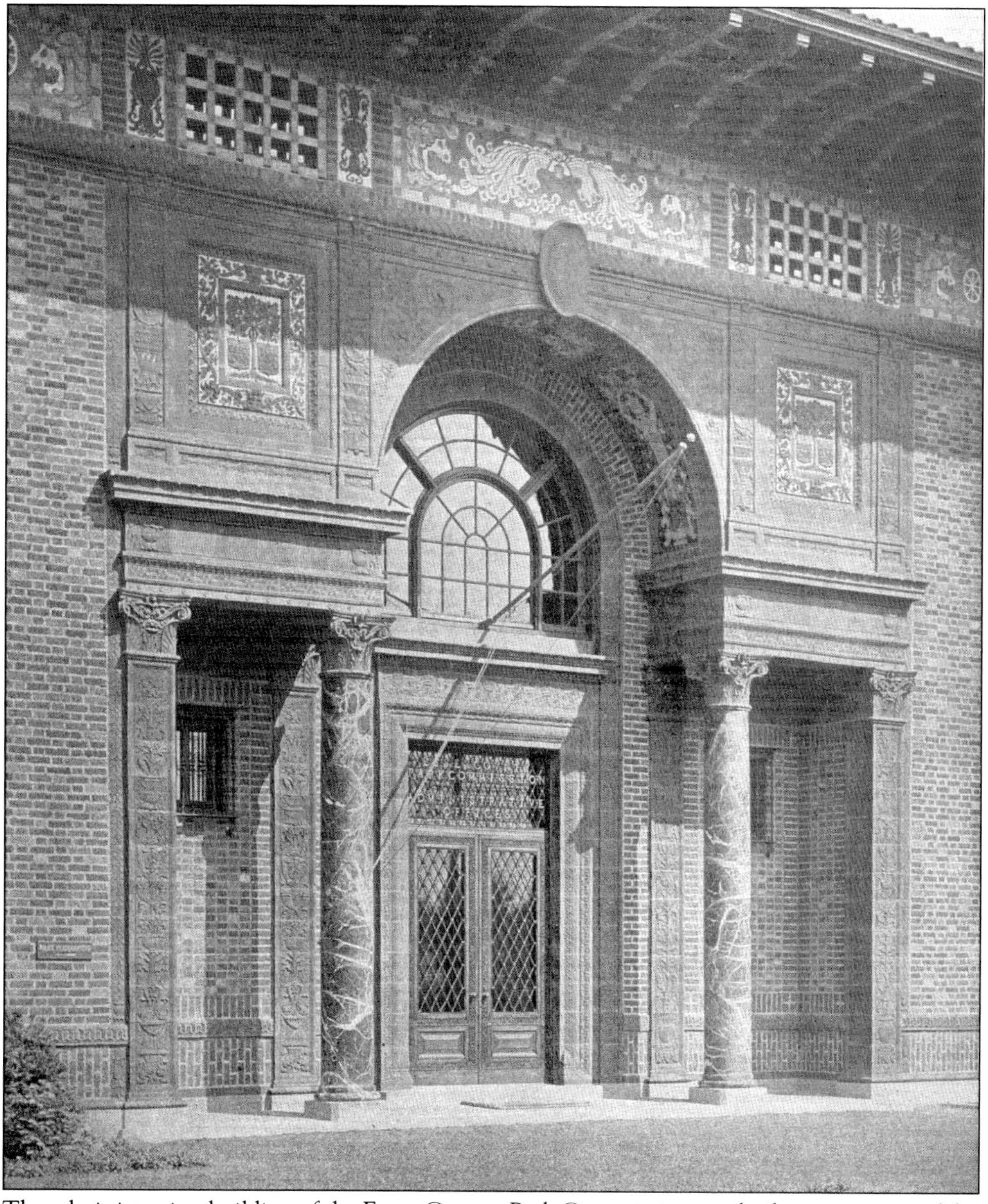

The administration building of the Essex County Park Commission was built on a portion of the land originally designated for Branch Brook Park. Constructed between 1914 and 1916 to the architectural design of H. Van Buren Magonigle, it features a Palladian window over the entry, surrounded by murals painted by Edith M. Magonigle. The symbol of the Essex County Park Commission, the oak leaf, is embedded into the stone on either side of the arched entryway. In 1977, this building was historically recognized through its placement on the New Jersey and National Registers of Historic Places. (Essex County Parks Historic Documents Library.)

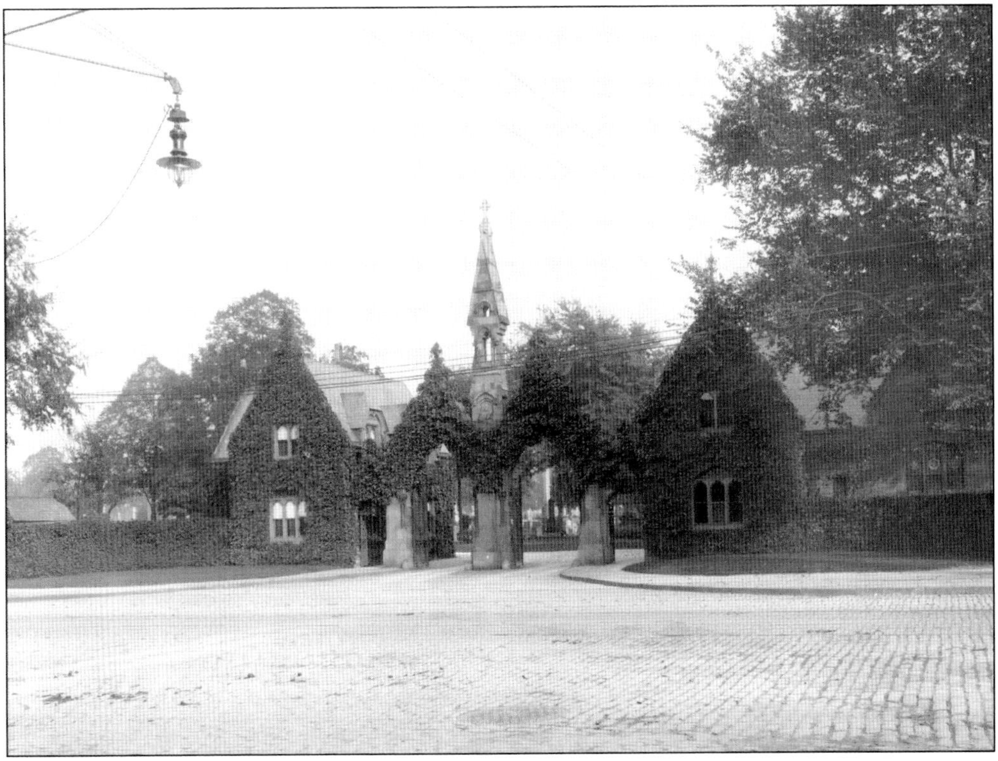

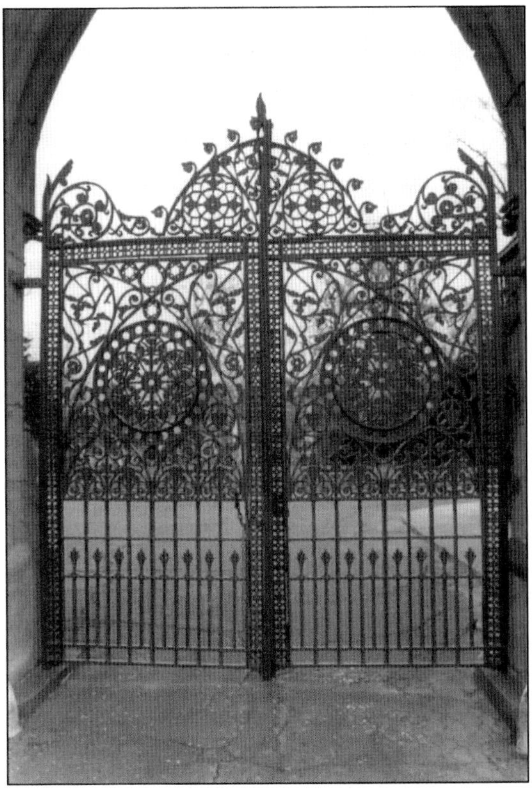

Planned in 1844 as a picturesque, landscaped garden similar to Boston's Mount Auburn and Brooklyn's Green-Wood, Mount Pleasant Cemetery is the final resting place for many of Newark's prominent families. Laid out following the contours of the terrain, roadways are named after species of trees, such as Ash, Elm, and Poplar, and paths after native plants, such as Ivy, Honeysuckle, and Primrose. The 36 acres of landscaped grounds are entered on Broadway through a massive gateway of Belleville brownstone designed by Thomas Stent and built in 1877 in the Victorian Gothic style. The ivy-covered gateway (above) has wings flanking the gabled carriage portals for a keeper's residence and cemetery offices. When closed, the wrought iron gates (left) resemble a lacelike pattern of scrolls with rounded pediments along the top and are considered one of the more spectacular features of the entry. (Above, NPL; left, NR.)

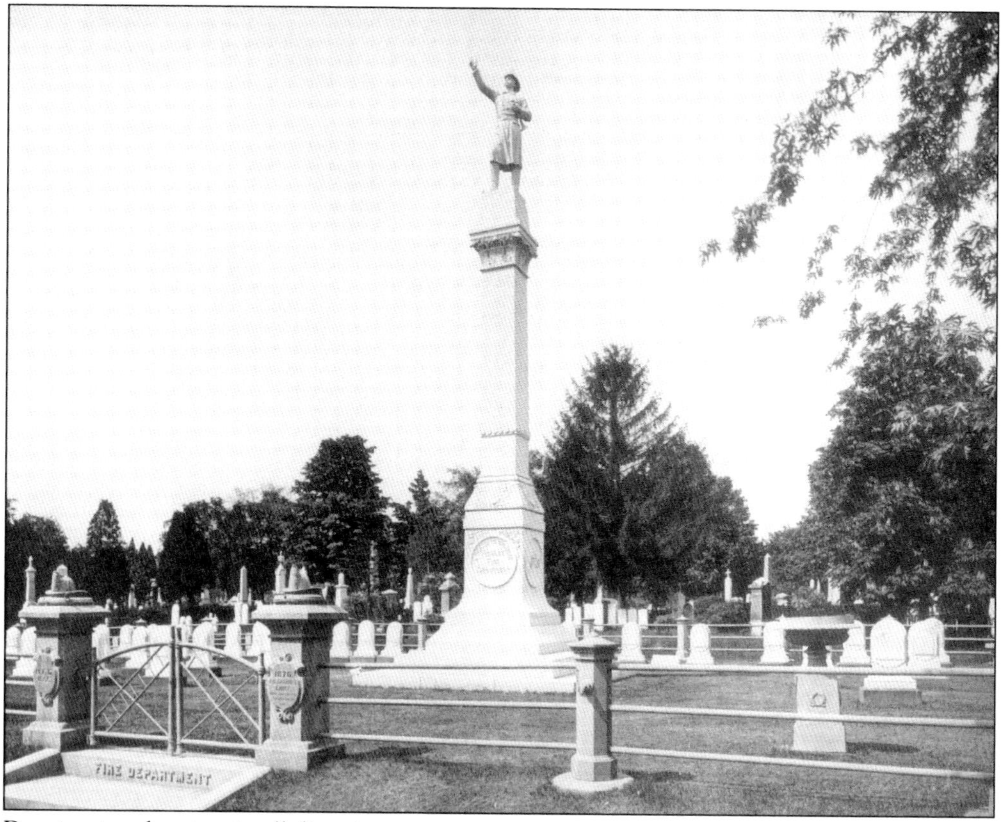

Dominating the view in all directions is the 35-foot Firemen's Monument unveiled in 1888 as "A Tribute to the Dead of the Newark Fire Department." The sculpted seven-foot fireman in full dress uniform towers over the memorial plot, surrounded by stone gateposts capped with fire helmets. Designed by George Brown and Company of Newark, it is one of the finest and most distinctive memorials of its type in the country. (NCC.)

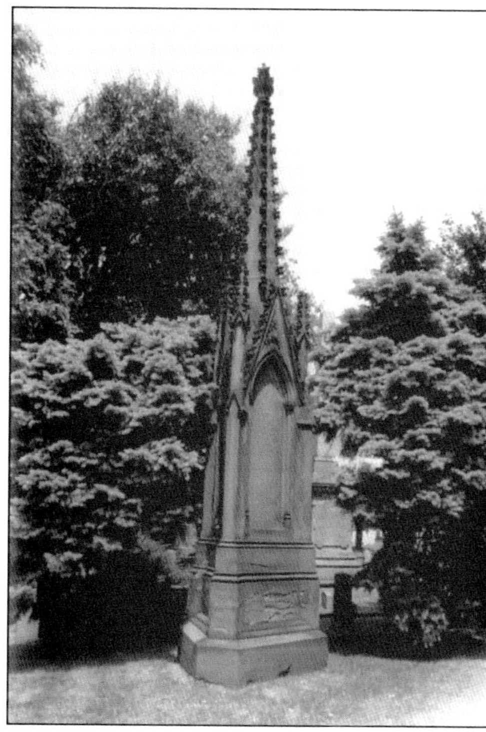

Constructed in 1854 at a cost of $1,500 as a tribute to the establishment of Mount Pleasant Cemetery, this monument reflects the Gothic Revival format and motifs. The triangular brownstone monument is rendered as an attenuated, triangular spire, edged with narrowly spaced crockets and surmounted by a handsome foliated finial. The cemetery was placed on the New Jersey (1987) and the National (1988) Registers of Historic Places. (NR.)

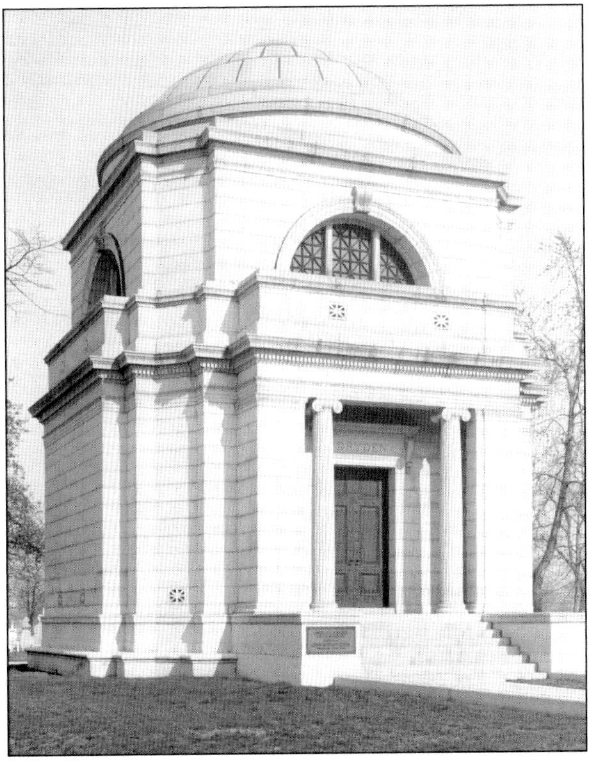

The largest and most prominent mausoleum in the cemetery belongs to John Fairfield Dryden, founder of the Widows and Orphans Friendly Society, now known as Prudential Financial. Dryden was also elected to and served in the US Senate from January 29, 1902, to March 4, 1907. Born in Maine, he died in Newark in 1911 at the age of 72 with an estate valued at $50 million. (NPL.)

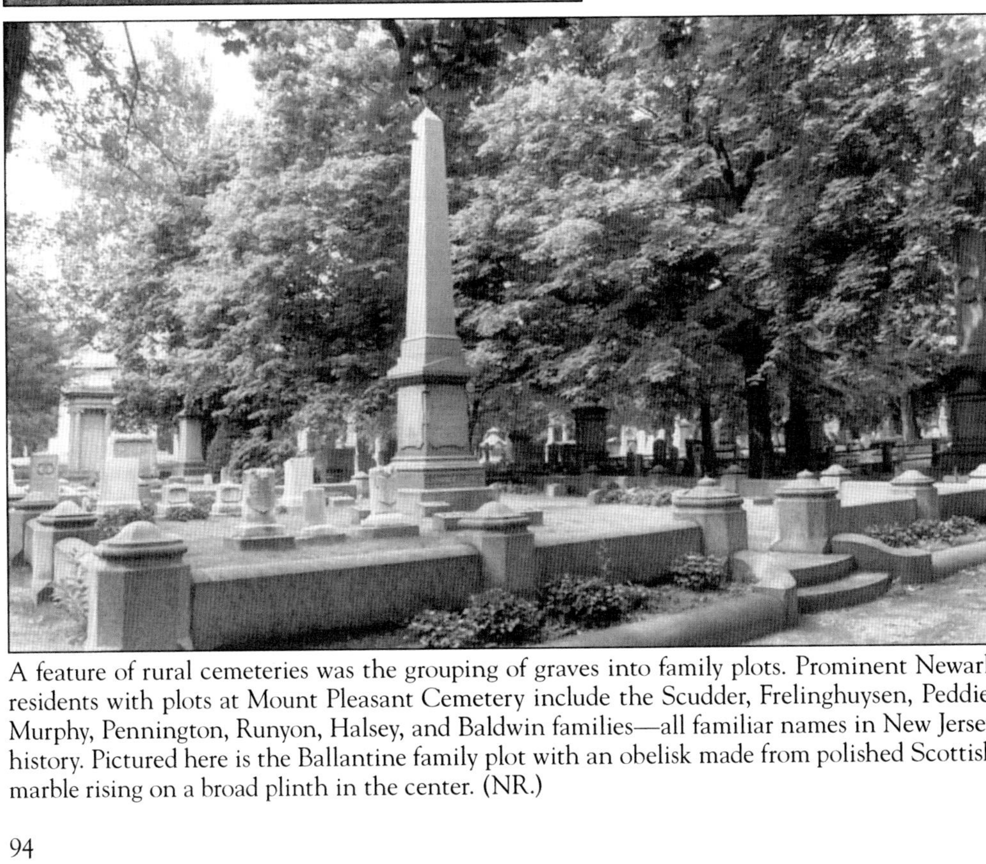

A feature of rural cemeteries was the grouping of graves into family plots. Prominent Newark residents with plots at Mount Pleasant Cemetery include the Scudder, Frelinghuysen, Peddie, Murphy, Pennington, Runyon, Halsey, and Baldwin families—all familiar names in New Jersey history. Pictured here is the Ballantine family plot with an obelisk made from polished Scottish marble rising on a broad plinth in the center. (NR.)

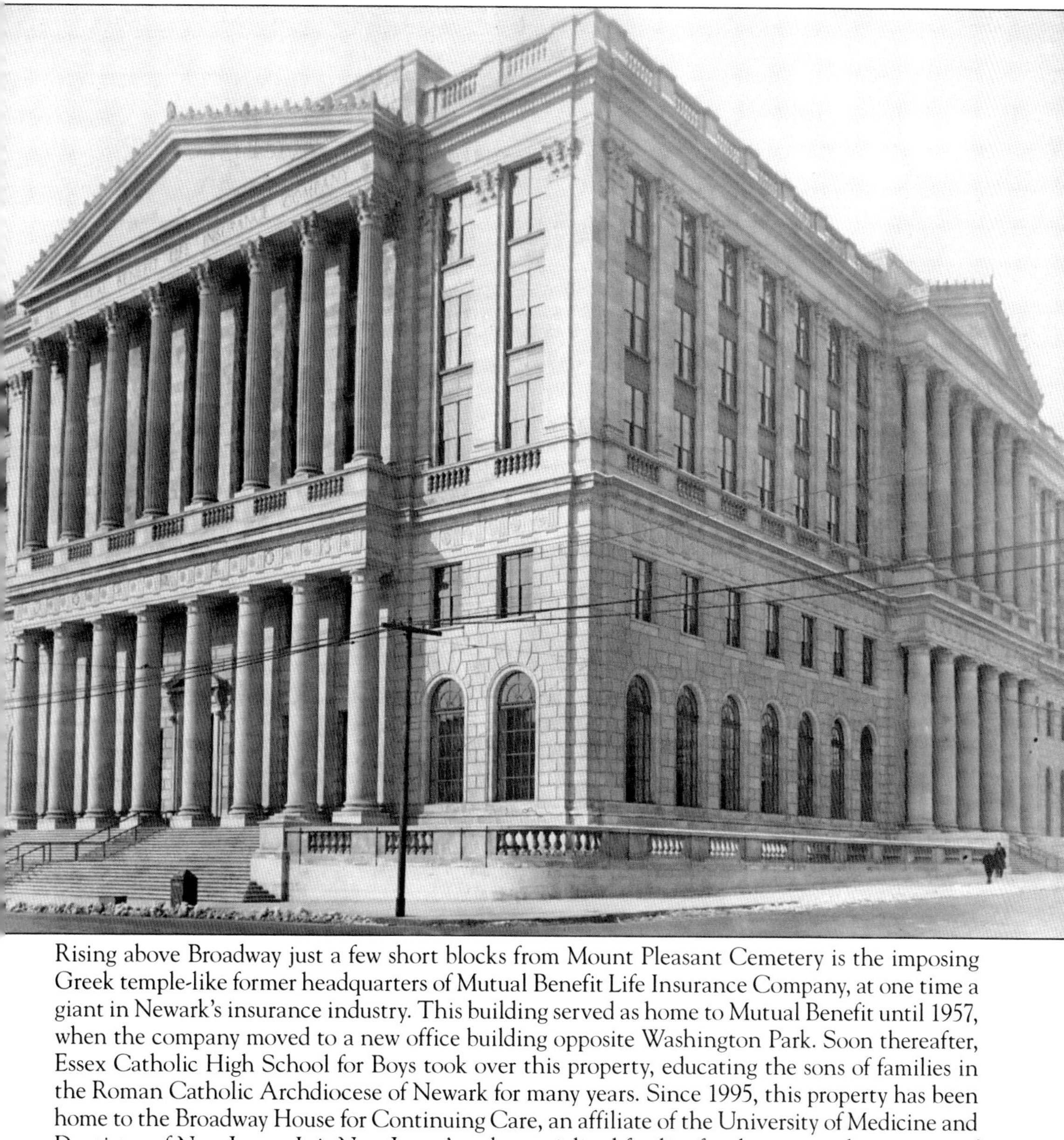

Rising above Broadway just a few short blocks from Mount Pleasant Cemetery is the imposing Greek temple-like former headquarters of Mutual Benefit Life Insurance Company, at one time a giant in Newark's insurance industry. This building served as home to Mutual Benefit until 1957, when the company moved to a new office building opposite Washington Park. Soon thereafter, Essex Catholic High School for Boys took over this property, educating the sons of families in the Roman Catholic Archdiocese of Newark for many years. Since 1995, this property has been home to the Broadway House for Continuing Care, an affiliate of the University of Medicine and Dentistry of New Jersey. It is New Jersey's only specialized facility for the care and treatment of those living with AIDS and HIV. In 2009, the Newark Preservation and Landmarks Committee recognized Broadway House with the Donald T. Dust Award for its adaptive reuse of the building while respecting its historical integrity. This building was placed on the New Jersey and National Registers of Historic Places in 1983. (NPL.)

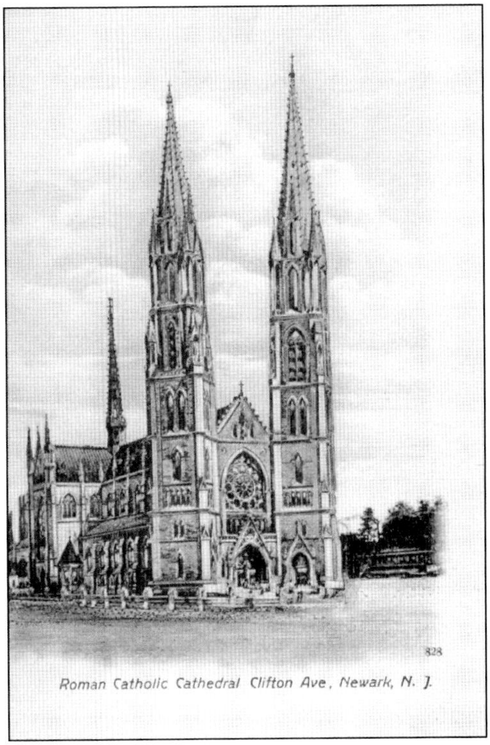

The vision for a cathedral for Newark's Roman Catholic Archdiocese was proposed in 1859 by the Most Reverend James Roosevelt Bayley, Newark's first Catholic bishop. The site, selected and purchased in 1871 with concurrence of architect Jeremiah O'Rourke, is bounded by Park Avenue and Sixth Street on one of Newark's highest elevations. This original design was much different from what was ultimately built. (CL.)

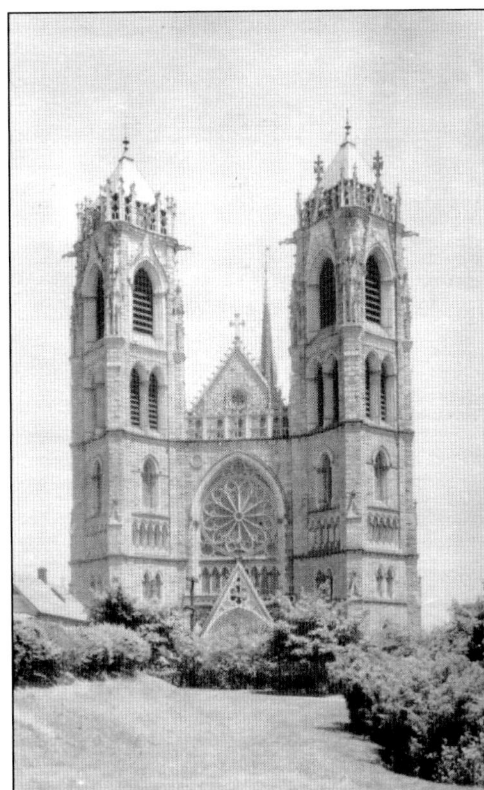

In 1897, O'Rourke introduced another plan, and massive fundraising was launched. By 1902, the walls reached 50 feet, and the tiers of the front towers were under way. But it was not until October 1954 when Archbishop Thomas M. Boland dedicated the cathedral. Its French Gothic style was enhanced by Isaac Ditmars and completed by Paul C. Reilly, with towers soaring 275 and 300 feet, respectively, and flanking the entrance. (CL.)

The cathedral is a work of art. Fashioned by local first-generation craftsmen, their work is recognized in separate chapels dedicated to the Irish-English, Polish-Slovak, German, and Italian populations in Newark. The jeweled beauty of the three rose windows came from the studios of Franz Zettler in Munich. Prof. Gonippo Raggi and his staff in Rome executed the marble altars, the woodwork, and the massive bronze doors of the cathedral's entrances. (NR.)

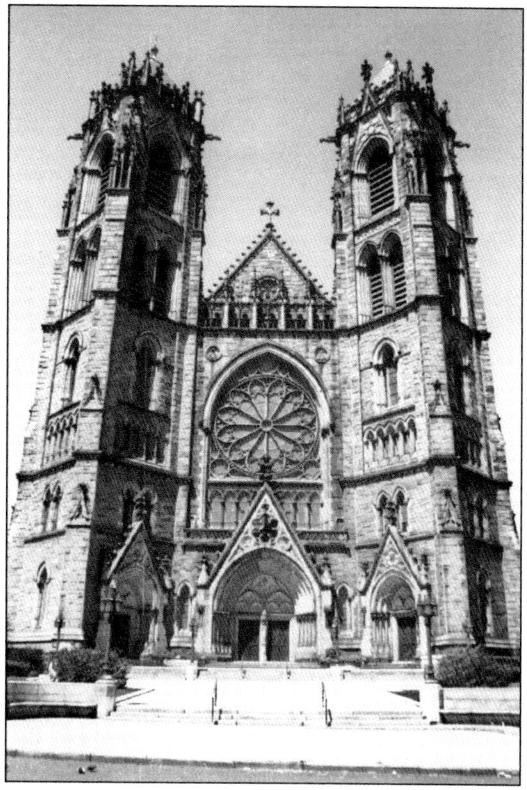

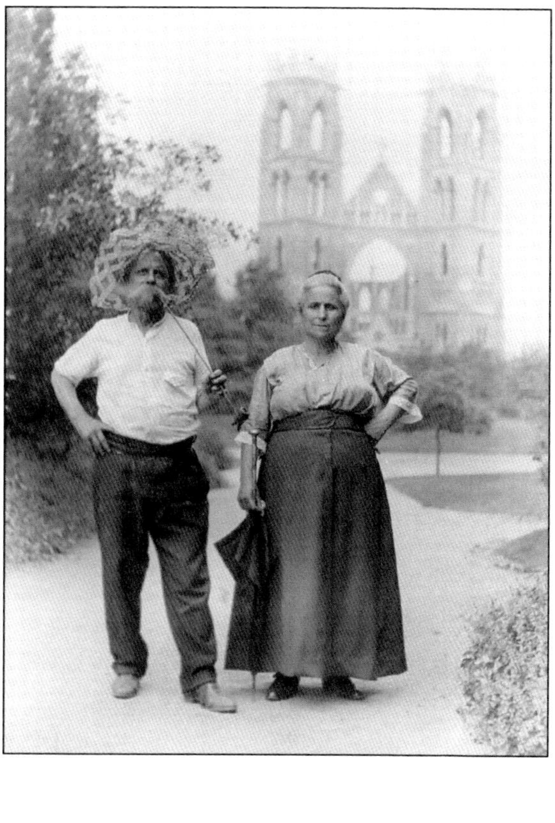

Andrew and Carmella Napolitano stroll through Branch Brook Park in front of the partially constructed cathedral. The stained-glass windows have not yet been installed, and the front facade and incomplete walls stand without a roof over what would become one of the most beautiful cathedrals ever built. This photograph originally appeared in *Newark's Little Italy: The Vanished First Ward* by Michael Immerso, 1997. (NPL.)

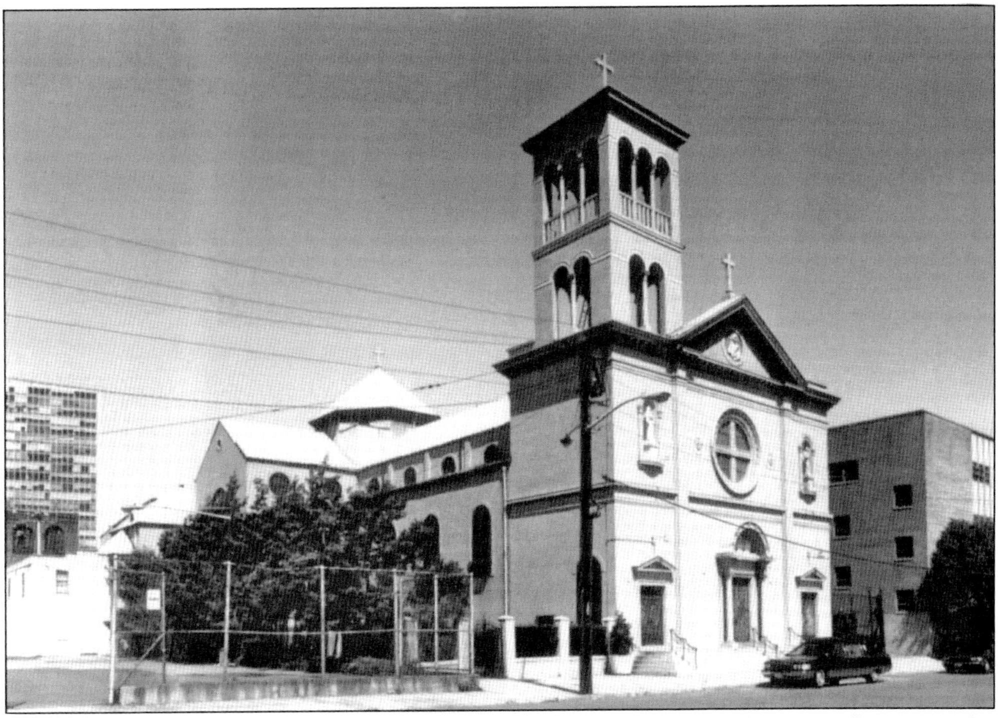

St. Lucy's Church is all that remains of Newark's Little Italy. Established as a parish in 1891, the present church was built in 1925. Its Old First Ward Museum received the 2013 Donald T. Dust Award for outstanding building preservation and the Charles F. Cummings Award for local history from the Newark Preservation and Landmarks Committee. St. Lucy's was placed on the New Jersey and National Registers of Historic Places in 1998. (NR.)

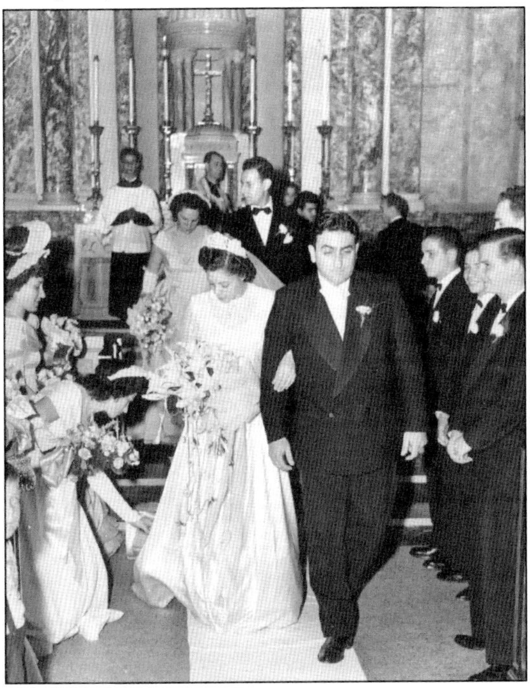

After World War II, weddings were an almost daily occurrence at St. Lucy's Church. Pictured on their September 12, 1948, wedding day are Joseph Falco and Angelina Romano Falco. Walking down the aisle in front of St. Lucy's elaborate altar, Angelina's wedding dress caught on the runner, but her attendants Henrietta Avalone (left) and Antoinette Bottone (right) quickly came to the assistance of the bride. (Angelina Falco.)

Six

From Horses to Engines

It can be argued that as new modes of transportation develop, the way of life changes forever. The slow but efficient (and ecologically friendly) Morris Canal was shut down by the railroads. Woodside was forced to change once it had been annexed by Newark and its streets paved and streetcar tracks installed, but modes of local travel had already been changing for a while.

Stagecoaches are often associated with the West, but in the 1790s, stagecoach service began between Newark and New York City. At first, it only ran once a day with a six-passenger maximum, but eventually it was making 8–10 trips daily with a maximum load of 15. In 1834, there were commuter horse wagons, and steam locomotives began pulling passenger cars in 1835. The horse train trolley was an essential factor in the suburban migration; by 1870, Newark had seven routes, including Mount Prospect Avenue. Woodside and Forest Hill were being traversed by the Newark and Bloomfield Horse Rail Road, with stables at Orange Street.

The year 1890 brought the first electric trolley car, which soon took over the city's streets, creating a confusion of horse-drawn buggies, delivery wagons, and electric streetcars. And of course, next would come the automobile.

Woodside and Forest Hill also had good access to the commuter railroad service into New York City via the Greenwood Lake Line that had two stops on Verona Avenue. By 1908, there was service from Hudson River tunnel trains.

Many Forest Hill residents owned their own carriages and horses, which they kept in carriage houses, or if they did not have a carriage house or staff to maintain the horse and its equipment, then they would house them in the horse barns on Van Wagenen Street. This prompted construction of the 77 Steps, a flight of stairs from Mount Prospect Avenue down to Woodside Avenue. Or maybe William Clark built the 77 Steps so he could easily walk down to his factory on the Passaic River. Eventually, when the wealthy families converted to automobiles and retired their horses, they were faced with the question of what to do with their carriage houses.

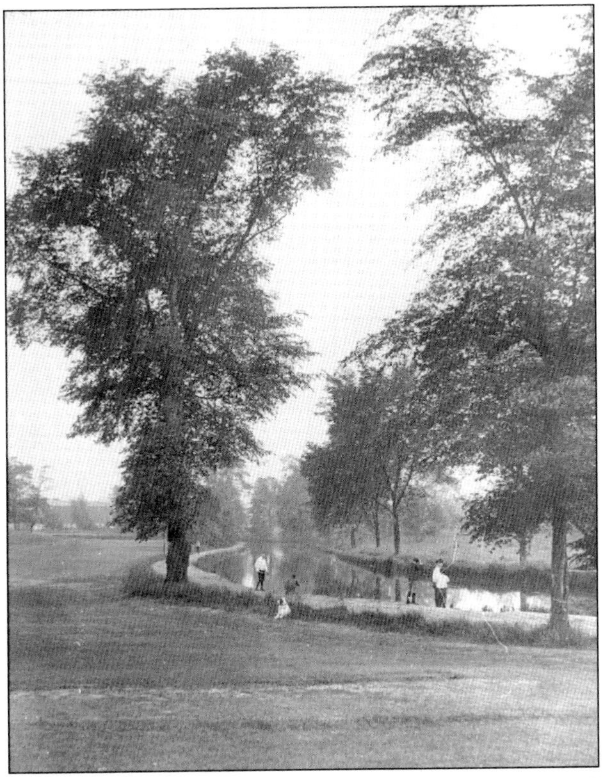

Construction of the Morris Canal was completed in 1836. It stretched from Phillipsburg to Jersey City and was 102.3 miles long. Like all transportation canals, it was an engineering marvel, and some of its locks and planes are still visible, and a few still operable. Its most important use was to ship coal from the Pennsylvania mines to the large cities in eastern New Jersey, where it could be easily transported to New York City. The growth of railroads doomed the slower shipping pace of the Morris Canal, and it gradually ceased operations completely. Local residents would spend their leisure time along the length of the canal, fishing during mild weather and ice-skating when the canal was frozen. (Both, NPL.)

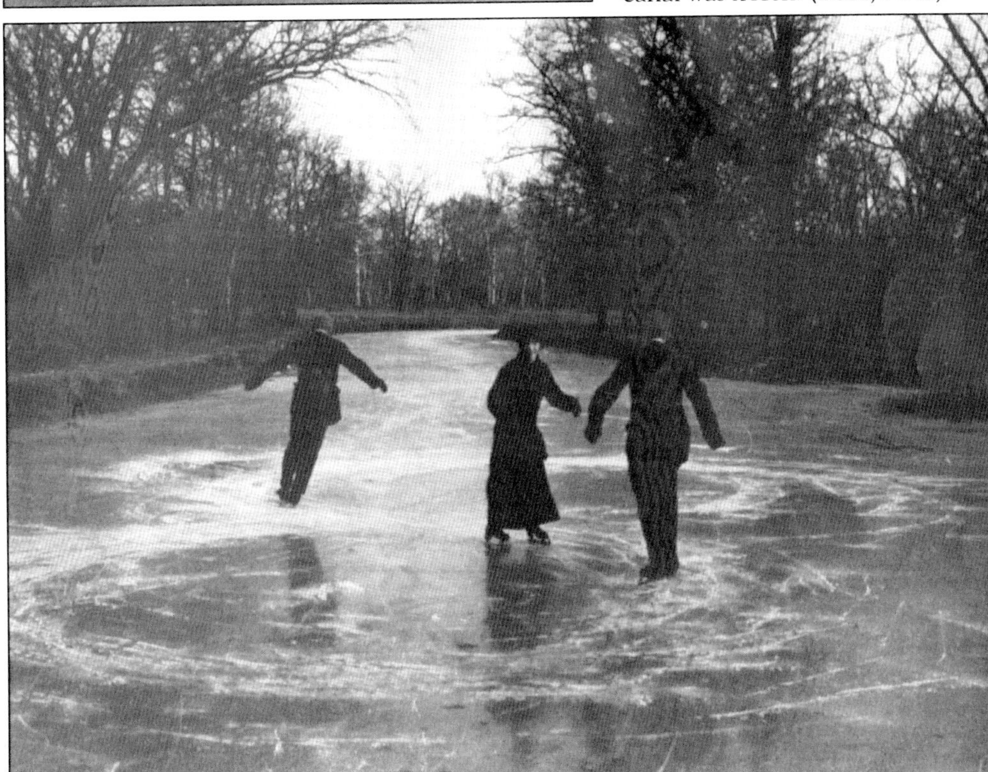

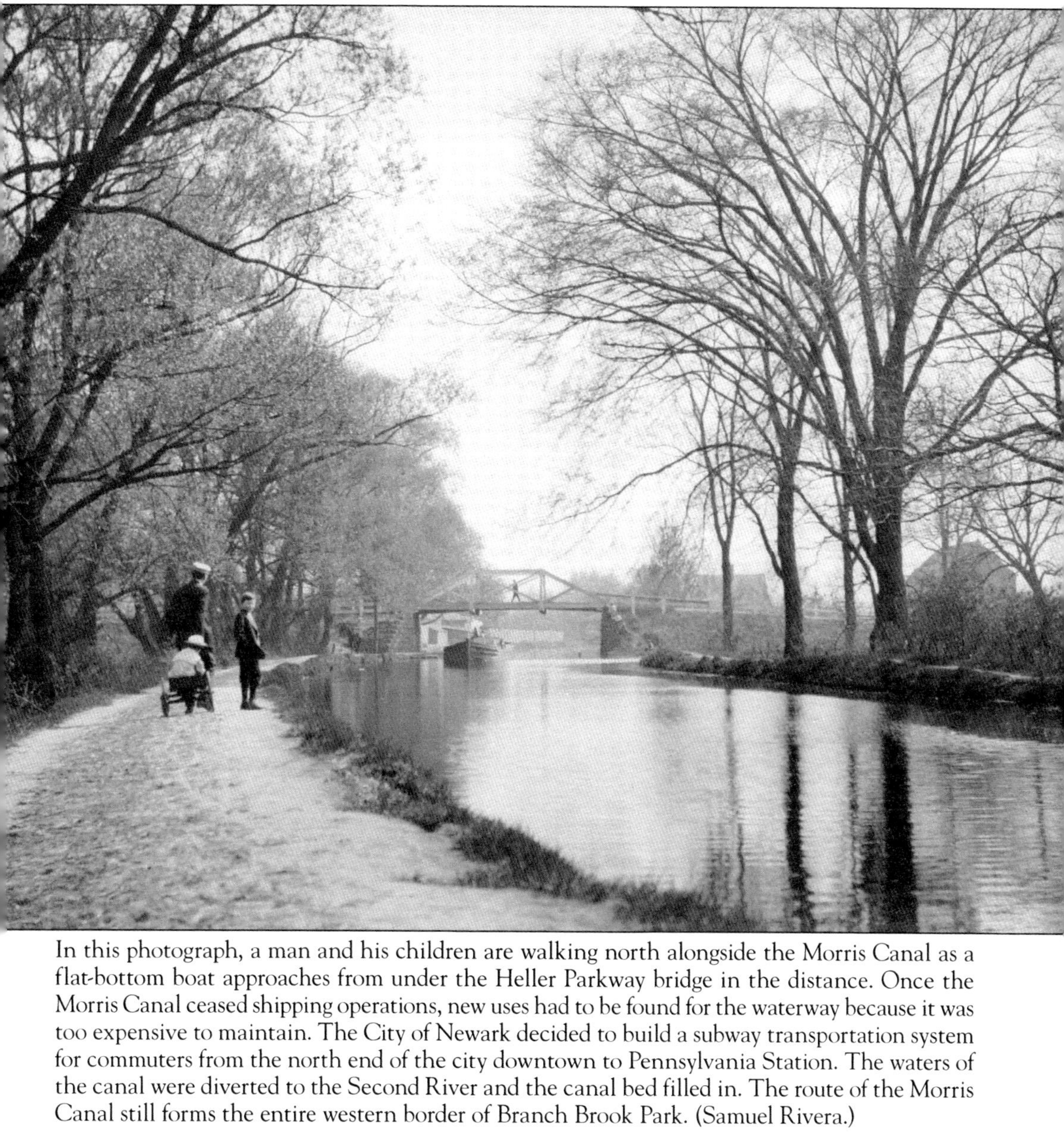

In this photograph, a man and his children are walking north alongside the Morris Canal as a flat-bottom boat approaches from under the Heller Parkway bridge in the distance. Once the Morris Canal ceased shipping operations, new uses had to be found for the waterway because it was too expensive to maintain. The City of Newark decided to build a subway transportation system for commuters from the north end of the city downtown to Pennsylvania Station. The waters of the canal were diverted to the Second River and the canal bed filled in. The route of the Morris Canal still forms the entire western border of Branch Brook Park. (Samuel Rivera.)

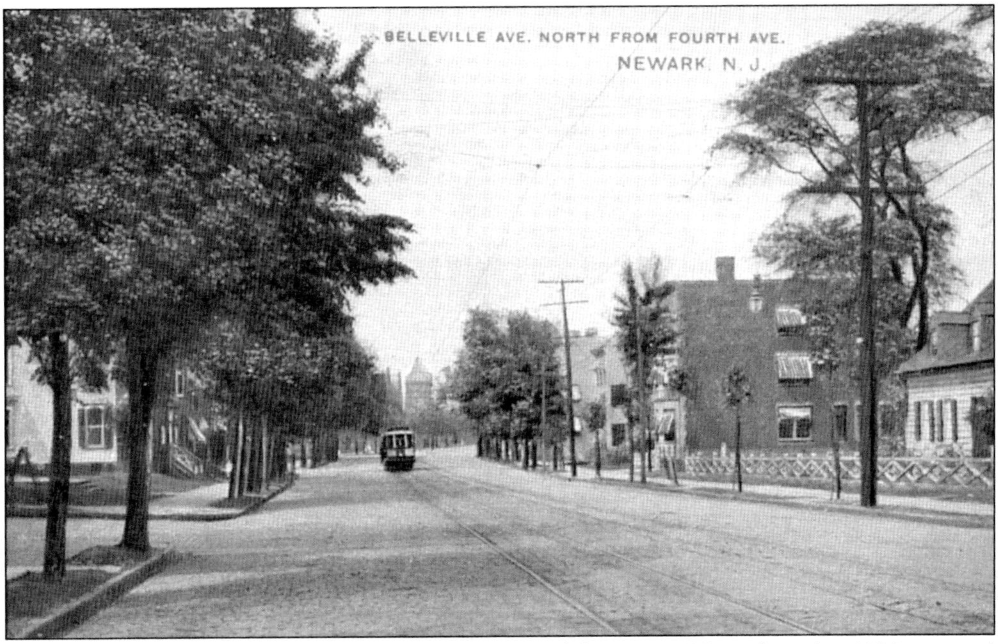

A streetcar is traveling down Belleville Avenue toward downtown Newark in this 1909 postcard view. Belleville Avenue was the main thoroughfare up to and through Woodside, and while residents decried the loss of their rural atmosphere, they came to appreciate the ease of commuting and shopping via regular streetcar service. Belleville Avenue was renamed Washington Avenue and is now called Broadway. (CL.)

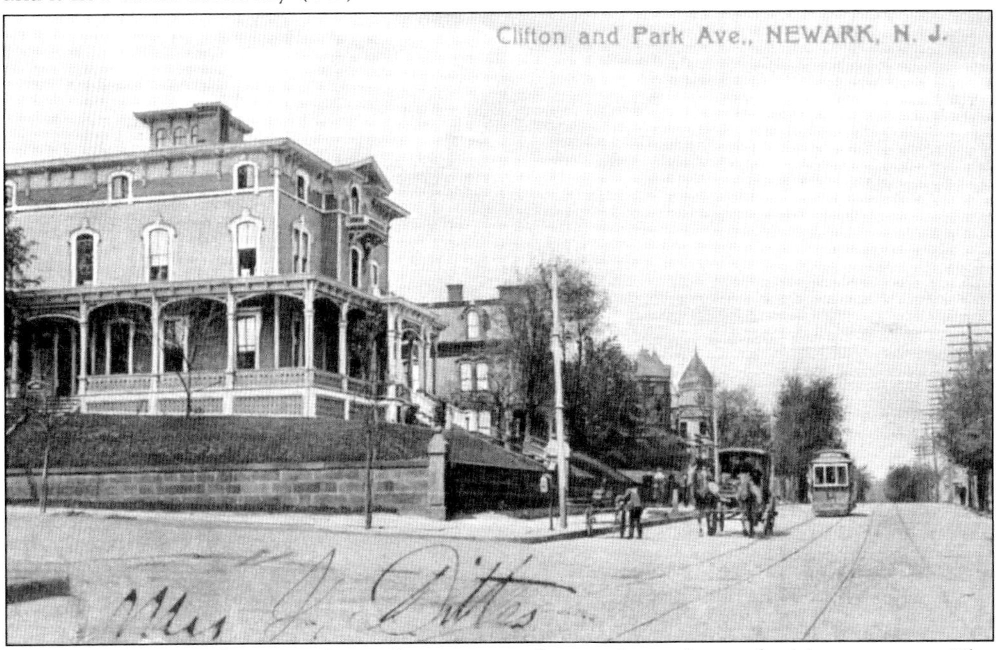

In this 1910 postcard scene, a horse-drawn wagon has to share the road with a streetcar. The grand house seen on the left at the intersection of Clifton and Park Avenues was used as the Crippled Children's Hospital. As the need for such services increased, a large brick structure was built at the same intersection. (CL.)

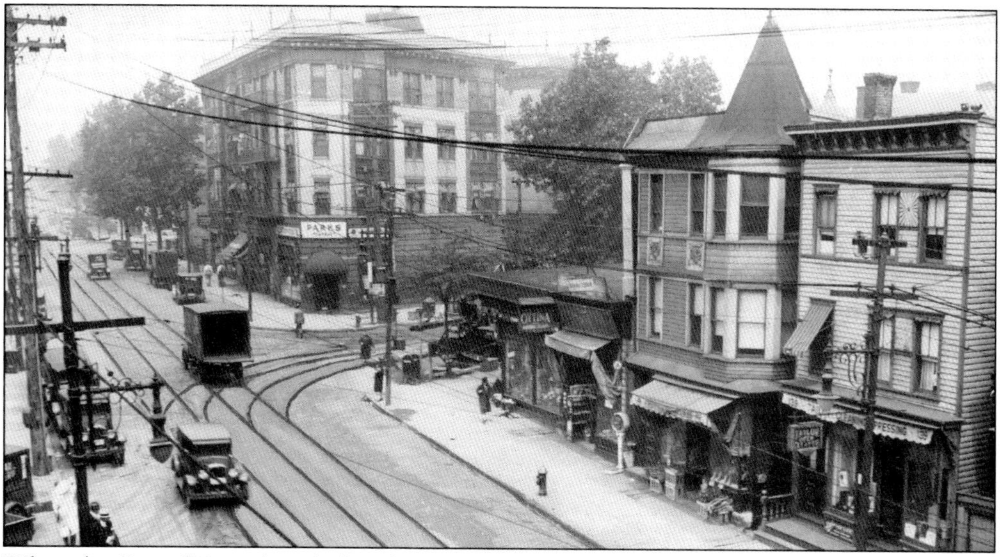

When the City of Newark took this photograph in conjunction with a study to determine where street-widening projects were needed most, this intersection of Bloomfield and Mount Prospect Avenues probably qualified, as these streets were both major thoroughfares. Note the profusion of streetcar tracks and the heavy truck and automobile traffic. (NPL.)

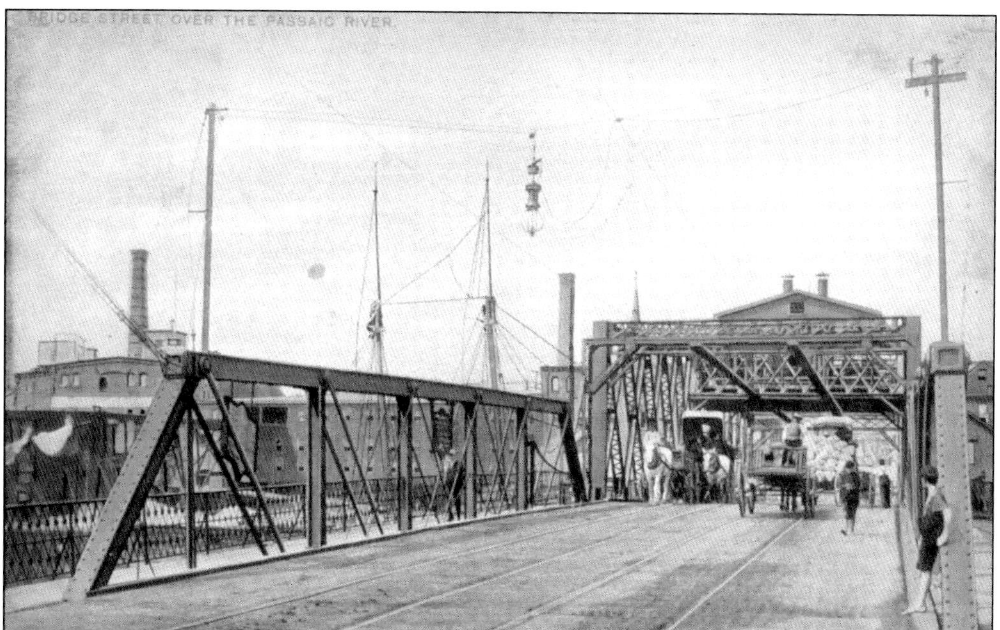

Both horse-drawn and pedestrian traffic on Bridge Street are seen crossing over the Passaic River, just south of Woodside, in this 1908 postcard view. This bridge was a major link from Newark to Harrison and Kearny. As manufacturing businesses spread up the Passaic River, delivery trucks competed with commuter vehicles for space on the road. (CL.)

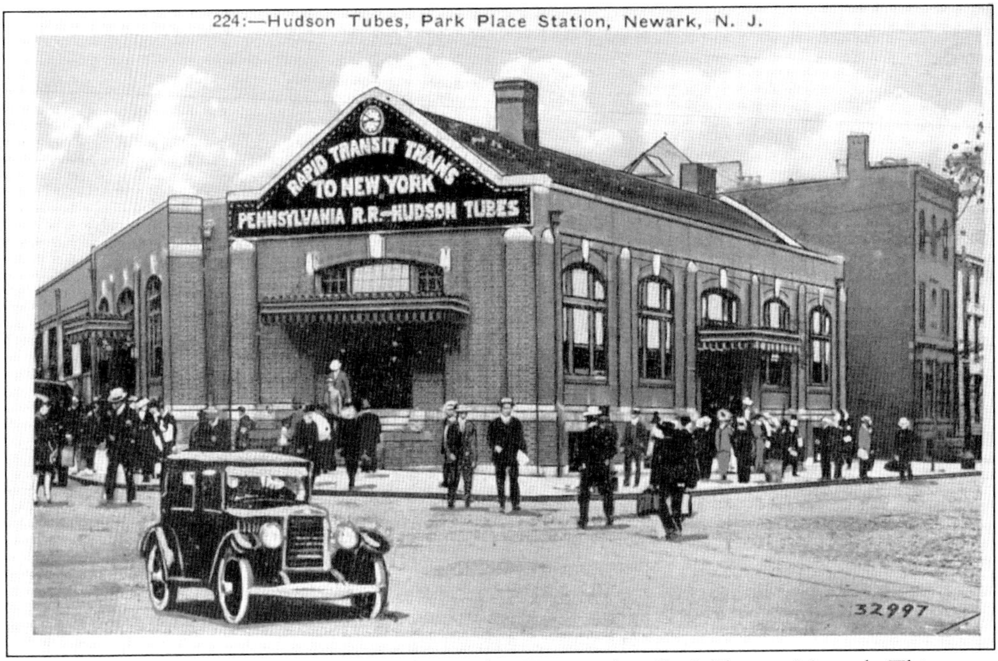

This early-1900s postcard shows the Hudson Tubes Terminal on Park Place in Newark. This was a subway-like means of travel under the Hudson River from Newark to Manhattan. Today, it is the PATH (Port Authority Trans-Hudson) train that departs from Newark's Pennsylvania Station, travels along the same tracks as the old Hudson Tubes, and in Jersey City, divides into separate lines to Midtown Manhattan and Wall Street. (CL.)

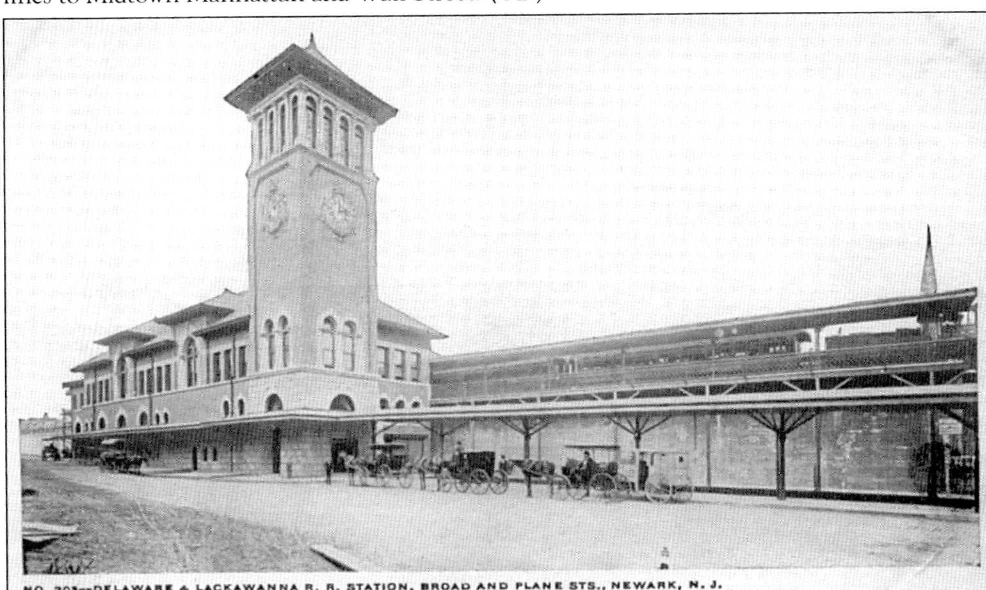

The clock tower on the Delaware & Lackawanna Railroad Station (now Newark's Broad Street Station) dominates the northern end of downtown. A hub for New Jersey Transit lines that connect the suburbs with New York City via the Midtown Direct Service into New York's Pennsylvania Station, this station was placed on the New Jersey and National Registers of Historic Places in 1984 through a thematic nomination of operating passenger stations. (CL.)

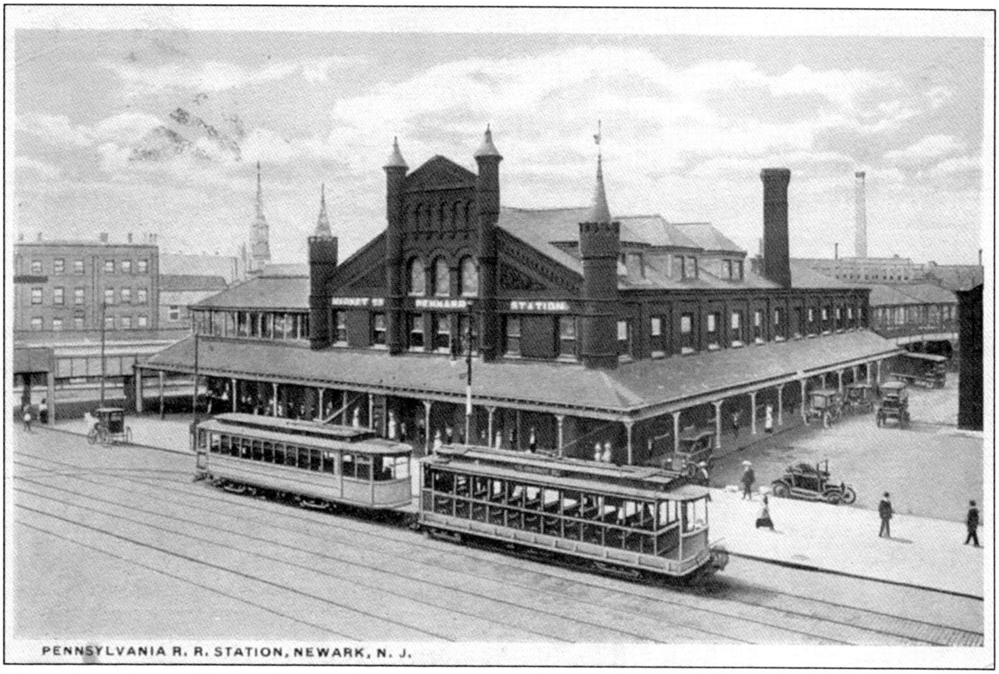

Newark's original Pennsylvania Station is depicted here showing the arrival of passengers on streetcars and horse-drawn carriages. From the earliest days of rail travel, Newark has always been a stop on the Pennsylvania Line along what is now known as the Northeast Corridor. The 10-minute trip from Newark to Manhattan is a benefit to commuters but presents competitive disadvantages to Newark's businesses. (CL.)

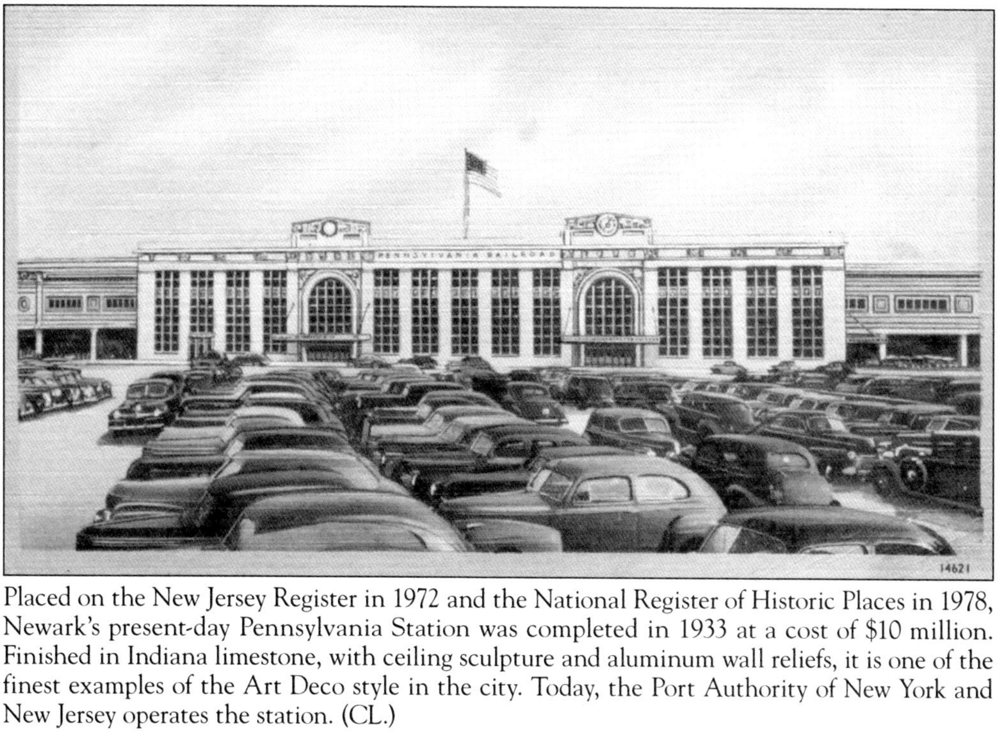

Placed on the New Jersey Register in 1972 and the National Register of Historic Places in 1978, Newark's present-day Pennsylvania Station was completed in 1933 at a cost of $10 million. Finished in Indiana limestone, with ceiling sculpture and aluminum wall reliefs, it is one of the finest examples of the Art Deco style in the city. Today, the Port Authority of New York and New Jersey operates the station. (CL.)

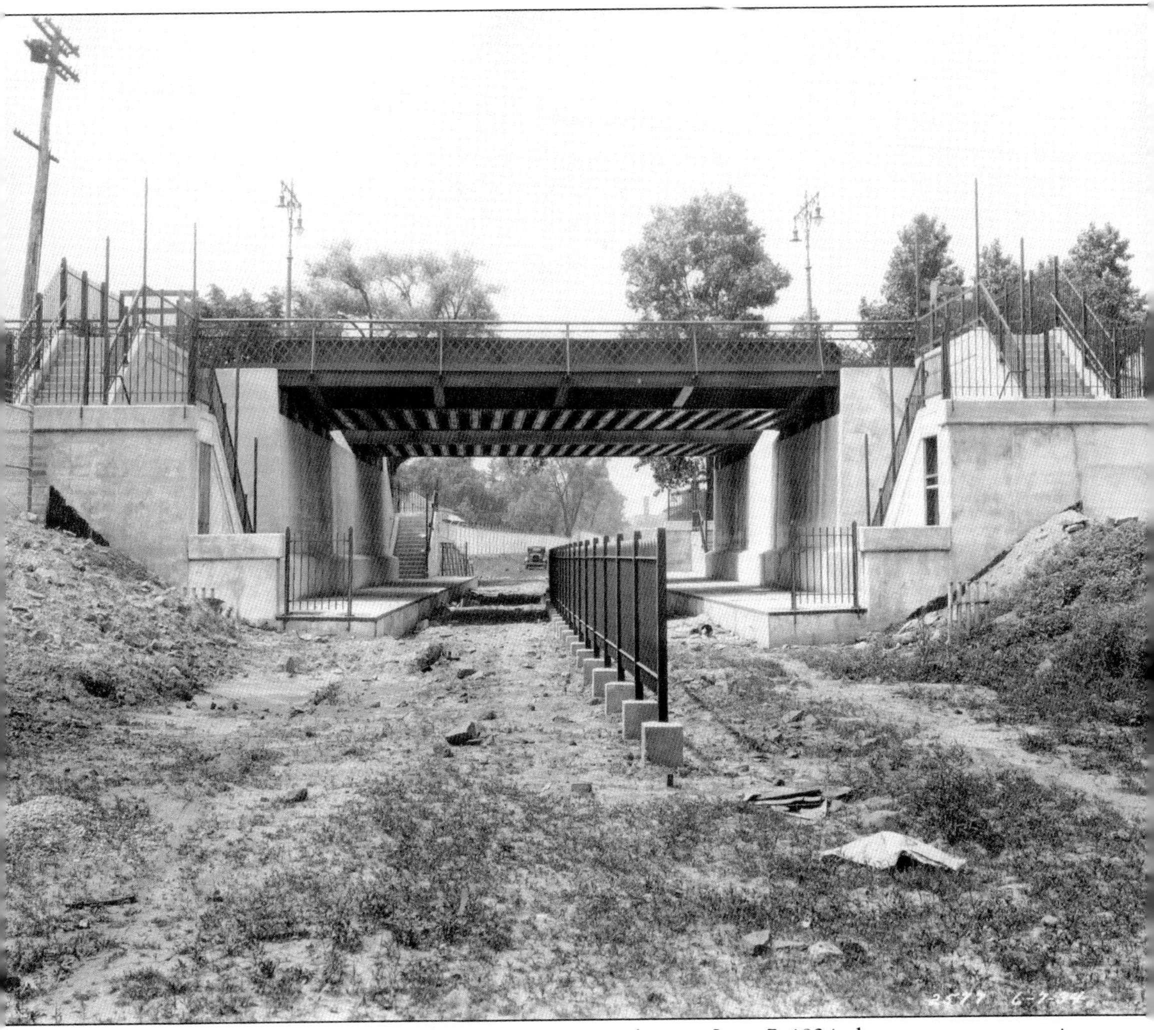

This photograph and those on the opposite page, taken on June 7, 1934, document construction of Section 6 of the city railway from Orange Street to Heller Parkway. Here the new roadbed is being prepared for the subway line. It is easy to envision that, just a few years earlier, this area was filled with the water of the Morris Canal. In the foreground are the beginnings of the fence to separate the northbound and southbound lanes. The stairways descending to both platforms have already been constructed for what would become the Heller Parkway (running perpendicular overhead) station. This subway system would greatly cut commuting time from Forest Hill to the business district in downtown Newark, terminating at the station for the Hudson Tubes to continue on to New York City. The cars have been modernized and the system upgraded, and it is still in use today as the Newark Light Rail. (NCC.)

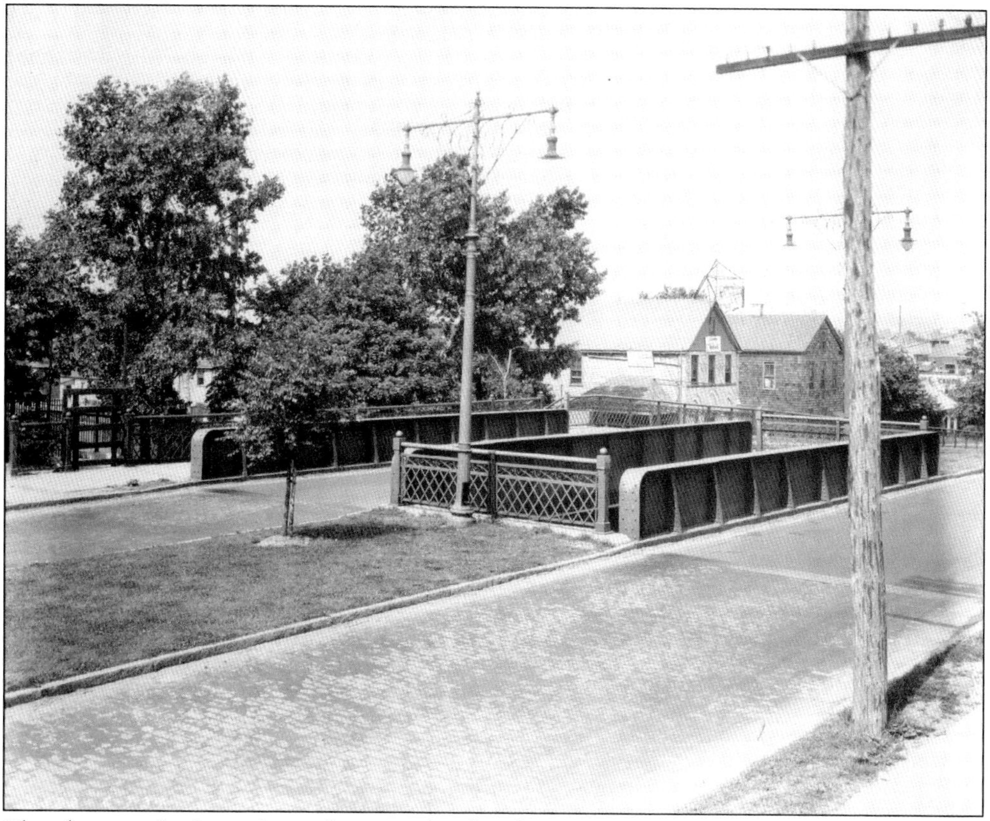

The photograph above shows the top side of Heller Parkway where it passes over the subway tracks in 1934. Today, the center median is gone, as well as the old-fashioned streetlamps. This street is heavily traveled by those coming and going from Forest Hill and Branch Brook Park. The photograph below shows the southwest stairs leading down from Heller Parkway to the station platform. This station is now closed, replaced by a ramp leading from Heller Parkway to the Branch Brook Park station, one block north. (Both, NCC.)

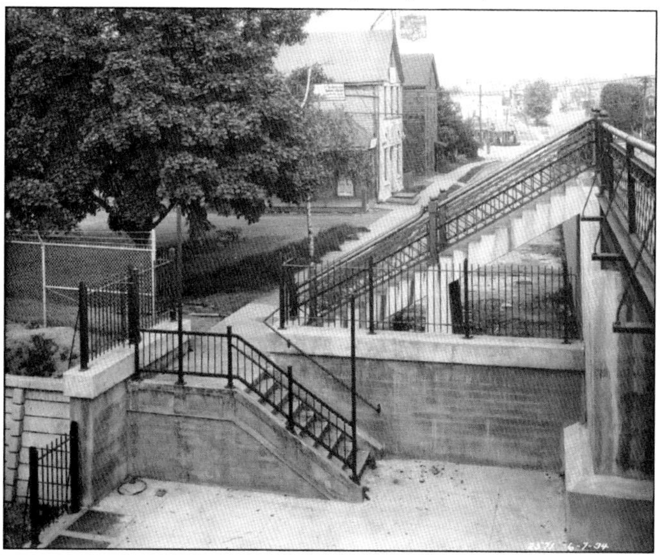

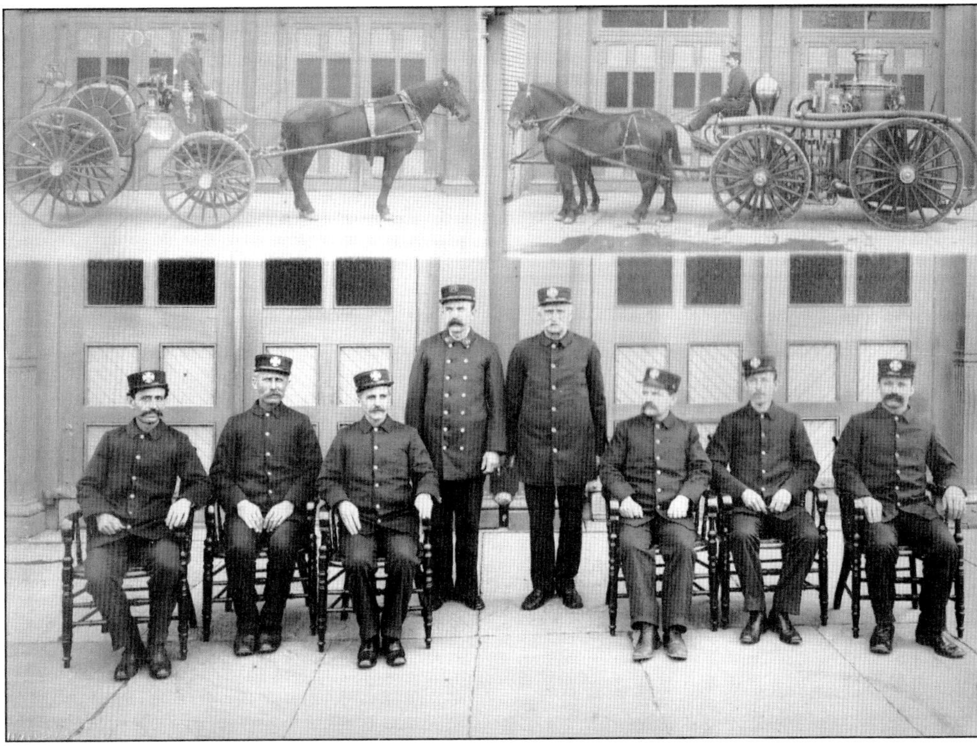

Pictured here is an 1891 photography montage of Newark Fire Department's Engine Company No. 9 on Summer Avenue, several blocks south of the Forest Hill neighborhood. The firefighters are seen wearing their dress uniforms, as they would for an inspection. Of particular interest is the inclusion of a hose carriage built in 1882 and the steam engine built in 1862, along with their teams of fire horses. (Jack Banahan.)

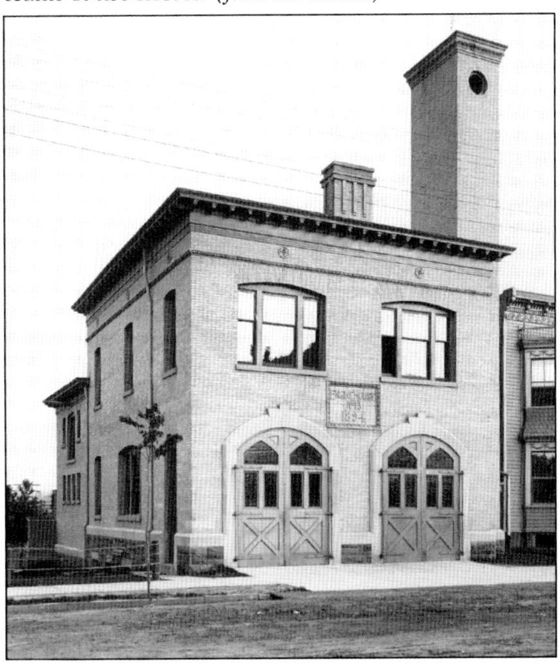

Built in 1894, Engine Company No. 13 was the closest firehouse to the Forest Hill neighborhood, and thus it was charged with being the first to respond. It remained at the corner of Summer Avenue and Halleck Street until 1967, when a new firehouse was built on Mount Prospect Avenue. The Summer Avenue location was ideal when the neighborhood was known as Woodside, as mostly farms dominated what is today called Forest Hill. (NPL.)

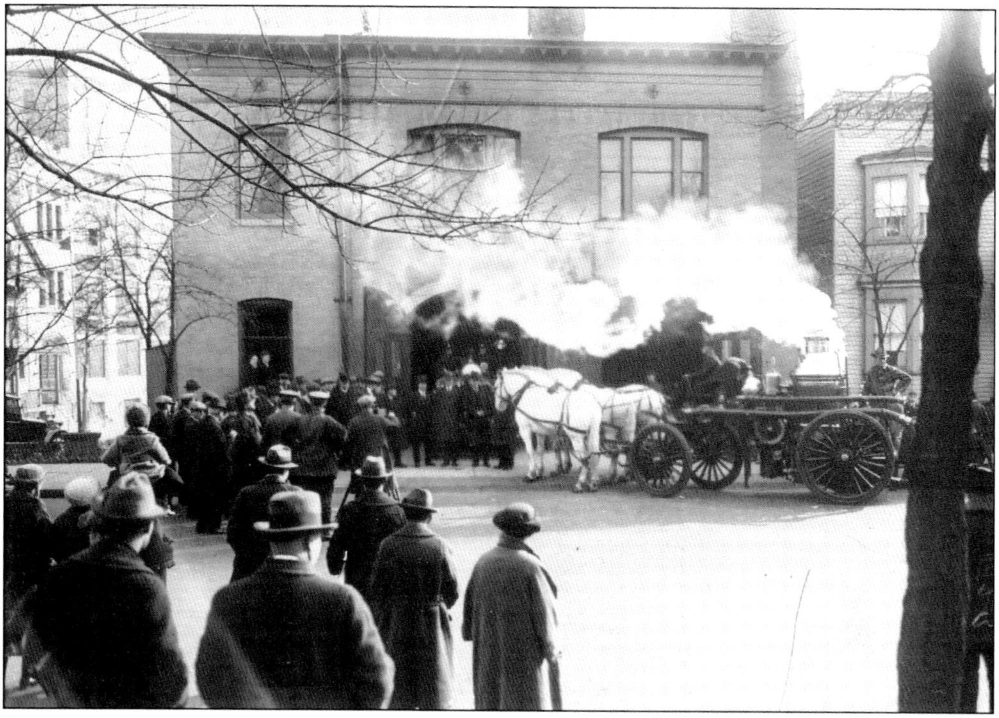

Engine Company No. 13 was the last firehouse in the city with fire horses. But all good things must come to an end, and in the winter of 1923, crowds from the neighborhood gathered for what has been billed as "the Last Run." This team of pure-white horses returned to the firehouse as the steam engine billowed into the sky. (NPL.)

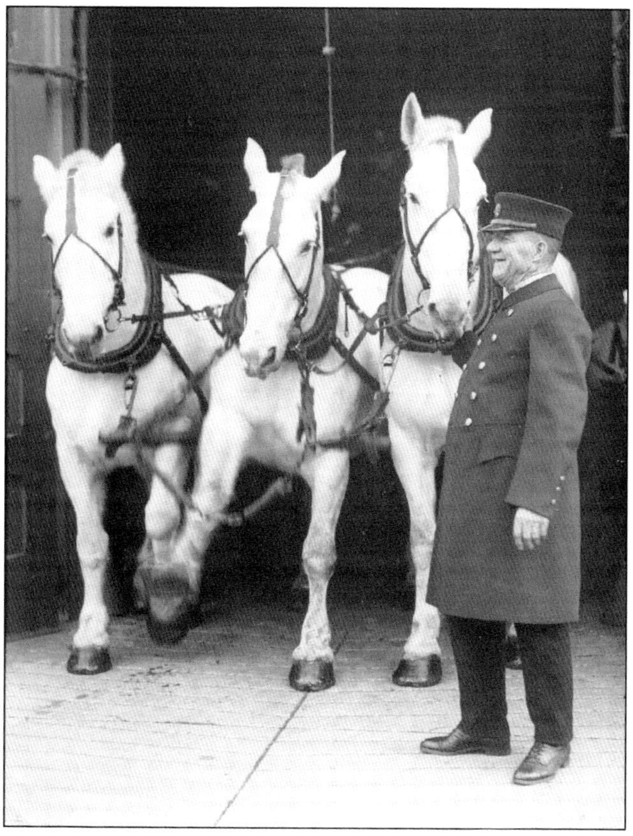

A critical moment for every firefighter was hitching up the horses that would carry them to the scene of a raging fire. Seen here with Chief McDermott is the team of horses that braved fires with the men of Engine Company No. 13. Jerry, Pet, and Baby served the fire department well and were essential to protecting Newark's citizens from imminent danger. (NPL.)

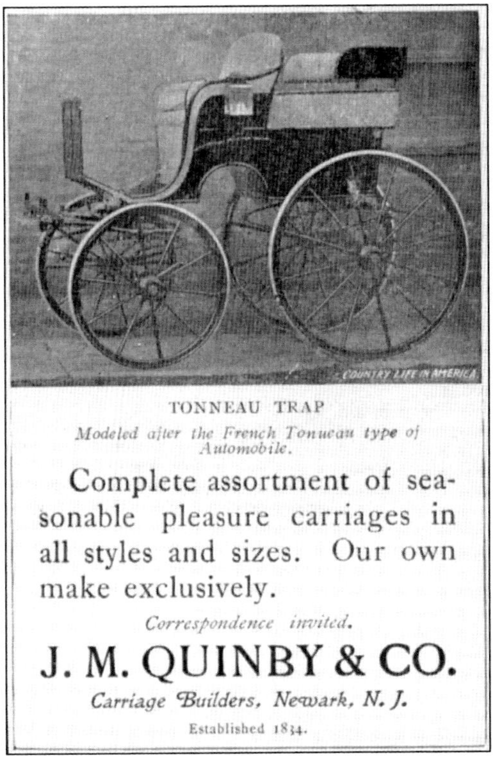

Before the advent of motorized vehicles, Newark was home to dozens of carriage makers. The oldest was J.M. Quinby & Co., established in 1834. Since automobiles were manufactured in central locations such as Detroit, one wonders how long all of these carriage makers managed to survive. (CL.)

Not everyone could afford an automobile, particularly during the Depression. This 1934 advertisement for the Mount Prospect Garage reveals the owner's ingenuity, still providing horses for hire with carriages and for riding. Those with means, however, had to decide what to do with their carriage houses, which were too large for automobiles. Many of these structures were torn down and replaced with small garages; others were converted into separate residences. (CL.)

KE. 2- 3654 DEl. 3-5922

Acme Coat, Apron, Towel Supply Company

HARRY QUINN, Mgr.

260 Chestnut St. Kearny, N. J. 481 Johnston Ave. Jersey City, N. J.

HUmboldt 3-9607

WILLIAM J. BLOCK

Newspapers and Magazines Delivered
Greeting Cards - Stationery
Cigars and Candy

177 BLOOMFIELD AVENUE
NEWARK, N. J.

HUmboldt 2-1617

MARJEAN . . .

Hairdresser

667 MT. PROSPECT AVENUE
NEWARK, N. J.

Hours: 9 A. M. to 6 P. M.
Monday, Friday, 9 A. M. to 8.30 P. M.

MT. PROSPECT GARAGE

671 MT. PROSPECT AVENUE
NEWARK, N. J.

CHARLES J. EARL, Prop.

To Hire: Horse and Buggies, Pony Carts
Saddle Horses
By the Hour, Day or Night

Seven

Residents of Note

The city of Newark claims many famous people, such as Stephen Crane, author of *The Red Badge of Courage*, and Samuel A. Ward, composer of *America the Beautiful*, as well as more recent popular figures like Savion Glover, Whitney Houston, Frankie Valli, and Sarah Vaughan.

Among Forest Hill's notable residents were two men who rose to the highest levels of the judicial and legislative branches of the federal government. Justice William J. Brennan Jr. was appointed to the US Supreme Court in 1956 and served until 1990. At the start of his legal career, he lived in a Forest Hill home two doors down from where one of this book's coauthors lives today.

Born Pelligrino Rodino Jr. to Italian immigrant parents in Newark, Peter W. Rodino Jr. was elected to the US House of Representatives in Newark's 10th Congressional District in 1949. After retiring from office, he returned to the practice of law and taught at Seton Hall Law School. The coauthors remember Rodino ushering at Sunday Mass when they were children.

Other famous Forest Hill residents featured here are Dorland J. Henderson, preservationist and engineer; Lucy Karr Milburn, activist and poet; Richard H. Ranger, inventor and Academy Award winner; and Madame Maria Jeritza, international opera soprano.

Another notable person is actor Jack Warden (1920–2006), who attended Good Counsel High School. He began his acting career in 1950 and went on to have roles in 59 movies (including *From Here to Eternity*) and 55 television productions (including *Brian's Song*). While there are many remarkable individuals who have called Forest Hill home, there are also those who have become notorious for one reason or another, such as dominatrix Monique Van Cleef and the phony doctor who famously buried a deceased plastic surgery patient in his Forest Hill front yard.

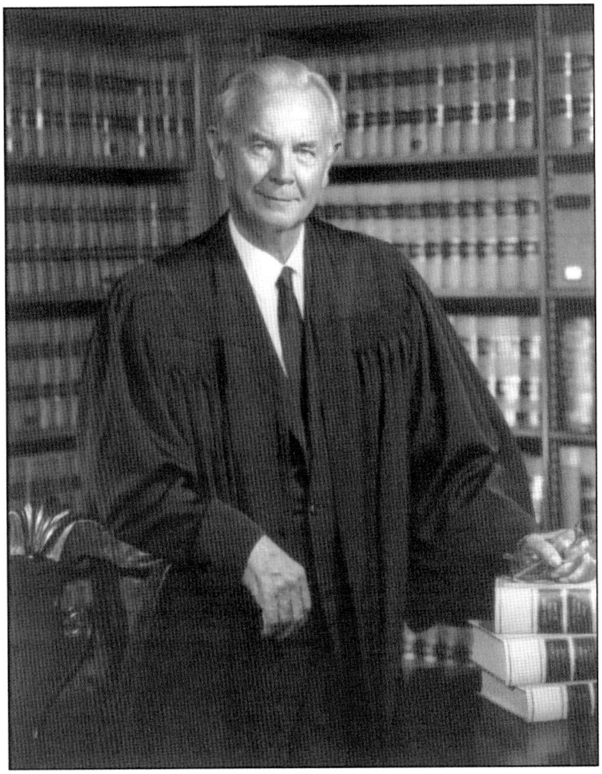

Republican president Dwight D. Eisenhower elevated Democrat William J. Brennan Jr. from the New Jersey Supreme Court to the US Supreme Court in 1956. Born in Newark in 1906 and a graduate of Barringer High School, Justice Brennan's decisions in the landmark cases of *Griswold v. Connecticut*, relating to privacy, and *Penn Central Transportation Co. v. New York City*, saving Grand Central Terminal, have made an indelible impact. (LC.)

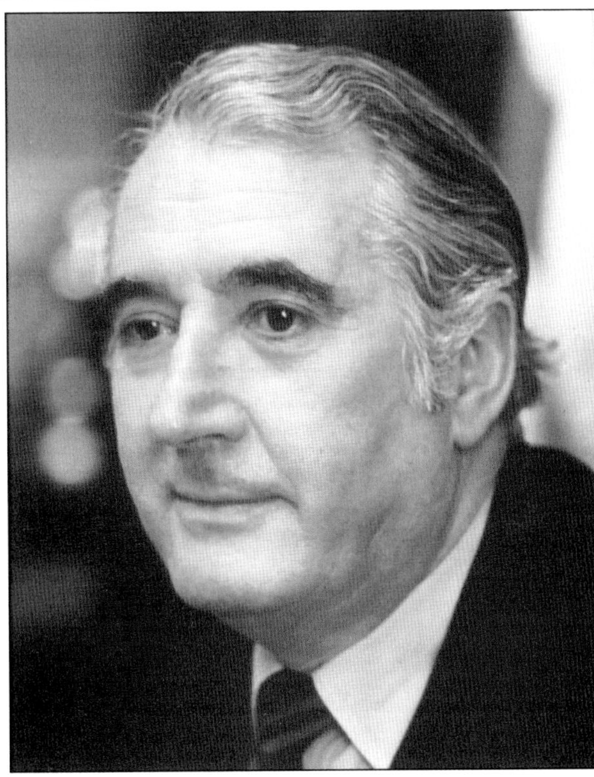

Representing Newark's 10th Congressional District for 40 years, Congressman Peter Rodino sponsored legislation to make Columbus Day a national holiday. He became chairman of the House Judiciary Committee in 1973 and is most remembered for chairing the Nixon impeachment hearings in 1974. Rodino negotiated those difficult proceedings with class and dignity. He continued to chair the committee until his retirement in 1989. His death came at age 95 at his home in New Jersey. (NPL.)

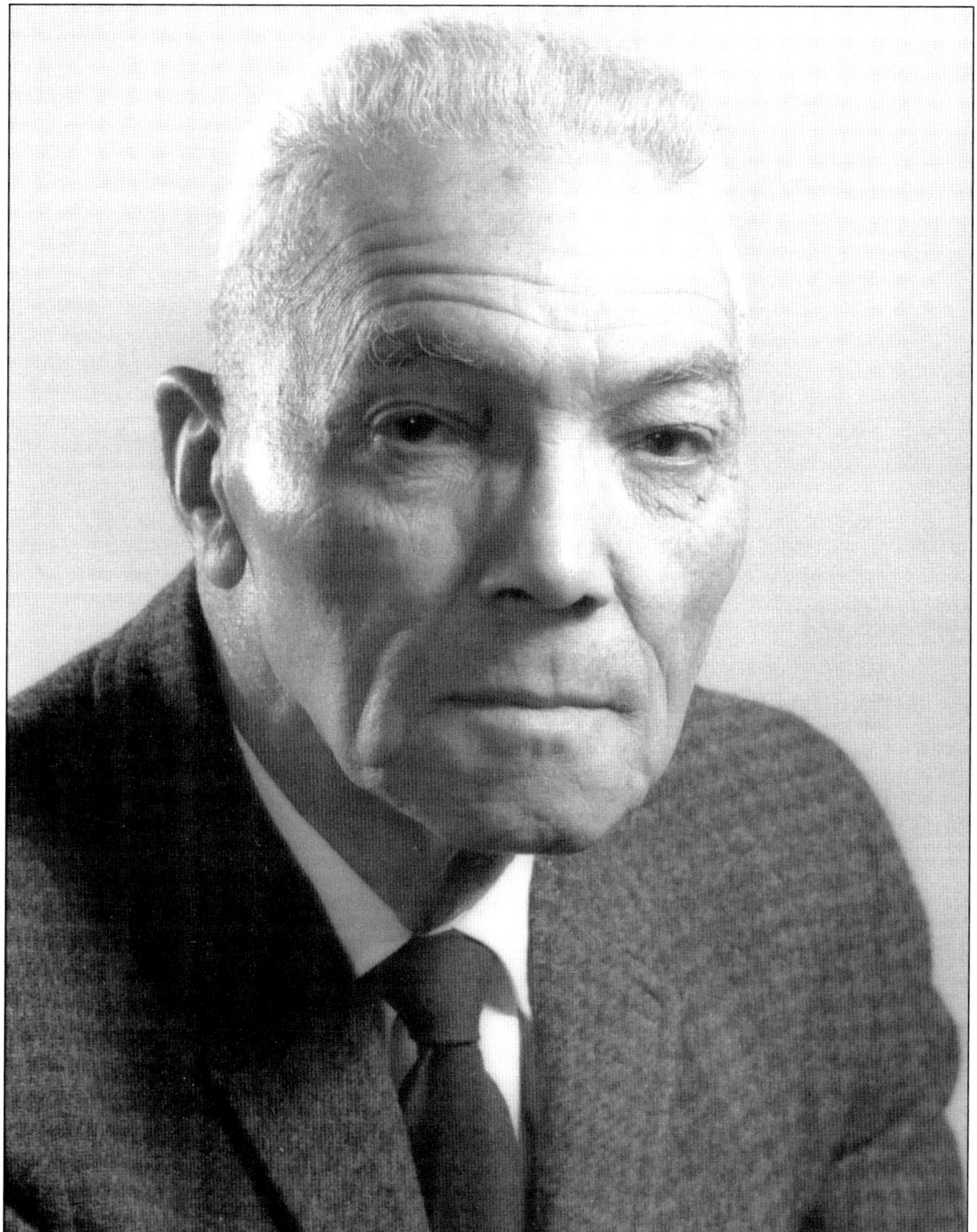

As half of Newark's prominent preservation couple, Dorland J. Henderson (better known as D.J.), also had a distinguished career as an engineer for the New Jersey Department of Transportation. Born in Indiana in 1898 and educated at Purdue University, D.J. was directed in 1958 to design a low-level lighting system for the Manahawkin Bay Bridge. The horizontal lighting he designed to be embedded in the railings of the span would later be described as "a string of pearls across the bay." At the rededication ceremony for the Manahawkin Bay Bridge in 1992, Commissioner Tom Downs thanked D.J. for his design, stating, "A good design is forever." Today, bridge spans across the country use D.J.'s design for lighting the roadway, eliminating the need for overhead poles and lighting. (NPL.)

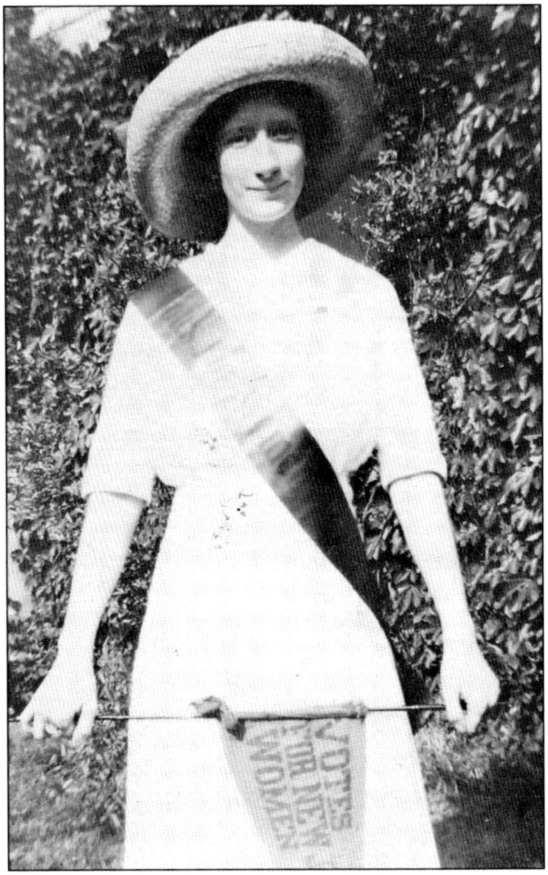

Lucy Karr (1895–1998) was born in Newark and lived in the same house in Forest Hill for almost her entire life. She graduated from Newark's Barringer High School and from Barnard College. In 1918, she married Richard Milburn, a neighborhood boy. She and Richard had two children, Anne and Richard. Lucy Karr Milburn was a lifelong activist. In the photograph at left, she is shown with the banner and sash she wore when she and her mother, Minnie Schneider Karr (below), marched to Washington, DC, in support of women's suffrage. (Both, Samuel Rivera.)

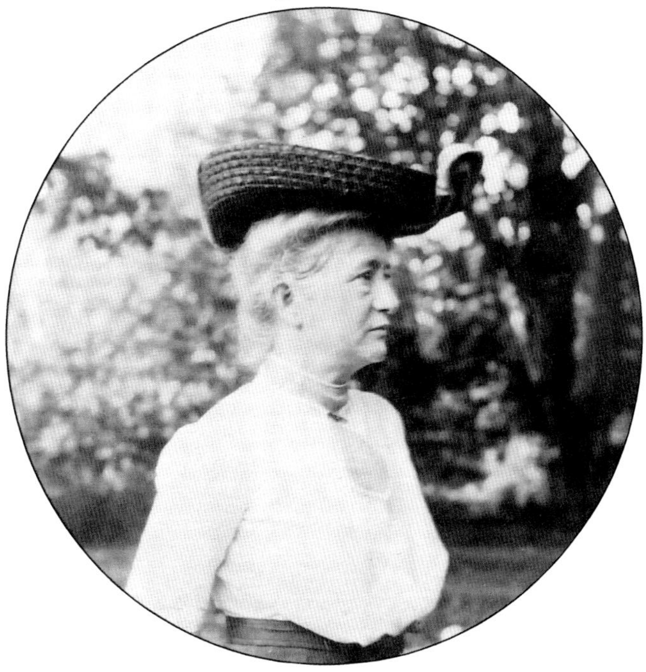

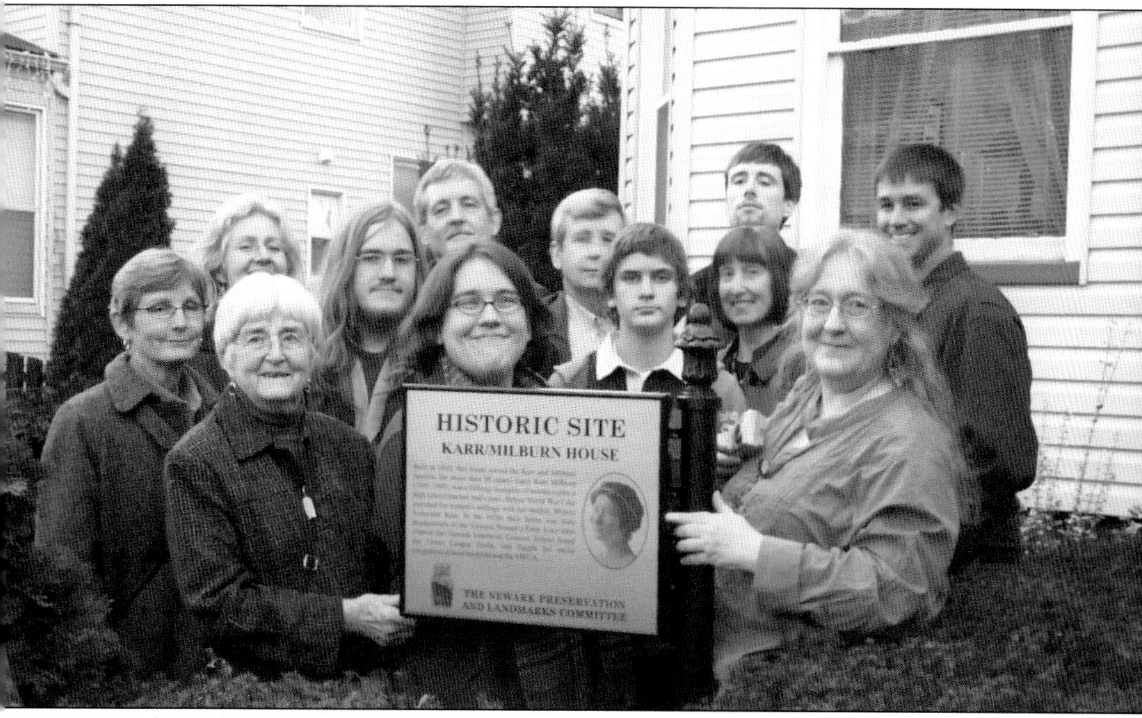

During the early 1900s, the Karr-Milburn home in Forest Hill served as the state headquarters of the National Women's Party (NWP). In later years, Lucy served as president of the Newark Interracial Council and was one of the founders of the Urban League Guild. Her work with these groups included successful campaigns to permit African American doctors to practice in Newark city hospitals and the racial integration of the YMCA swimming pool. Through the efforts of Samuel Rivera, current owner of the Karr-Milburn house, the Newark Preservation and Landmark Committee installed a plaque in 2008 designating the house as a historic site. As shown here, several descendants of Lucy Karr Milburn came for the unveiling of the plaque. (Samuel Rivera.)

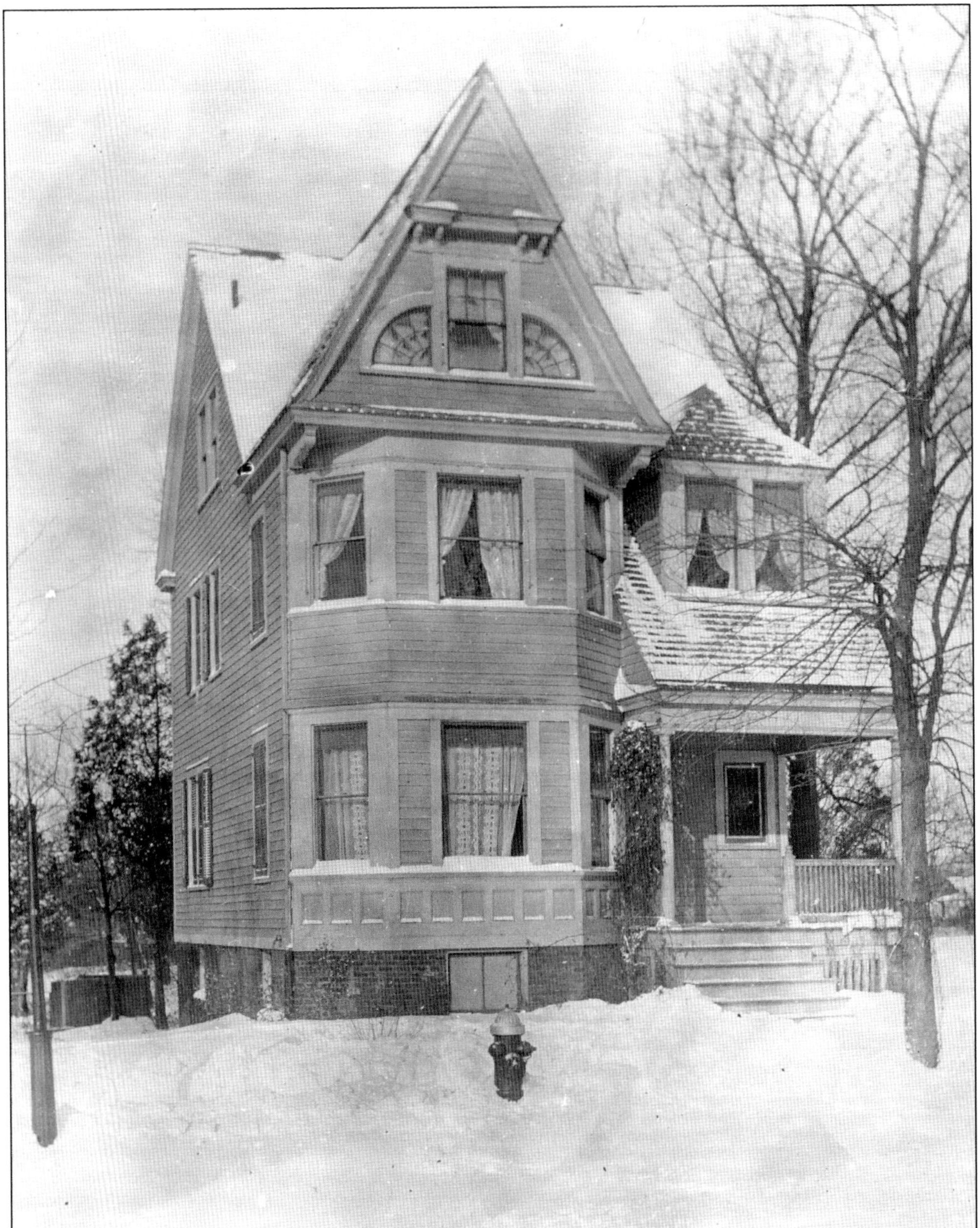

Lucy Karr Milburn, a poet, privately published several of her collections. She loved her DeGraw Avenue home (shown here) and was heartbroken to leave it when her family convinced her to move into an assisted-living facility when she was in her early nineties. One of her poems from her later years, "The Incurable Rhymester," is particularly apt. "Old Homestead" is excerpted as follows: "Four generations have called her 'home,' / And a fifth felt free to come, . . . / But now signs point to a curve in the road, / And beyond the bend, the End. / The old house will pass to other hands, / Likely from Spanish-speaking lands." The Rivera family purchased the home from her estate. (Samuel Rivera.)

Lucy Karr Milburn (right) was a Quaker and lifelong member of the Montclair Monthly Meeting of the Religious Society of Friends. In 1960, she wrote the definitive history of that congregation. The photograph below shows a gathering of the members to dedicate a new building. Lucy is seen front and center, in the light-colored coat, with her mother, Minnie Karr, on her left. In her later years, when Lucy could not always get to her Montclair Monthly Meeting, she would attend the Forest Hill Presbyterian Church. The night before she moved out of her Forest Hill home, she asked the Presbyterian pastor, the Reverend Ed Clydesdale, to spend the evening with her so she would have someone with whom to share her memories. Another poem from *The Incurable Rhymester* collection begins as follows: "Not every Clydesdale is a horse. Ed is a pastor, kind and caring." (Both, Samuel Rivera.)

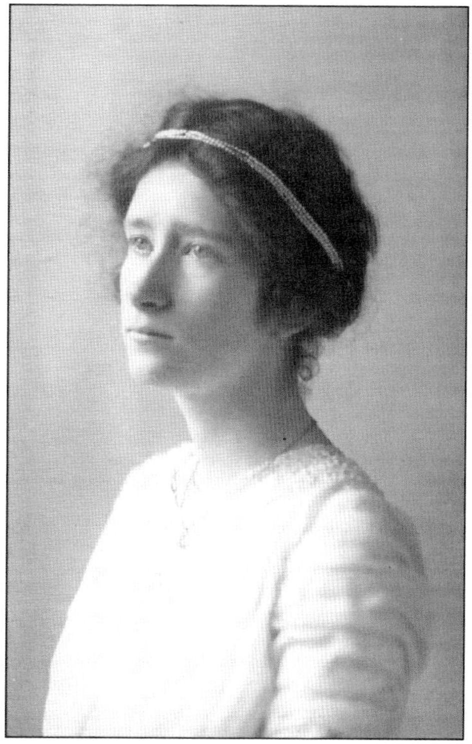

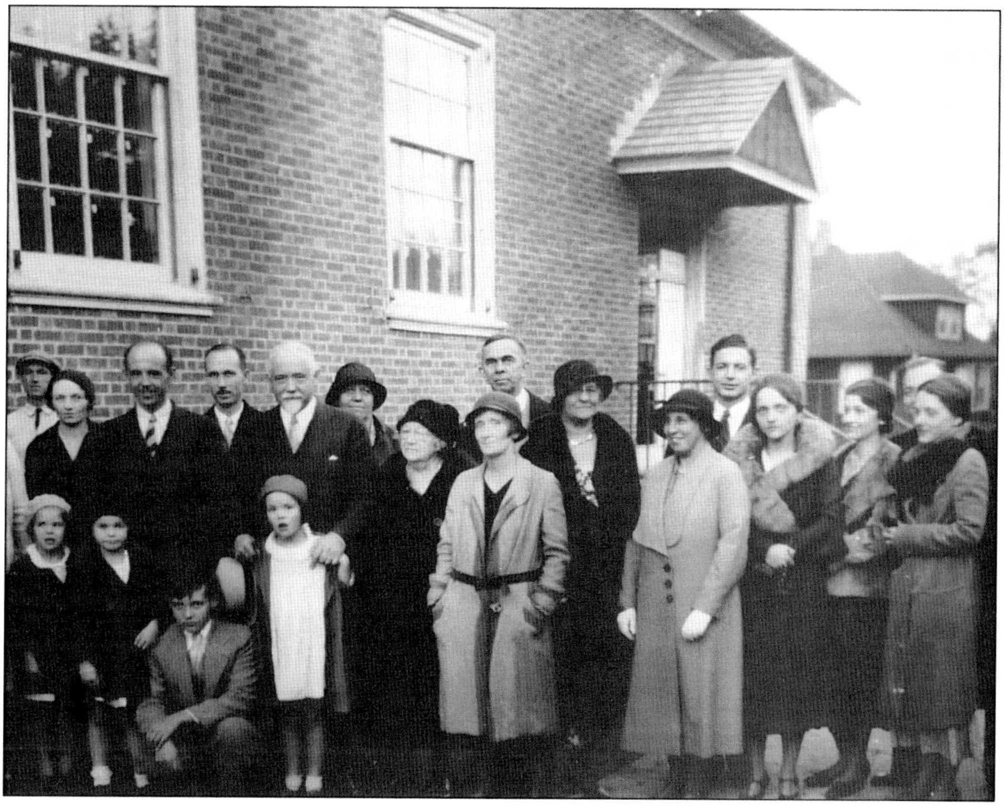

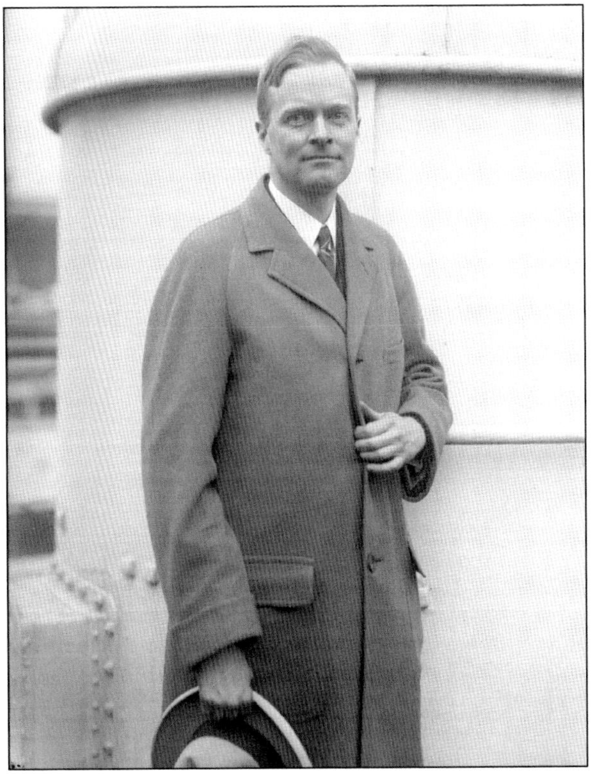

As it happens, Lucy Karr Milburn's son Richard was a protégé of Forest Hill resident Richard H. Ranger (1889–1962), an engineer and inventor pictured at left. In 1956, Ranger received an Academy Award for Technical Achievement for developing a synchronous sound system. He also invented an electric organ and held many other patents. His company, Rangertone, Inc., is still in operation today. (LC.)

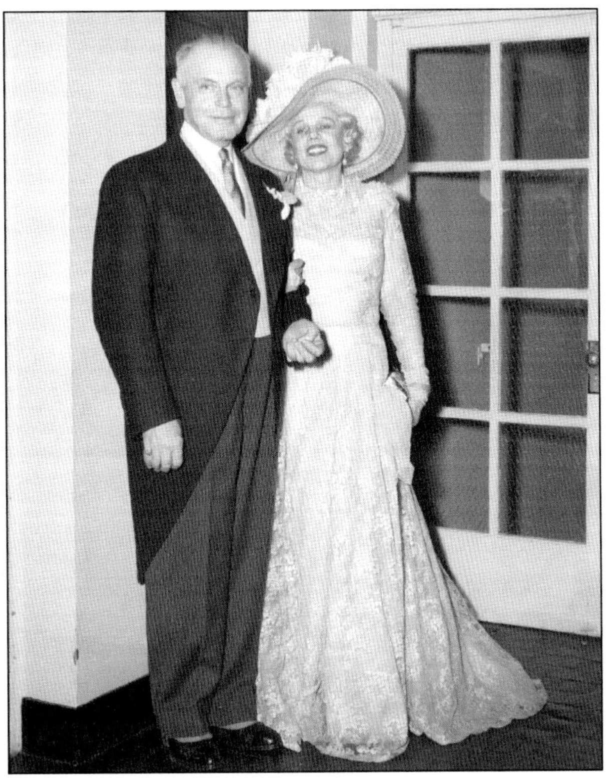

Maria Jeritza (1887–1982), "the Moravian Thunderbolt," rose to fame with the Vienna Opera. She was under contract at the Metropolitan Opera from her 1921 debut through 1932, and again in 1951. Her fame was such that she appeared on the cover of *Time* magazine in 1928. In 1948, Madame Jeritza married Newark businessman Irving Seery. Shown here on a glamorous outing, they lived in a gated estate in Forest Hill. (NPL.)

Eight

A Preservation Success Story

Awareness of the significance of Newark's historic neighborhoods and landmarks became apparent in the early 1970s. Newark had become the poster child for all that was wrong with America's cities, but the committed citizens who made Newark their home knew differently.

The Newark Preservation and Landmarks Committee (NPLC) was founded in 1973 to save and restore Newark's heritage of irreplaceable structures and sculptures. In 1975, the Newark Cherry Blossom Festival nominated Branch Brook Park to the New Jersey and National Registers of Historic Places. The Newark Museum demonstrated its faith in Newark by putting its resources behind the restoration and public opening of the Ballantine House in time for the country's bicentennial.

Subsequent to the National Register designation in 1978 of the James Street Commons Historic District, the Forest Hill Historic District nomination was prepared and shepherded through the process by the NPLC in 1990. The Forest Hill Historic District comprises a 56-block area in Newark's North Ward. Even before register designation was granted to Forest Hill, the Forest Hill Community Association was founded in 1984 as a touchstone for the neighborhood. This chapter includes a descriptive map of the Forest Hill neighborhood that can be used for a walking tour to view the Properties of Distinction throughout the historic district.

In response to the growing interest in preservation of its historic sites, the City of Newark adopted a Historic Preservation Ordinance in 1990, creating the Newark Landmarks and Preservation Commission with authority to designate historic sites and to review planned construction, alterations, repairs, maintenance, and demolition affecting those sites.

Since the Forest Hill Historic District is strictly residential, its residents rely heavily on the businesses in the area of Mount Prospect Avenue for everything from banking to hardware supplies, to prescription refills, to restaurants and fast food, as well as a multitude of professional services. The Mount Prospect Partnership acts as a liaison for residents, businesses, and government leaders on matters affecting Mount Prospect Avenue and its surrounding streets.

All these groups are committed to maintaining the health and vitality of Newark's North Ward.

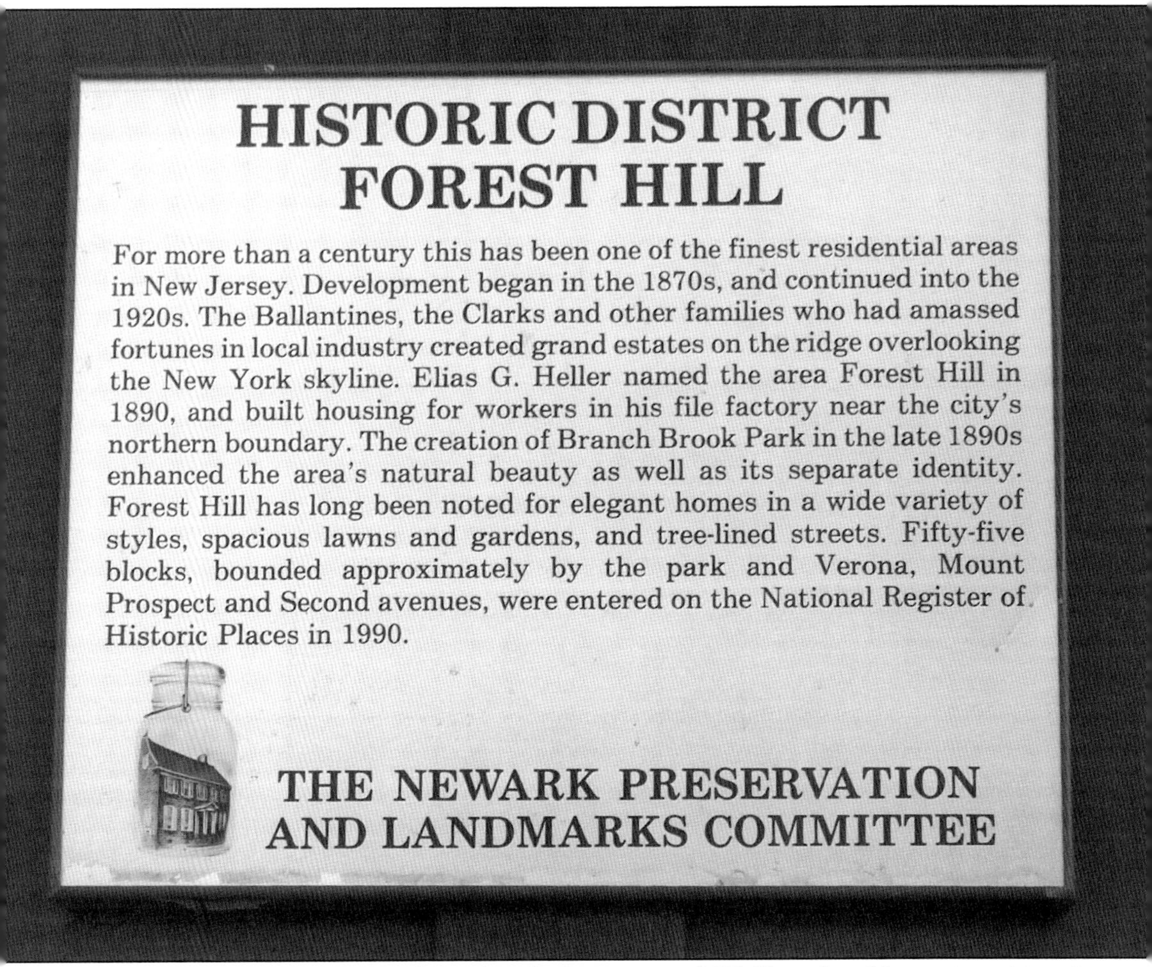

The Newark Preservation and Landmarks Committee (NPLC) is the oldest private historic preservation group in the city of Newark, serving as a citywide advocate for the preservation of Newark's historic and cultural resources. The committee's activities include preparing nominations of properties to the New Jersey and National Registers of Historic Places, intervening on behalf of threatened landmarks, implementing educational initiatives, promoting the importance of historical preservation, and collaborating with other nonprofit groups. The NPLC adopted a depiction of the Plume House in a mason jar as its logo, showcasing the property considered to be the oldest in the city, built around 1710 as a Dutch Colonial farmhouse. Once Forest Hill received its National Register listing, the NPLC installed this plaque in 1990 at the Ballantine Gates. (Photograph by Catharine Longendyck.)

www.fhcanewark.org
Newark
New Jersey
FOREST HILL
COMMUNITY ASSOCIATION

The Forest Hill Community Association (FHCA) was founded in 1984 and incorporated in 1986. The mission of FHCA is to improve the quality of life for all in Forest Hill by continuing to foster close relationships among residents of the community through various initiatives. Among the first initiatives was the successful effort to secure a place for Forest Hill on the National Register of Historic Places. Other popular FHCA initiatives have included annual home and garden tours as well as a variety of social events. Today, residents depend on the FHCA website (www.fhcanewark.org) for all the latest news and events. Shown below is the sign erected by the FHCA on Heller Parkway at DeGraw Avenue as a guide to the historic district. (Above, Forest Hill Community Association; below, photograph by Israel Ehrisman.)

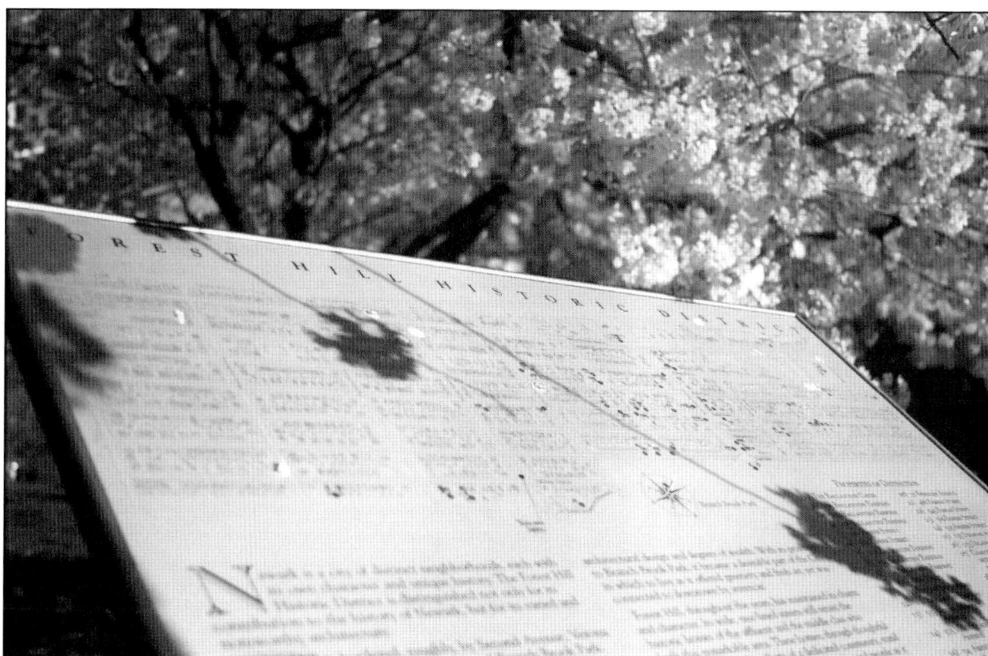

F O R E S T   H I L L   H I

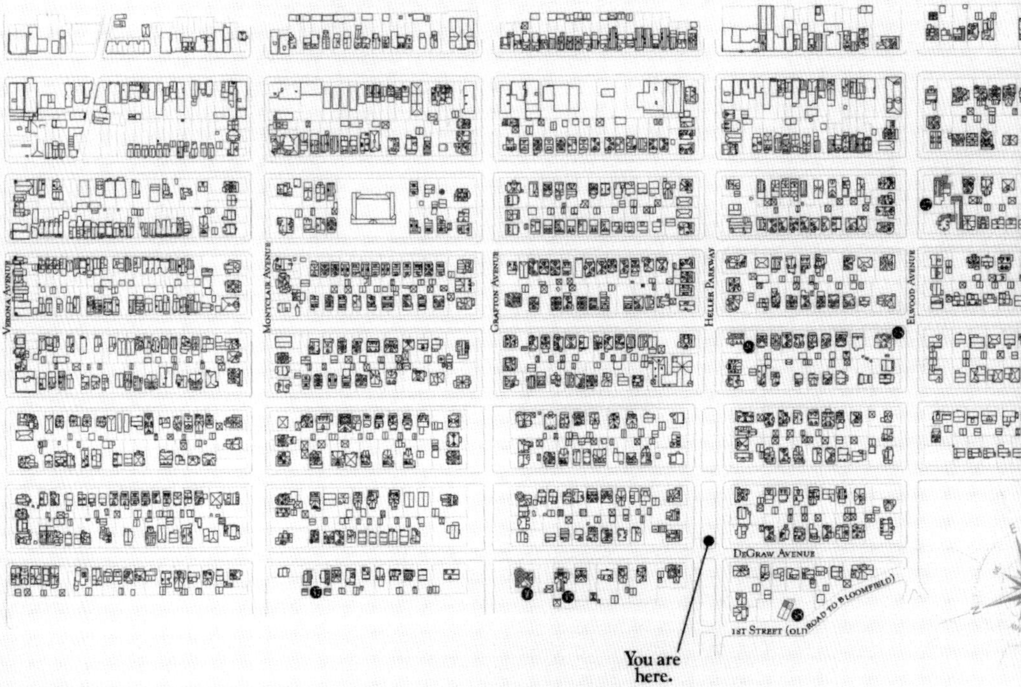

Newark is a city of distinct neighborhoods, each with its own character and unique history. The Forest Hill Historic District is distinguished not only for its contribution to the history of Newark, but for its varied and noteworthy architecture.

Forest Hill is bordered, roughly, by Second Avenue, Verona Avenue, Mount Prospect Avenue and Branch Brook Park. During its early years, most of Forest Hill was owned by three prominent families of industry: The Hellers, the Ballantines and the Clarks.

Between 1880 and 1925, many notable Newarkers built their residences in Forest Hill, exemplifying a full range of architectural design and degrees to Branch Brook Park, it becam in which to live as it offered gre connected to downtown by stre

Forest Hill, throughout the ye and character. Its wide, tree-line historic homes of the affluent a built this remarkable area. Thes preservation and the efforts of a today as reminders of the City's continues onward as one of the City of Newark.

www.fhcanewark.org
Newark New Jersey
FOREST HILL
COMMUNITY ASSOCIATION

The Forest Hill Historic District was entered on the New Jersey Register of Historic Places and the National Register of Historic Places in 1990. This plaque was made possible through generous contributions from members of the Forest Hill Community Association.

Reproduced above is the aforementioned guide to the Forest Hill Historic District. (Forest Hill

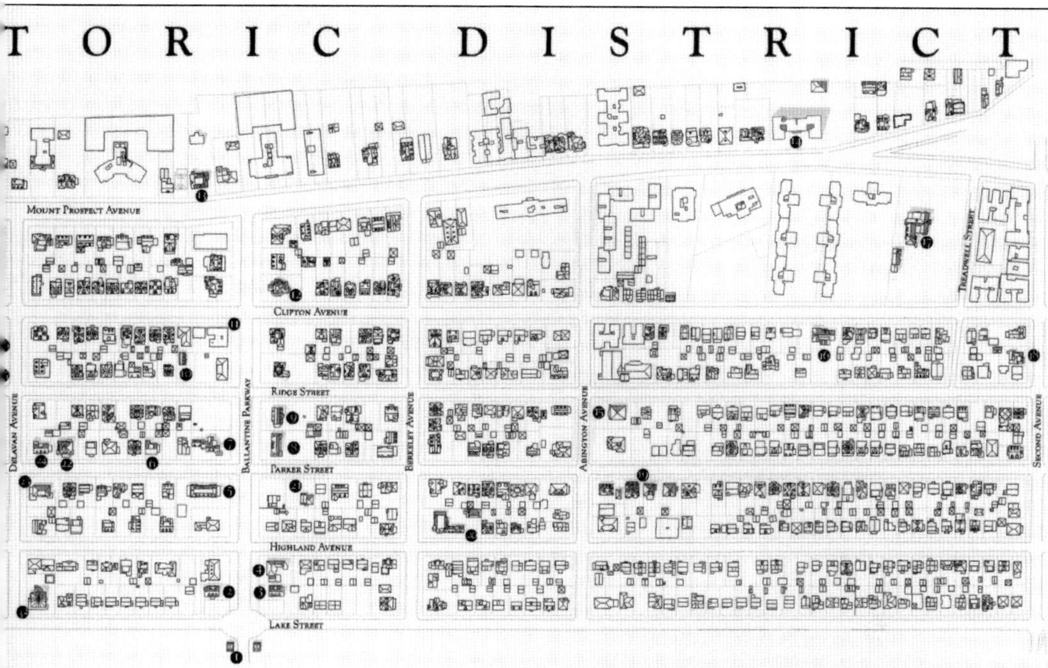

ıch Brook Park

With its proximity
e part of the City
fresh air, yet was

intained its charm
ill retain the
dle class who
ırough thoughtful
community, stand
, and people as it
borhoods of the

Community Association.)

Properties of Distinction

1) The Ballantine Gates
2) 255 Ballantine Parkway
3) 254 Ballantine Parkway
4) 246 Ballantine Parkway
5) 510 Parker Street
6) 525 Parker Street
7) 225 Ballantine Parkway
8) 224 Ballantine Parkway
9) 214 Ballantine Parkway
10) 511 Ridge Street
11) 197 Ballantine Parkway
12) 190 Ballantine Parkway
13) 533 Mount Prospect Avenue
14) 375 Mount Prospect Avenue
15) 54 Abington Avenue
16) 432 Clifton Avenue
17) 346 Mount Prospect Avenue
18) 121 Second Avenue
19) 390-396-400 Parker Street
416 Parker Street
20) 70 Berkeley Avenue
21) 486 Parker Street
22) 545 Parker Street
23) 560 Parker Street
24) 555 Parker Street
25) 235 Delavan Avenue
26) 233 Delavan Avenue
27) Complex at Elwood Avenue between Clifton Avenue and Ridge Street
28) 233 Elwood Avenue
29) 98 Heller Parkway
30) 571 Parker Street
31) 566 Parker Street
32) 300 Delavan Avenue
33) 649 Lake Street
34) 655 Lake Street
35) 776 DeGraw Avenue
36) 290 Grafton Avenue
37) 834 and 840 DeGraw Avenue
38) The Sydenham House on Old Road to Bloomfield

September 2008

Promoting
Business and Community

MOUNT PROSPECT
PARTNERSHIP

The Mount Prospect Partnership (MPP) is a community-based, not-for-profit organization promoting business and community. It serves as a catalyst for the revitalization of its neighborhood and Newark's North Ward to support the area's economic revival and increased quality of life for its residents, business owners, and visitors. MPP facilitates development by acting as liaison among interested parties. It holds community events for local residents, such as Christmas tree lighting programs, visits from Santa Claus, and a vintage car rally. The partnership also sponsors volunteer community cleanup days. Through its ongoing efforts, the security and cleanliness of the Mount Prospect Avenue area has been greatly improved. (Mount Prospect Partnership.)

YOUR DRUGGIST IS MORE THAN A MERCHANT

Try the Drug Store First

The modern housewife must constantly exercise unusual care in the selection of drugs and spices.

Our pride in selling is our selecting the qualities that are always best and freshest.

We carry a full line of spices, cake coloring and pure extracts.

LISS' PHARMACY

DEPENDABLE DRUG STORE SERVICE

Mt. Prospect, Corner Montclair Aves. Newark, N J

Telephone Branch Brook 4749

This advertisement for Liss Pharmacy appeared in 1925, when the Liss family lived in Forest Hill. The business is still located on the corner of Mount Prospect and Montclair Avenues, although the store and building have been enlarged and upgraded. (Michael Sheehan.)

HUmboldt 2-0397

WEBER'S

General Hardware Store

Paints - Oils - Glass - House Furnishings

Electrical and Plumbing Supplies

836 MT. PROSPECT AVENUE
NEWARK, N. J.

HUmboldt 2-1617

MARJEAN HAIRDRESSER

Miss Mathilda, Prop.

Permanents of Distinction

Hair Cutting Our Specialty

667 MT. PROSPECT AVENUE
NEWARK, N. J.

HUmboldt 2-3854

DR. STEPHEN L. MICONE

Dental Surgeon

872 BROADWAY

At Verona Avenue NEWARK, N. J.

RUDOLF'S
BLUE MIRROR BAKERY

Melchior Gajeski, Prop.

512 BROADWAY
NEWARK, N. J.

Specialty

WEDDING and BIRTHDAY CAKES

"Pure Whipped Cream Goods"

Weber's Hardware, originally founded as Mount Prospect Hardware in 1917, ran this advertisement in 1946. A few years ago, the business relocated to a storefront next door to its original site. Mr. Weber sold the business several years ago but still comes in to help out around the store. (CL.)

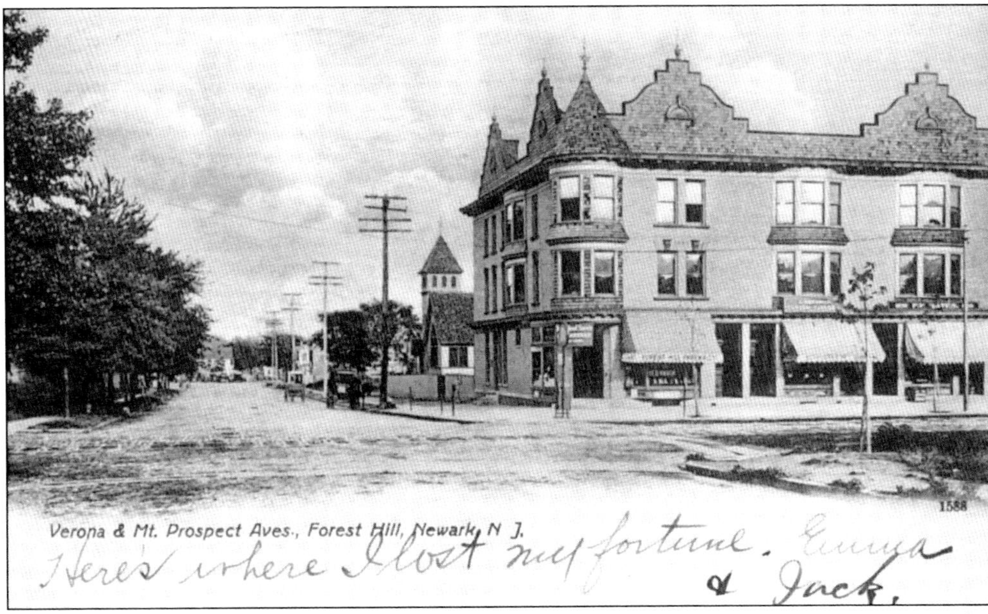

The Mount Prospect business district extends north to approximately Verona Avenue. This postcard from 1906 shows the intersection at that time; the building pictured still stands at this location. Directly across the street was the main Heller factory. (CL.)

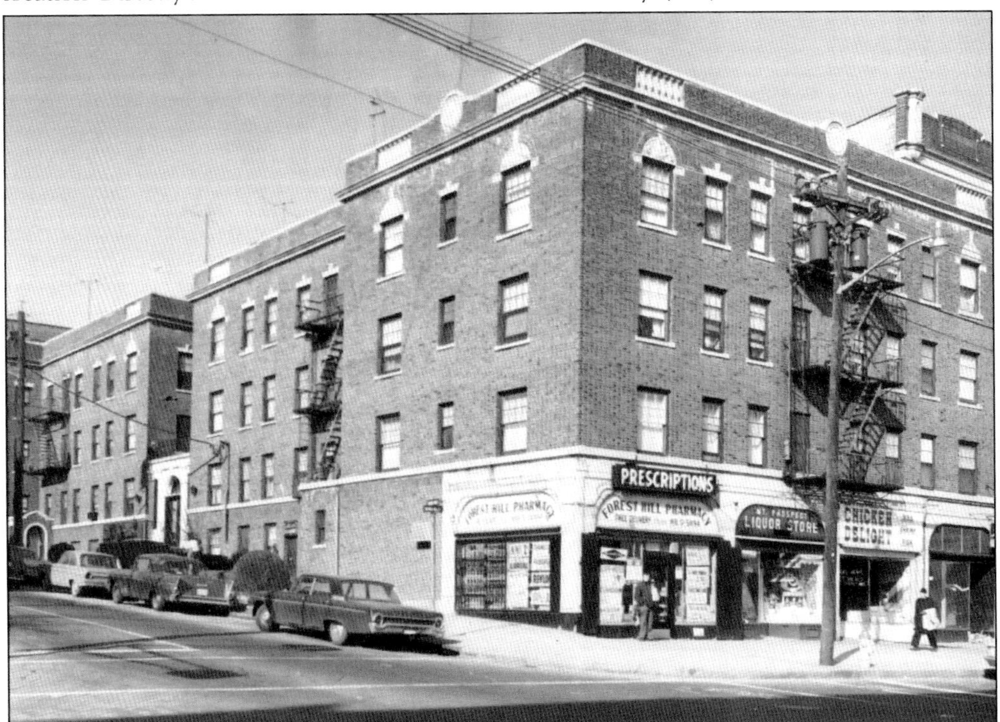

Just outside the Forest Hill Historic District, about one block south of the Clark Mansion, there is another, smaller business area. This 1965 photograph features a drugstore capitalizing on the Forest Hill name. (NPL.)

Bibliography

Art Work of Newark, Illustrated. The W.H. Parish Publishing Co., 1892.

Atkinson, Joseph. *The History of Newark, New Jersey.* Newark, NJ: William B. Guild, 1878.

Fidelity Trust Company. *Historic Newark.* Boston, MA: Walton Advertising & Printing Company, 1916.

Forest Hill Association. *About Forest Hill: A Strictly Residential Suburb.* Newark, NJ: W.H. Shurts, *n.d.*

Heller, Wilma Phillips. *The Name's the Same: History of Heller Parkway.* Thesis, Newark State College, 1961.

Hine, Charles Gilbert. *Woodside, The North End of Newark, NJ.* New York, 1908.

Hopkins, G.M. *Combined Atlas of the State of New Jersey and the City of Newark.* Philadelphia, PA: G.M. Hopkins & Co., 1873.

Leary, Peter J. *Essex County, NJ, Illustrated.* Newark, NJ: Press of L.J. Hardham, 1897.

National Register of Historic Places. Nomination of [various Newark, NJ, Landmarks and Historic Places]. Washington, DC: US Department of the Interior, National Park Service, various dates.

Newark City Directories. Newark, NJ, various dates from 1861 to 1926.

Shaw, William H. *History of the Essex and Hudson Counties, New Jersey.* Philadelphia, PA: Everts & Peck, 1894.

Street and Ward Map, City of Newark, New Jersey, 1910.

Urquhart, Frank J. *A History of the City of Newark, New Jersey.* New York: Lewis Historical Publishing Co., 1913.

———. *A Short History of Newark.* Newark, NJ: Baker Printing Company, 1908.

Zakalak, Ulana. *Nomination of Forest Hill Historical District, Newark, New Jersey.* Newark, NJ: The Newark Preservation & Landmarks Committee, 1989.